DIVINE REVELATION
AND THE LIMITS OF
HISTORICAL CRITICISM

Divine Revelation
and the Limits of
Historical Criticism

WILLIAM J. ABRAHAM

OXFORD NEW YORK TORONTO MELBOURNE

OXFORD UNIVERSITY PRESS

1982

Oxford University Press, Walton Street, Oxford OX2 6DP

London Glasgow New York Toronto
Delhi Bombay Calcutta Madras Karachi
Kuala Lumpur Singapore Hong Kong Tokyo
Nairobi Dar es Salaam Cape Town
Melbourne Auckland

and associate companies in
Beirut Berlin Ibadan Mexico City

Published in the United States by
Oxford University Press, New York

British Library Cataloguing in Publication Data
Abraham, William J.
Divine revelation and the limits of
historical criticism
1. Revelation
I. Title
231.7'4   BT127.2
ISBN 0-19-826665-0

Library of Congress Cataloging in Publication Data
Abraham, William J. (William James), 1947-
Divine revelation and the limits of historical
criticism.
Includes index.
1. Revelation.   2. History (Theology)   I. Title.
BT127.2.A27   231.7'4   81-22441
ISBN 0-19-826665-0   AACR2

Typeset by DMB (Typesetting) Oxford
and printed in Great Britain
by The Thetford Press Limited
Thetford, Norfolk

To
Timothy Fletcher,
Siobhan Elizabeth,
and
Shaun Wesley

PREFACE

My work on this book has been a labour of love made possible by the encouragement and advice of many friends and teachers. I want to thank Maurice Wiles whose questions and searching comments have been a spur to much reflection on my part. I especially want to thank Basil Mitchell whose criticism has been invaluable and whose own work has been for me a model of elegance and rigour. It is certainly not their fault that so many blemishes remain.

I gratefully acknowledge the work done by Sonya Vasilieff in typing, the patience and support of my wife, Muriel, throughout the time spent on this project, and the encouragement of my witty and stimulating colleagues in the School of Religion at Seattle Pacific University during the final stages of the work. Among the latter Eugene Lemcio, Frank Spina and Robert Wall deserve a special word of thanks.

CONTENTS

INTRODUCTION

IT is a commonplace observation that revelation is fundamental in any articulation of Christian theism, so much so that it has a secure position in the structure of all systematic theologies that purport to be Christian. It is equally uncontroversial to say that many contemporary theologians have been uneasy with if not hostile to traditional thinking in this area. In other words, traditional conceptions of revelation have fallen on hard times, and as a result the search is on for an account of revelation that will be fully acceptable today.

The reasons for this state of affairs are legion. Undoubtedly one is the continued development and spread of fundamentalist evangelicalism.[1] In this tradition revelation and inspiration tend to be so run together that the commitment to inerrancy which is entailed, on this view, by inspiration is associated with traditional conceptions of revelation. The problems generated by this interpretation of inspiration are notorious. Not surprisingly they become associated with classical doctrines of revelation, and thus those who reject the prevailing orthodoxy on inspiration automatically reject traditional thinking on revelation.[2] However, the reasons for hostility to traditional conceptions of revelation go much deeper. Chief among them is the settled conviction that traditional conceptions of revelation are incompatible with modern developments in history and science. Traditional thinking on revelation has involved an unashamed commitment to 'supernaturalism'. On this view, God really did intervene in the past. He spoke to the prophets; He brought Israel out of Egypt by a miracle; He became incarnate in Jesus Christ. It was through events such as these, through direct acts in the world in the past, that God made Himself known to mankind. It is now widely believed that such a conception of revelation is quite literally incredible given the canons of judgement that must be exercised today. These canons have been forged in the development of history and science and are now indispensable for an adequate reading of the Bible. Thus tension, and even hostility, develops between traditional conceptions of revelation and the 'modern man'. The one is believed to be incompatible with the other. Through time this has become standard orthodoxy among theologians who would consider themselves progressive and truly modern, so much so that it is often not considered worthy of reasoned argument. It has become part of the air that we breathe in academic theology.

In such circumstances it is only natural that fundamentalist evangelicalism should flourish in the churches and among many students. On the one hand it is a safe haven to which the threatened believer can retreat. Herein is to be found an unashamed commitment to a full-blooded supernaturalism that at first sight, at least, seems to preserve the riches of the gospel and the content of the great classical Christian heritage. On the other hand, fundamentalist evangelicalism is a convenient club with which to assault traditional Christian thinking on revelation. After all it is not difficult to identify the problems that inerrancy poses. Chief among these is the enormous difficulty in taking seriously critical historical study, a 'sacred cow' of modern theological study. So by focusing on the problems of fundamentalist evangelicalism, it is not difficult to discredit at the same time traditional conceptions of revelation. Having done so, the search for an alternative account of revelation can begin. By this time the student or believer has been sufficiently softened up to receive what is offered. In such circumstances any account of divine revelation that eschews reference to divine intervention will be a welcome relief. The rejection of divine intervention would mean the removal of a burden for the believer that calls for celebration.

No doubt there is an element of caricature in my analysis. What it highlights, however, is a fundamental issue for the contemporary Christian theologian. On the one side there is the classical Christian heritage which has seen some kind of divine intervention as an essential ingredient in any comprehensive account of revelation. On the other side there is the conviction that the contemporary theologian, if he is to be really honest and at home in recent developments, simply cannot appropriate the classical heritage at this point.

We should note immediately that this conviction is a philosophical conviction. I say this not to discredit it but to identify its character. It is a thesis about the compatibility of traditional Christian belief with contemporary canons of judgement in history and science, and even to state this with any degree of sophistication demands the exercise of philosophical judgement. The thesis is a philosophical one that calls for philosophical scrutiny. As such it deserves not just careful attention but sympathetic consideration, especially on the part of those whose minds and hearts find peace in the great classical heritage of Christian reflection and teaching. In many respects that heritage has been loath to come to terms with new data and fresh discoveries, as is always the temptation of those who have developed an appreciation for tradition. It is not too much to say that traditionalists do have reason to feel guilty. Certainly they should have learnt enough from the past treatment of figures like Galileo and Darwin to have repented of any theological triumphalism by now. As we all know, this is easier said than done.

There is a real danger, however, that past guilt will precipitate a readiness to believe that when conflict between the tradition and fresh developments in this or that field of enquiry is announced, then the tradition is not to be trusted. There is no guarantee that this is so; each case must be weighed on its merits. This is especially so when the issue at stake is philosophical in nature. With the advent of any particular historical or scientific proposal that conflicts with some doctrine or other, the issue is relatively straightforward: if the particular proposal is well grounded in evidence, there is little doubt as to what course a rational believer should take. To be sure, it may take time to work through the full implications for various aspects of doctrine, but at least one knows what to do in principle. However, philosophical issues are notoriously more difficult to appropriate, partly because the relationship between philosophy and theology is a matter of endless dispute, but more importantly, because the evidence for and against the philosophical thesis purported to call for drastic reformulation of Christian doctrine is invariably contested. In this instance a body of agreed evidence to resolve the philosophical issue in one direction rather than another is just not available.

In such instances it is very tempting to accept uncritically that option which best chimes with one's initial intuitions and leave it at that. Or perhaps the choice seems so obvious that it does not call for further reflection. Whichever way one goes, there are likely to be scholars who will be able to back up our particular choice with what looks like cogent reasoning. This is not so, however, in the case under review. On the whole the best literature in the field has taken the view that the traditional Christian doctrine of revelation is incompatible with the exercise of critical historical and scientific judgement. At the moment the onus is clearly on the traditional believer to argue for the viability of his position. He must meet this challenge; silence would indicate intellectual defeat.

In this book I shall mount an argument on two fronts. First, I shall argue that a traditional understanding of revelation is essential to the overall coherence of Christian theism, and that to abandon it is to abandon something of enormous significance. Secondly, I shall argue that one can be committed to this as a modern theist without in any way commiting intellectual suicide. One can, in fact, also be fully committed to the canons of judgement that are an essential part of modern history and science.

Those who have read or are aware of my earlier book, *The Divine Inspiration of Holy Scripture,*[3] will recognize that this is a sequel to that book. I argued therein that it was utterly essential to separate revelation from inspiration. When this was done it was possible to develop an account of inspiration which was at home with the general conclusions that historians have reached about the origins and the content of the Bible. Because of the endemic tendency among theologians to confuse inspiration with revelation it was impossible to avoid some comments on the nature of the revelation. In this book I shall continue the reflection which began at that point. The reader should therefore be aware that, although this is an independent enterprise, it has continuity with my proposal about inspiration. In both books I aim to develop a contemporary statement of doctrine; in the former case I proposed an account of inspiration, in the present one I deal with revelation. In both cases I aim to do justice to the development of historical study as applied to the Bible; in *Inspiration*

I sought to do justice to the conclusions that historians have reached, in this book I intend to do justice to the canons of judgement that historians must rely on in their work. I hope that my work will be viewed as a deliberate contribution to the renewal of the evangelical tradition as expressed in the Reformers, and more especially in the thought of John Wesley. I also intend my work to be seen as an attempt to resolve issues which any theologian in our day must face; and I hope to seek and find the truth independently of any banner or label under which it may fly.

What I have to say is timely not just because I address a question which cries out for analysis and resolution in its own right, but because there is at present serious questioning about the role of historical study within theology as a whole. A number of voices in recent years have expressed deep concern about the limits of historical study. Perhaps most notable of all is the recent work of Brevard S. Childs in Old Testament study.[4] I share some of the misgivings that Childs and others have expressed, and I believe that an exaggerated emphasis on history has cut us off from a full theological reading of and appreciation for scripture. Yet I detect in some quarters a desire to be rid of history as a nuisance and a hindrance.[5] Certainly Childs cannot be accused of this, but there are those who would only too gladly welcome any scholarship that would confirm the prejudice that there still is against the historical study of the Bible, a prejudice, by the way, that is by no means confined to fundamentalists. In such circumstances a study of some of the limits of historical criticism is bound to be of value. At the very least it should help make us suspicious of any attempt to turn the clock back and forget the work that has been done in historical criticism.

I want no reader to gain the impression that I believe historical study to be illegitimate in theology. On the contrary, I am convinced that not only do we need history in its own right but that we cannot read the Bible without it. Moreover, evangelical scholars have hardly begun, in my view, to absorb the results of the historical study of scripture. When they do so the contribution that they may make, not only to the evangelical heritage but to the whole Church of Christ, is incalculable.

However, I am convinced that historical study does have limits in theology. These need to be recognized and identified with care, and we may then be able to rid ourselves of the obsession with historical reason that characterizes contemporary theology. We have become so committed to the importance of historical study in theology that we have lost sight of the crucial significance of philosophical theology for the welfare of theology as a whole.

No doubt there are many reasons why philosophical theology has had a poor innings in many theological circles of late. Logical Positivists within philosophy on one side, and Barthians and speculative metaphysicians within theology on the other, have forged a strange coalition to inhibit much interest in the philosophical side of classical Christian theism. There are welcome signs of renewal, at least in Britain.[6] But there is a long way to go. I hope this book will indirectly help us to see how important philosophy is to theology. In due time we can then make the necessary changes that this entails in the training of future theologians.

This concern explains why my primary focus is on the impact of history rather than science on theology. There is little to suggest that theologians have sold their intellectual souls to scientists in return for the benefits of a scientific mode of reasoning. There is however ample evidence to convince me that the only form of reasoning in which most theologians are at home is historical reasoning. For example, ask the average theologian how to evaluate the Gospels historically, and he will detain you for hours, keeping you spellbound by explaining the wonderful methods that New Testament historians have developed. Ask him, however, to explain why he accepts the theological content of the Gospel, and he will either shake his head in incomprehension or lapse into an uncritical fideism or tell you to what church he belongs. We are trained too exclusively in historical reason, and this is one reason why I want to focus on the limits of historical reason. However, as we shall see, there is a clear logical connection between scientific and historical modes of reasoning, so it would be remiss to omit this element entirely. By including it I hope to kill two proverbial birds with one stone. On the one hand I hope to undercut the claim that by omitting science, I would not have dealt fully with the challenge presented by historical study. On the other hand I hope to overturn the view that commitment to divine revelation as traditionally understood is incompatible with the canons of scientific judgement as we know them today.

This book divides naturally into two parts; in the first four chapters I shall outline and define what I deem to be a traditional understanding of divine revelation. In this account commitment to divine intervention of a substantial sort is unavoidable. I shall argue that God is made known by special acts of revelation in the world without which any comprehensive account of His will and purpose would be weak and inadequate. Let it be noted at this point that I do not intend to argue in any strong sense that God has so acted in order to reveal himself. I shall indicate why I think this is in fact true, but it is not my primary concern. That is to argue for the retention of special revelation on the grounds that without it the tradition as a whole lacks coherence. This of course does constitute a reason for believing in it, but only for committed Christians—however for the purposes of this work I have assumed commitment to Christianity, and thus identification with its traditions, as to do otherwise would increase its scope far too widely.

In chapters five to eight I shall argue that it is possible to believe in special divine revelation without any sacrifice of critical judgement in either history or science. I shall analyse and criticize the arguments of those who think it does involve a sacrifice of the intellect to believe in special divine revelation. In the course of this the proper nature and limits of historical enquiry will be revealed, and a vision of a complex relationship between theology and history should emerge; the two interact in a way that will surprise us, and yet I hope the interaction will be seen to be obvious, given what has gone before in chapters one to four.

1
DIVINE REVELATION AND DIVINE SPEAKING

SUSTAINED and systematic interest in the nature of revelation is a modern development in Christian theology, which arose out of the Enlightenment critique of classical Christian theism. In that critique interest centred less on the nature of revelation than on its necessity. The deists, who raised the key questions in this field, argued that God could be sufficiently known in creation. There was no need, in their view, for any special revelation, for creation in itself could reveal all that the religious believer could desire. If special revelation was to be allowed within this scheme, its role was secondary; at best it simply republished in story form the truths that were essentially made available in creation.

Not surprisingly the traditional definitions of special revelation reflect this background. Invariably they focus on the informative content of special revelation; revelation is generally defined as the unveiling of those truths which are unavailable to reason in creation as a whole. Uniformly this is brought about on God's side by means of divine speech. *The Catholic Encyclopedia* expresses this succinctly in its definition of revelation: 'Revelation may be defined as the communication of some truth by God to a rational creature through means which are beyond the ordinary course of nature.'[1] This concept of revelation was at one time so influential that it has left its mark on standard dictionary definitions. Thus the opening section of the *Oxford English Dictionary* entry perceives revelation as 'the disclosure or communication of knowledge to man by a divine or supernatural agency'. The influence of this concept is also reflected in its general acceptance by both Protestant and Roman Catholic orthodoxy in the nineteenth century and in the fact that it is now known in theological literature generally as the 'propositional' theory of revelation.

Most recent theology has reacted vehemently against this idea of revelation. Indeed the reaction has been so successful in winning adherents that outside fundamentalism it is difficult to find anyone who espouses it. The story of this change is by now well known, and there is no need to rehearse the details.[2] Suffice it to say that the emphasis in recent years has fallen on the mighty acts of God in history—it is through His acts that God makes Himself known to mankind. To be sure if this revelation of God is to be communicated, it will have to be put into sentences which express propositions, but this is not denied by those who are unhappy with the claim that revelation is propositional. Thus Ninian Smart writes:

What they mean is that revelation is God's self-disclosure in human experience and in history, as recorded by the Bible. It is God revealing Himself in the history of the Jews, in the experience of the prophets, and in the person of Christ. The historical events, the religious experiences, Jesus—these are not statements, they are what the statements of the Bible are about. They are not propositions: they are what Biblical propositions refer to.[3]

Despite the demise of neo-orthodoxy this alternative analysis of revelation has not yet collapsed. Two sorts of problem have brought it under considerable strain. On the one side there has been extensive historical work that has challenged the view that the Bible as a whole speaks only of mighty acts of God in history. On the other side there has been some important philosophical work that has either rebutted some of the charges made against the propositional view or challenged the coherence of any proposal that focuses on the mighty acts of God as the exclusive bearer of divine revelation.

Despite this I cannot detect any great enthusiasm for a return to the traditional propositional theory. The exception to this is of course to be found in the third volume of C. F. H. Henry's work on systematic theology, *God, Revelation and Authority*,[4] which represents the crystallization of recent evangelical theology as developed in America. But here of course it would be inappropriate to speak of a return to a propositional theory, for Henry belongs to a tradition that never abandoned it in the first place.

My own feelings about the propositional theory are mixed. My basic unease derives from the fact that fundamentalists have skilfully used the emphasis on propositional revelation to underscore an account of inspiration that is both confused and dangerous. It is confused because it has constantly treated divine inspiration as a species of divine speaking; it is dangerous because it constantly uses an inferred doctrine of inerrancy to call a halt to proper study of the Bible.[5] Moreover, I am not convinced that the term 'propositional' has served us well as a focus for discussion. With the use of the term it is very easy to be distracted into side issues, especially if one is aware of the philosophical debate about propositions. The real issue lies elsewhere, and the theological literature in the field bears this out. Thus those who argue about propositional revelation rarely touch on whether propositions are to be taken as sentences, states of affairs, or timeless nonlinguistic entities. Despite this, I am very sympathetic to a doctrine of propositional revelation for the simple reason that I think it captures an essential ingredient of any comprehensive account of divine revelation. That ingredient, I have argued elsewhere, is the view that God has spoken to particular individuals to reveal His intentions and purposes.[6] In what follows I intend to articulate the underlying assumptions which generate this conviction and to defend it from some objections that have recently been made against it. In so doing I hope that the reader will clearly understand that I have no desire to give even indirect support to many of the attitudes and convictions held by those who have kept alive an emphasis that I deem extremely important.

Our reflection on divine revelation must begin neither with the Bible, nor with religious experience, nor with any purported claim to divine revelation, but with those everyday rules that govern the use of the term in ordinary discourse. Other starting-points could be used, but as a matter of logic reference to the meaning of revelation in everyday discourse must come first, because it is in this context that we initially learn the rules governing the meaning of the word. Indeed it is because we already have some awareness of revelation in the human context that we can apply it outside that context and speak of divine revelation.

In everyday language the main location of discourse about revelation is in the arena of interpersonal relations. It is primarily people who reveal themselves, although by no means exclusively. For the theist it is this human context that is of crucial significance. God, after all, is defined as a trans-cendent person, analogous to human agents; hence when the theist speaks of divine revelation the activity of human reveal-ing serves as the model for conceiving that revelation.

We sense immediately a certain awkwardness. It is odd to speak of a person simply revealing, in the same way as we speak of a person writing or walking or whistling. The latter verbs stand on their own, complete, so to speak. The verb 'reveal' does not; it is invariably used reflexively: 'x reveals himself or herself'. Even then it is odd to use it in isolation or on its own; thus used it is too vague and obscure to be informative. Why is this? It is because the concept of reve-lation is polymorphous. Revealing is an activity that is accom-plished in, with, and through other acts and activities. Without a context in which these acts are specified, the word is mean-ingless. One reveals oneself by speaking, by writing, by per-forming this or that act. Another way to explain this is to say that revelation is an 'achievement verb'. As Ryle expresses it: 'in applying an achievement verb we are asserting that some state of affairs obtains over and above that which consists in the performance, if any, of the subservient task activity'.[7] Thus when we say that Dr Smith cured patient Jones, Jones must not only be treated in various ways by Dr Smith but he must also be well again as a result of the activity of Dr Smith. Likewise when we say that Smith revealed himself in what he said at any given time, he must not only have said something, but he must also have unveiled or made known something that was previously unknown to those who were listening. It is not enough that Smith has performed certain tasks; he must through those tasks have achieved the goal of making himself known.

To be sure, sometimes we borrow achievement verbs to signify the corresponding task performances, especially where the hope of success is good. But this does not undermine the difference in logic that separates achievement verbs from task verbs. And that difference is to be located in the particular achievement or success that is over and above the performance through which it is gained. For example, winning a race is done through running the race and coming in first. The task in both cases is from a physically point of view identical: it involves the same physical exertions and activity. The difference is to be located in the achievement brought about by the same physical activity: in winning the person must come in first. Likewise with revelation, where revealing oneself is identical with certain tasks such as speaking, and yet is different. To say that Smith revealed himself in what he said is to say that he made something known about himself through what he said, i.e. he achieved revelation through a subordinate activity.

This point is so important that it deserves to be fleshed out by another example. Consider the verb 'to educate'. When we say that A is educating B, we do not thereby imply any specific activities, yet education cannot take place independently of specific activity. A educates B by talking to B, marking B's essays, supervising B's travel plans to a foreign country, scolding B for his slovenly work-habits, etc. Education is not something that is done after these activities are complete; it is done through them. What makes these activities educational is that they also result in certain achievements—through these activities A passes on to B something that is worth while in such a way that B appreciates what is passed on and relates what is passed on to a wider cognitive perspective. The element of achievement makes education akin to reform. As R. S. Peters points out: 'Education relates to some sorts of processes in which a desirable state of mind develops. It would be as much of a logical contradiction to say that a person has been educated and yet the change was in no way desirable as it would be to say that he had been reformed and yet had made no change for the better.'[8] The parallel with the concept of revelation is obvious. Agents reveal themselves through various actions and activities, and these actions and activities are marked off by their bringing it about that something previously unknown is now known. Any analysis of revelation that ignores these facts is ignoring the fundamental logic of the concept. My strategy in all this is to focus on the common conditions that govern the use of the term 'revelation' in those everyday contexts where we first learn to use it.

Why is all this important? To begin with, this analysis provides a framework from within which to develop a comprehensive doctrine of revelation. Divine revelation must not be approached in independence from delineating the divine activity through which God reveals Himself. To pick out any one act or activity as the essence of revelation is to miss the total picture, yet this is what has happened in the history of the doctrine of revelation.[9] One generation focuses on divine creation as the bearer of revelation; another in reaction focuses on divine speaking to prophets and apostles; another focuses on Jesus Christ as the bearer of revelation; another highlights the supreme significance of the inner illumination of the Holy Spirit; yet another argues that revelation comes only at the end of history. It is futile to play these off against one another as if one was generally more important than the other, or as if offering a doctrine of revelation involved the acceptance of one and the rejection of the other. In the classical Christian tradition all have a place. What unites each element to the other is a narrative of God's action that stretches from the creation to the end. Particular acts or activity of God such as creation, speaking to the prophets, the incarnation, can be isolated for special attention as revealing this or that about God, but the relation that exists between revelation and the acts through which it takes place makes it inappropriate to argue that any of these is the essence of revelation.

This way of construing the underlying unity in the various emphases of the Church's reflection on revelation can be contrasted with other ways of providing a unified perspective. Especially noteworthy at this point is the suggestion of Gabriel Moran.[10] Drawing on the phenomenological tradition of modern European philosophy, Moran has suggested that revelation should be construed as a continuing process in which God encounters man at a pre-conceptual level. Revelation involves a pre-predicative comprehension of truth. This revelation is then bodied forth in concepts, words, and other objective expressions. These are very important, indeed they are essential for revelation to occur, but they presuppose a kind of pre-conceptual experience which cannot be described by drawing on conventional subject-object distinctions. It is this experience that is at the heart of revelation.

Moran's analysis of revelation, as he himself would admit, is by no means complete. However as it stands it is questionable whether it will really help to make sense of the great variety of ways in which divine revelation can surely take place. For example, Moran remains faithful to the classical commitments that stress revelation in creation, in the incarnation, and in the lives of the apostles. But it is not clear how reference to some kind of pre-conceptual experience illuminates the revelatory character of either creation or the incarnation. Besides, it is difficult to make sense of the experience to which he appeals. Surely to identify any experience we have to use words of some sort to describe it; experience does not occur 'raw': it always comes conceptually cooked in one way or another. Perhaps there is simply an unbridgeable gulf here between the analytic and phenomenological traditions in modern philosophy, but I can only confess that I find Moran's assumptions about experience unintelligible. I think he has isolated a traditional emphasis on the internal witness of the Holy Spirit as one element in the total set of divine activity that brings about revelation, and then proceeded to make this the essence or pre-condition of all revelation. Against this it is much simpler to recall that revelation by definition is a polymorphous concept, and then resist any attempt to make the task-verbs through which it is achieved the essence of the matter.

Besides providing a framework for viewing the various kinds of revelation holistically, this approach suggests a way to proceed in order to assess what is at stake if special revelation is abandoned by the Christian theist. It suggests that we must look in some detail at those acts of God which constitute special revelation. Thus we must ask what is lost from the content of Christian theism if we give up the belief that God spoke to the prophets and apostles, that He became incarnate in Jesus of Nazareth, or that He performed a miracle such as the resurrection. Clearly all these lie at the heart of special revelation as it has been traditionally formulated.

Turning to the place of divine speaking in revelation, what I find especially surprising is the key role it plays in the total process of revelation. This emerges when we reflect on the privileged position it has in human contexts where we speak of revelation. Thus it is obvious that people reveal an enormous amount about themselves by telling us their inner thoughts, their intentions, reasons, and purposes, their secret plans and aspirations. Just imagine what it would be like if everyone were struck dumb. Clearly it would be very difficult indeed to know what people were doing and to know their overall intentions and purposes from their actions. To be sure we would not be completely in the dark, for we could rely on people's body-language to determine what they were doing. But this avenue is limited, for any particular bodily movement can be seen as several different acts. Thus the raising of an arm can be construed as sending a signal, bidding at an auction, attempting to gain attention, registering a vote, practising a muscle exercise, volunteering for work, waving at a friend, etc. The bodily movement by itself is quite insufficient to determine what is going on. Usually we rely on the context to read what is taking place, but if this fails the easiest way to find out is to ask the person. If he tells us what is going on this generally settles the matter for us.

This is crucial in the case of God. God by definition does not have a body; there is nothing equivalent therefore to our bodily actions by means of which we can begin to gues at what He is doing or what He intends. In His case we are even more dependent on His speaking to us than we are in the case of human agents. Incorporeal agents who do not speak are like invisible men who are dumb. We are rightly very suspicious of those who profess to know what they are doing. This is not to say, however, that we are exclusively dependent on divine speaking. As we have seen, revelation can indeed take place through other actions. Thus classical Christian reflection has spoken, for example, of divine revelation in nature and in history. But this in no way detracts from the point that we are to a great degree dependent on divine speaking if we are to have any substantial account both of what God is doing in nature and in history and of His intentions and purposes in acting in creation and in history. This argument has recently been set forth by Basil Mitchell.

Although if I do not know you I can learn a certain amount about you by observing and responding to your behaviour, unless I am *very* familiar with the work you do and the way you live I am likely to find this somewhat ambiguous. And even if I have this kind of background knowledge and you behave always as someone of your sort might be expected to do, I can have no warrant for supposing that *this* bit of behaviour rather than *that* represents your distinctive character and intentions. If, however, you talk to me about yourself and tell me what you are trying to achieve, and if some of your behaviour is evidently directed to your avowed ends, then I can use the clues thus provided to interpret behaviour of yours which has not been explained to me. Similarly men can discover 'sermons in stones, books in the running brooks' if in some way other than by contemplation of nature they have been given an inkling of the character and purposes of the author of nature. This is one point which emerges clearly from Hume's Dialogues. If we had some *independent* knowledge of God the contemplation of nature is capable of reinforcing it. Of itself it remains ambiguous.[11]

That which is suggested by philosophical considerations about the logic of revelation is confirmed by the biblical traditions. Paul, for example, points out that the Church is 'built upon the foundation of the apostles and prophets'.[12] In fact Paul himself can be seen as a paradigm case of what it is to be addressed by God. He claims authority for his message not on the basis of his own insights or genius but on the basis of his own call to the apostolate and the communication of the divine will by direct revelation.[13] In this regard Paul sees himself and his ministry as similar to those of the prophets in the history of Israel. In both cases there is an awareness of a special disclosure of the divine will that is received as a message from God. I am suggesting that these elements in the tradition be taken with radical seriousness.

The modern reader naturally feels puzzled by this suggestion. What is it to take this element seriously? Do you mean, it will be asked, that we are to read these at face value? Are we really to believe that God actually spoke to Paul or to Jeremiah? And if we do, are we to construe this as involving audible voices, as is the case in human speaking? There are a number of issues here that must be separated and treated sensitively. Thus, for example, we must be reminded that in the case of the Old Testament prophets it is not always possible just to turn to the text and pick out this or that 'word from the Lord' and treat it automatically as a case of divine speaking. The quest for the historical Amos or Hosea is not that simple. There has clearly been a complex process both within and without the canon that must be approached with great care. There are fewer problems with Paul in that we do have firsthand sources to which to turn, but even then these are not intended primarily as biographical literature which would tell us all we might like to know about his encounter with God and the means God used to speak to him. In other words in no way do I want to foreclose the complex historical issues that confront us in the study of the text. The text cannot be read at face value, especially in the case of the Old Testament. There has been a complex development of interpretation, reinterpretation, editing, and collecting which must be taken seriously.

Despite this we cannot ignore the possibility that somewhere behind the present traditions God really did communicate to particular people to disclose His will. The material itself insists on this, as is clearly reflected in the case of Paul. How, then, is this divine activity to be construed? We have good grounds for a measure of agnosticism at this point. We can of course speculate in terms of visions, of voices of one sort or another, or even of some kind of non-verbal communication similar to telepathy. Certainly I see no reason to conclude that God must use any particular vehicle to communicate a message or word to people. If people can send messages without using voices, clearly God will have no trouble with this. Nevertheless we must acknowledge that it is extremely difficult to insist on any particular, detailed account of how God speaks to people. Any general statement is unlikely to cope with the various cases that one meets. Besides, we just do not have the necessary evidence to reach a decision in many cases. Whereof we must be silent, thereof we should not speak, but at the same time we cannot avoid positing some form of direct communication if we are to make sense of the data as a whole.

It is precisely this element that is resisted by those who feel that it involves an unnecessary stumbling-block for the modern mind. From this perspective the obvious move to make is to reinterpret talk about divine speaking as either a culturally conditioned or a dramatic way of expressing the results of intense spiritual reflection on history and experience. On this view, what we really have in the prophetic and apostolic tradition is the deposit of sensitized human insight about the activity of God in the world. Alongside this a companion argument is developed to undercut the epistemological claim that speaking has a privileged position when it comes to determining the intentions and purposes of an agent. Thus Maurice Wiles invites us to consider the analogy of a great artist who expresses himself in his work.

Suppose we have a number of art critics interpreting the profound but difficult work of an artist no longer alive. We may feel that one of them is an 'inspired' interpreter, who sees into the intention of the artist's work as none of the others do. We may feel thoroughly confident about this even though we cannot check up by asking the artist (who is no longer alive) and even though no hitherto unknown correspondence turns up to confirm his interpretation. We are confident that he is right because when we look at the work under his guidance, we come to see what he has indicated (which we had not seen before) as something really there in the work.[14]

This is an ingenious suggestion, worthy of sustained reflection. Despite its attractiveness, however, I am not convinced by this proposal. First, it ignores the extent to which one's ability to interpret a great work of art depends on prior experience where proposed interpretations are at times matched with the artist's own avowals about his work. The matter is complex, but inductive considerations which involve appeal to the self-disclosure of the agents do surely play a part. Thus the analogy does not entirely undercut the role that direct communication has in those situations where we want to refer to the intentions of an agent.

Secondly, in the analogy proposed by Wiles there is no real correspondence to the content of the divine disclosure demanded by the theistic context. What the Christian minimally wants to say, for example, is that God has forgiven us our sins, that He has promised us eternal life, that He has acted to save us from spiritual bondage in the cross of Jesus Christ, etc. These are very specific claims about God. In contrast any claim about a great work of art will be very broad and is highly unlikely to have anything to do with the artist's intention, say, to forgive someone, make promises to someone, etc. To be sure, it will be possible to speak of the artist communicating a point or a vision or a mood; and we may well be convinced of this without any direct disclosure on the part of the artist. But much more is at stake when a prophet or apostle begins to spell out in rather precise terms what God is doing in history and in the personal life of that apostle or prophet.

Thirdly, the analogy also overlooks the fact that in a work of art we can at least point to it and weigh the evidence before us. We cannot come close to this in the religious situation. Here we want to speak of what God is doing in creation as a whole, in the history of Israel, in Jesus Christ, in the life of the community, in the life of apostles and prophets, and in our own lives. If we are reduced to 'inspired' interpreting in the latter case, then the task seems to me to be so precarious that a proper response would be one of agnosticism rather than any positive religious faith.

It is much more coherent to take seriously the element of direct divine disclosure as an integral part of the total theological proposal, especially when the tradition itself, despite its complexity, does insist on distinguishing at times between human insight and a word from God. The ancient world was well aware of the modern alternative, at least in the sense that the categories for expressing that option were clearly available. This is true of both the ancient Hebraic and Greek cultures.[15] Of course, whichever proposal one embraces there will be problems. What is at issue in the end is the balancing-out of the evidence as a whole. As I read it, it is simply impossible to replace the direct disclosure of God's will with surplus amounts of profound human insight. Divine revelation is not a pious way of doing justice to the genius of human discovery. It stands on its own as a marvellous expression of divine grace, mercy, and love. So God's word to the prophets and apostles is not just part of that wider activity of God that is the salvation of our souls. It is also the salvation of our theology and philosophy.

It is relevant to note how difficult it is for theologians to avoid falling back into a position that makes reference to divine speaking. This is seen especially in the work of those who have argued in recent times that the biblical traditions spoke only of revelation in history. I detect in their writings a sliding scale that begins at the point where nothing more is necessary for revelation than history. Consider, in this regard, Porteous as he speaks eloquently of the work of von Rad: 'Von Rad makes one feel that Hebrew history throughout the formative period right up to the rise of the Christianity was self-interpreting, the literature coming into existence as a witness to the events through which God was dealing with His people.'[16] At the bottom of the scale all we need is history. The history somehow is self-interpreting.

Moving up the scale, we find that history alone is not enough. A certain kind of religious experience or faith is also needed if it is to be read aright as involving divine activity. Hick can furnish a good example: 'the prophets were not formulating a philosophy of history in the sense of a hypothesis applied retrospectively to the facts; instead they were reporting their actual experience of the events as they happened'.[17] The problem with this is that it is no advance on history alone as a medium of revelation. The locus may have changed from history to experience, but we are not told how experience reveals the purposes of a transcendent divine agent any more than the events of history do.

Moving further up the scale, we are told that it is a special class of men, prophets and apostles, who license the interpretation of history as involving divine revelation. Alan Richardson will serve as a witness here: 'God has revealed himself in his mighty acts in history, as they have been interpreted by the prophets of the Old Testament and Apostles of the New Testament.' Surprisingly, however, we are not told why these men are in this privileged position. If God spoke to them and told them things not available to others, then at least we would have the beginnings of an answer. But precisely this is ruled out by Richardson. According to him, his view has 'the great advantage of not involving the notion of revelation as consisting in revealed propositions or revealed truths'. It is small wonder that there is a lapse back into the position of Porteous. Thus special revelation, for Richardson, comes 'through the prophetic history of Israel and its culmination in Christ'. The word of God may be through the prophets but it is really '*in* the events of the biblical history'.[18]

The next move up the scale reaches to the very threshold of the propositional view. Thus Wright says: 'As revelation the Biblical event was a happening in the time deemed of special importance because God's word was present within it, interpreting its meaning. The historical happening and its interpretation, the deed and the word of God as its commentary, these constitute the Biblical event.'[19] Unfortunately in this case it is not possible to determine whether Wright really does intend to speak of a genuine word from God. Thus in the paragraph from which this quotation is drawn he seems to equate the word of God with 'the body of "inferences" or assumptions that can be deduced from the events'. If this is really his intention then, of course, his position is best placed at the bottom of the scale with that of Porteous.

Undoubtedly it is Baillie who comes closest to acknowledging that divine speaking has an important place in the Bible: 'According to the Bible, what is revealed to us is not a body of information concerning various things of which we might otherwise be ignorant. If it is information at all, it is information concerning the nature and mind and purpose of God—that and nothing else. Yet in the last resort it is not information about God that is revealed, but very God himself.'[20] Granted, the concession to divine speaking is made rather grudgingly, and once made it is immediately withdrawn again, but it has nevertheless been made, and in so doing Baillie has borne unwilling testimony to its significance.

My argument, then, is that we should take the traditional emphasis on divine speaking with the utmost seriousness. It is only because God has spoken His word that we can have any assurance about what He has done in creation and history and about His intentions and purposes in acting in creation and history. Without His word, the alternative is not just a tentative, carefully qualified guessing at what God is doing, but a radical agnosticism. Against the backcloth of recent theological slogans about divine revelation, this constitutes a claim of substantial boldness. It may seem less unacceptable if we know why theologians rejected divine speaking so vehemently. Before commenting on this, two other remarks are in order.

First, it is to be noted that a theology without the concept of divine speaking has of necessity a God who cannot forgive, command, or make promises. The reason for this is that forgiving, commanding, and promising are performative utterances. To forgive someone their sins is to say sincerely to them, 'I forgive you your sins.' To command y to do x is to say to y, 'I command you to do x', or just to say to y, 'Do x.' To make promises is to say sincerely, 'I promise ...' To preclude God from speaking not only has serious implications concerning what can be known of God's actions, but also implies fundamental restrictions elsewhere in one's theism.[21]

Secondly, it is to be noted that prima facie there is nothing logically incoherent in the idea of divine speaking, as there is, for example, in the idea of God kicking a football or God washing His socks. These ideas are incoherent because the idea of kicking a football and the idea of washing one's socks are both logically connected to having feet. An agent who does not have a body could not therefore wash his socks. Not surprisingly, some philosophers[22] are tempted to suggest in addition to this that God cannot speak, for the concept of speaking is logically connected to agents using their vocal cords. In this, however, they are mistaken, for it is logically possible to conceive of someone communicating information without the use of vocal cords, and this is enshrined in dictionary definitions of telepathy. Thus the *Oxford English Dictionary* defines telepathy as: 'The communication of impressions of any kind from one mind to another, independently of the recognized channels of sense.' Much divine speaking could be construed as analogous to this.

In concluding this chapter it is appropriate to say something about why divine speaking was rejected so vehemently. A full answer would require a detailed historical analysis of the kind that cannot be pursued here. Here it is sufficient to point out that divine speaking was identified with a theory of propositional revelation that was extremely unfortunate in its associations, particularly those with what might be loosely termed fundamentalism. In the hands of the fundamentalist the Bible and propositional revelation enjoy a relation of strict identity. Thus one recent fundamentalist defines propositional revelation as simply 'the conceptual truth claim extractable from Holy Scripture'.[23] The association with fundamentalism is in itself unfortunate enough: it conjures up the image of a flat Bible dictated by a literalist God who gives inside information on the workings of nature and the details of history. It conjures up debates which descend to hair-splitting on the differences between, for example, the inerrancy, infallibility, immutability, and indefectability of scripture. It conjures up the image of the theologian as a kind of cake-mixer selecting ingredients from one end of the Bible to another in order to prove what was often either obvious or ridiculous or question-begging.

Such associations are greatly compounded by a strict iden-tification of propositional revelation and the Bible, because such an identification rules out the possibility of any genuine historical criticism. If God speaks every word of scripture then it is obvious that, God being who He is, He does not get things wrong.[24] The role assigned to historical criticism can therefore only be minimal. At a maximum its task is only to tell you what its authors, and thereby God, intended to say to the world. Any critical role, any radical criticism of its his-torical content, is ruled out *ab initio*. But if one thing is clear about those who insisted on a non-propositional conception of revelation, it is that they were particularly intent on defend-ing the indispensability of historical criticism. In this they are surely correct. The restrictions imposed by fundamentalism are quite intolerable.

That such restrictions continue to be made by those who advocate propositional revelation,[25] or that arguments in support of propositional revelation continue to be used to keep alive fundamentalist orthodoxy,[26] should not obscure the fact that some reliance on divine speech-acts is an indis-pensable feature of a theology that makes substantial claims about the purposes of God. Were the concept of divine speak-ing to be abandoned, the Christian religion would be under-going drastic reformulation. Those who claim to know what God is doing in creation, in history, or in a world to come, and yet do this without at some point relying on their own or someone else's claim to have had direct access to the mind of God as He has revealed it, are in the dark. Incorporeal agents who do not speak are like invisible men who are dumb. We rightly are very suspicious of those who try to tell us what they are doing. We should be equally suspicious when told that such agents forgive us our sins, command us to love our neighbour, or promise us eternal life in a world to come.

To express the matter thus is to say that theologians who make claims about God's intentions or purposes without having within their theistic commitments a concept of direct divine speaking are without warrants for such claims. In so far as they continue to make such claims, they are trading on the resources of a theological tradition which they have rejected.[27] This could also be expressed as a proposal about meaning. To claim that God reveals Himself to man but to reject the He reveals Himself by speaking to man is to so whittle away the analogy on which the concept of divine revelation is built that it must be seriously asked whether the concept of divine revelation has enough content to license its continued use. Revelation in the fully personal sense characteristic of personal agents has been abandoned.

2

DIVINE REVELATION AND MIRACLES

IN the previous chapter I focused on the overall structure of a contemporary doctrine of special revelation, and I argued that direct divine speaking to particular people was an indispensable step in the total process of revelation. If God does not speak, then it is not clear how we can know in any substantial way His intentions and purposes. This, in turn, is the warrant for taking very seriously the traditional emphasis on divine speaking and the biblical stress on the divine word to prophet and apostle. In this chapter I shall explore the role of miracle in revelation. How significant is it? What is at stake for the theist if he has to abandon this element of the tradition?

First, of course, one must be clear about what is meant by the miraculous, and I plan to clarify this by outlining an account of miracle that invests a high degree of significance in it. By examining this account I hope to offer some insight into the role that miracle has in a comprehensive analysis of special revelation.

It might naturally be objected that to distinguish the idea of God performing a miracle from the other acts of God under review is unnecessary or redundant. Are not divine speaking and divine incarnation themselves instances of miracles? Is it not sufficient therefore to rest content with discussing these as an adequate examination of miracle? This objection does indeed have force, but only if one is appealing to a rather broad concept of miracle. Such a concept is to be found both in ordinary discourse and in the writings of theologians, when the miraculous is identified as an event that the religious believer responds to in awe and wonder in that God is active in it. B. W. Anderson illustrates this idea of miracle concisely when he defines miracle as 'an unusual, marvellous event which testifies to God's active presence in the world'.[1] Such an event does not involve any disruption of the natural order, for what looks marvellous to the man of faith may be quite ordinary from another point of view.

The event which the faithful Israelite or Christian may regard as wonderful may, from another point of view, seem quite ordinary or may be regarded as an insignificant coincidence. Thus the miracle at the Red Sea may be attributed to a strong wind which drove back the shallow waters of the sea of Reeds, the manna and the quail are nothing more than phenomena familiar in the S wilderness of Palestine, or the crossing of the Jordan was facilitated by seismic activity which caused the waters to be dammed up temporarily ... But within the Biblical circle of faith the question is not whether the miracle happened according to a particular description but whether God was in the event, thus making it wonderful.[2]

Anderson sums up this concept of miracle: 'In a general sense, everything is miraculous to the man of faith insofar as it is touched by the hand of God ... But in certain situations God's action coincides with a critical moment in the life of a person or people, thus making it possible to speak of specific miracles.'[3] If this is the idea of miracle in mind when it is said that divine speaking and divine incarnation are miraculous, then it is true that miracle has already been covered. However, there are good reasons for challenging this view of miracle.

To begin with, this concept is vague and incomplete in so far as it is not clear what is meant by such phrases as 'testifying to God's active presence' or 'touched by the hand of God'. Such phrases might be given content by making them synonymous with the awe-inspiring, the marvellous, and the wonderful. But this is either inappropriate or still incomplete. It is inappropriate in that there are many events which evoke awe and wonder in people, as did Hitler in many of his followers, without testifying in any obvious sense to God's active presence. Evoking of awe and wonder can at best be a necessary but not a sufficient condition of being miraculous. To supply a further condition, appeal might be made to the role of faith in the response of awe and wonder. Thus only those events that evoke awe and wonder in the religious believer are miraculous. But this is either circular or probably false. It is circular in so far as the man of faith is identified precisely by his response of awe to God's active presence. Those who do not respond thus are characterized as lacking faith. If this is so then no light has been thrown on the phrase 'God's active presence'. Alternatively, the man of faith may be identified not in this way but by virtue of his verbally professing faith or belonging to certain public institutions such as the Church. But then it is probably false to say that what he responds to with awe and wonder testifies to God's active presence in the world. Religious believers thus identified have responded with awe and wonder to a win on the pools or to the rise of Hitler, but it is odd to claim that such events are either touched by the hand of God or testify to his presence.

Secondly, it is useful for the sake of clarity, if for no other reason, to draw a distinction between the two different types of wonderful events by means of a narrower concept of miracle than that provided by Anderson. Thus it is possible to distinguish between a mere marvel and a miracle in the following examples. It would be marvellous but not miraculous if a lion was to be seen in an Oxford quad and if the government were to solve our economic problems overnight. But it would be both marvellous and miraculous if a lion were to come through the keyhole of an Oxford college's door or if the government, merely by decree, were to make all sick people healthy. The distinction between these two classes of events is surely captured by noting that miracles violate laws of nature while marvels do not. Thus there is some merit in retaining this older but less popular definition of miracle, in that it preserves a distinction which is reasonably clear.[4]

Thirdly, and more importantly, it is helpful to draw on this less broad idea of miracle in the context of this discussion because it is clear that some of the acts traditionally attributed to God in the doctrine of special revelation were, if they occurred, violations of laws of nature. An example would be the resurrection of Jesus from the dead. Classically this has been understood as the return to a form of embodied existence on the part of a person who had been dead for three days. To treat this merely as a marvel may be an apologetic device which masks the extraordinary character of such an event and thus also masks problems that might be associated with justifying its occurrence.

If we rely on this view of miracle, it is clear that neither divine speaking nor divine incarnation need be construed as miraculous. It is not necessary to say that either of these acts of God implies the violation of any laws of nature. In other words, God could speak to someone and could become incarnate in the world without thereby having to disrupt the presently operating laws. Perhaps because of this it has been plausible to speak of such acts of God as being invisible rather than visible miracles.[5] But one must seriously ask whether it makes sense to speak of an invisible event which violates a law of nature, for must not events be necessarily of a public and visible character if they are to be identified as violations of natural law?[6] In any case, it is proper to challenge those who insist on treating divine speaking and divine incarnation as miraculous by asking them to specify what laws must, as a matter of logic, be violated therein. Until this challenge has been met, it is legitimate to examine the divine act of performing a miracle independently of divine speaking and divine incarnation.

The account of miracle to be expounded and scrutinized here is related to the claim that the instances of divine revelation instantiated in the acts of divine speaking and divine incarnation are not visibly identifiable in the world. Such acts are hidden and require some form of 'proof' or authentication if they are to be believed as having occurred. Miracles are said to offer support for such claims. Miracles, that is, are the signs whereby the credentials of an agent of God are to be secured. To abandon miracle would thereby entail the loss of significant warrants for special revelation, and as such would constitute a loss of major proportions.

This view of miracle was once commonly accepted in theology. Two of its most distinguished supporters were John Locke[7] and J. B. Mozley.[8] They differ somewhat in detail, but it is possible to derive from them an account of the role of miracles suitable for present purposes. This account accepts that what God has revealed of Himself in nature is severely limited. Nature reveals the wisdom and power of God, but beyond that it is mute.[9] If more is to be known of God then God must reveal Himself, and such revelation has been given to mankind through the prophets and through Christ. That God has thus revealed Himself is indicated by their being accompanied by miracles. Just why miracles prove that revelation has occurred is not altogether clear, but the central idea is that miracles manifest power that is divine: 'what shall be a sufficient inducement to take any extraordinary operation to be a miracle, i.e. wrought by God himself for the attestation of a revelation from him? And to this I answer, the carrying with it the marks of a greater power than appears in opposition to it.'[10] Locke considers superior power to be an easy as well as sure guide to divine revelation. Thus, concerning Jesus, he writes:

The number, variety and greatness of the miracles, wrought for the confirmation of the doctrine delivered by Jesus Christ, carry with them such strong marks of an extraordinary divine power, that the truth of his mission will stand firm and unquestionable, till any one rising up in opposition to him shall do greater miracles than he and his apostles did. For any thing less will not be of weight to turn the scales in the opinion of any one, whether of an inferior or more exalted understanding. This is one of those palpable truths and trials, of which all mankind are judges and there needs no assistance of learning, no deep thought to come to a certainty in it. Such care has God taken that no pretended revelation should stand in competition with what is truly divine, that we need but open our eyes to see and be sure which came from him.[11]

Focusing on this emphasis on power, we can see that the logic of this view of the role of miracle might be expressed summarily as follows. First, we can be reasonably assured of the natural powers that nature possesses. Secondly, events that go beyond the natural powers of nature, i.e. miracles, are acts of God because they reveal a power behind them that is divine. Thirdly, if a prophet or messiah tells us they have a revelation from God, we can discover the divine origin of their message by discovering that they are accompanied by miracles.

As it stands this account of miracle is subject to several significant qualifications.[12] To begin with, it presupposes belief in God and is not meant to establish belief in God, for both Locke and Mozley presuppose that classical natural theology is possible.[13] Furthermore, certain limits are set to the content of any putative revelation. For Locke, revelation could not involve any new simple ideas which had not been derived from sensation or reflection; nor could it contain anything that was contrary to our clear intuitive knowledge; nor could it contain anything trivial. For Mozley, miracles could not oblige us to accept any doctrine which was contrary to our moral nature or to a fundamental principle of religion.[14] Moreover, there is no desire to rule out the use of other considerations in the testing of claims to revelation. Locke allows appeal to the indirect and direct avowals of Jesus in his teaching. However, he is generally very suspicious of such avowals in his remarks on 'enthusiasm'. Mozley allows the intrinsic nature of the revelation and its results in the Church to carry weight, but such evidence is only indirect and is, in any case, dependent on the argument from miracle.[15] Nor does the use of miracle as a test rule out the possibility of doubt in certain cases.[16]

Recent discussion of the relation between miracle and revelation has found this account so unsatisfactory that it is rare to find it examined in any detail. It would be no exaggeration to say that it is not even taken seriously. The assessment of John Dillenberger is not untypical. He writes: 'The defence of Christianity through miracle and prophecy in the 17/18th century sense is an unfortunate chapter in the history of Protestant theology. It was already a mistake to discuss theological questions as if they were on the same level as the knowledge of nature. It was but a short and fatal step from understanding the messianic claims in categories appropriate to nature to rejecting them because the knowledge of nature made them appear incredible. On the old path, no new directions were possible.'[17] Two relatively recent objections against it are worthy of consideration. It has been objected that the very thought of asking for a justification of a claim to possess a revelation is a betrayal of faith. Thus Reinhold Niebuhr writes: 'Christ cannot be known as the revelation of God except by faith and repentance; but a faith not quite sure of itself always hopes to express its scepticism by establishing the revelatory depth of a fact through its marvellous character. This type of miracle is in opposition to true faith.'[18] Niebuhr is making three separate claims: there is a positive thesis as to how Christ is to be known as the revealer of God—it is 'by faith and repentance'. There is a judgement about the motivation for the claim that Christ is the revealer of God—it is sought by those who have 'a faith not quite sure of itself'. Finally, there is a judgement about the use of the conception of miracle resorted to—it is 'in opposition to truth faith'.

This last claim is perhaps outside the sphere of philosophical theology, in that it is not the task of philosophy to decide what counts as true faith within a particular religious tradition. Suffice it to say that it is difficult to castigate the piety of either Locke or Mozley, and that both were prepared to offer an analysis of faith that they considered religiously acceptable.[19] The other two claims, however, merit some comment.

Concerning the motivation behind the search for credentials of revelation, it is surely correct of Niebuhr to point out that some people have sought such credentials for the simple reason that they were unsure that those who purported to possess such revelation did actually possess revelation. However, it is obviously untrue that this motive constitutes the only possible motive for such a search. Thus it is conceivable that a person may believe that Christ reveals God, and be subjectively sure of this, but still seek a justification for this claim. And he may seek it for a variety of reasons, say, because he is a philosopher who does such things because of the intellectual pleasure to be gained; or because he is an evangelist trying to encourage other people to take seriously this claim to revelation (an end which may be realized in some quarters if he can offer a justification for his claim); or because he believes on epistemological grounds that it is legitimate to give reasons for his theological beliefs; or because he believes that failure to test claims to revelation may lead to the embracing of serious error.[20] To see all attempts to offer a justification for the claim that Jesus is revealer of God as motivated by a faith not sure of itself is a vast oversimplification of the issue.

The remaining claim of Niebuhr is also difficult to affirm. This can be seen by asking how Christ is established to be the revelation of God by faith and repentance. It is obvious on a moment's reflection that the experience of repentance does not certify or give ground for the claim that Christ reveals God. The appeal to faith is also a dubious one. Commonly faith can mean either trust, as in faith in God to keep His promise to forgive, or a system of religious doctrine, as in the Protestant faith, the Mormon faith, etc.[21] Neither of these lends support to the contention that Christ is known as a revealer of God. Trust in God does not do so because it would be odd to say that one knows that Christ reveals God because of one's trust in God. This might plausibly be emended to read that one knows that Christ reveals God because one trusts God when He says that Christ reveals Himself. We may now be approaching an answer, but only the beginnings of one in that credentials are now needed for identifying this further revelation of God, and thus we are off again in the search for credentials for revelation. To answer this in terms of trust is to set out on an infinite regress. To analyse the appeal to faith as an appeal to faith in the second sense identified is openly circular, in that the claim at issue is itself a doctrine of the Christian faith.

This may seem a rather wooden interpretation of the concept of faith. Over against this account some construe the appeal to faith as an appeal to the personal religious life of the believer, or perhaps his past religious experience, say in conversion, when God, by His Spirit, is said to give the believer an internal assurance that Christ reveals God.[22] Even if it is granted that this consideration is to be given some weight in an argument to establish that Christ reveals God, it is not at all established that this alone certifies as true the proposal that Christ reveals God. To put all the weight on this is surely to have weak foundations, if it constitutes foundations at all.[23] Moreover, it is surely appropriate to ask how one is to identify that act of God whereby He gives such internal assurance. In other words we still need further credentials that will enable us to identify this further act of personal revelation which shows that the purported revelation in Christ really is revelation.

Another significant objection to the foregoing account of the relation between miracle and revelation is offered by Tennant. According to him, this account is vitiated by the fact that what is to count as a violation of a law of nature is determined by the science of the day. Being culturally relative, the miracles of one generation cease to be miracles in another generation. To one generation the stigmata of St. Francis were miracles, to another generation the stigmata were the natural results of certain preceding natural conditions. What one generation saw as both marvellous and beyond nature, another would see as merely marvellous, for science has given a naturalistic explanation of their occurrence. If science can conceivably account for stigmata, it is bold to set limits to its capacity, for 'it is not absurd for the scientific imagination to entertain the possibility even of resuscitating life in an organised body from which life has been but recently parted'.[24] Although we have, in this account, a clear definition in thought of what a miracle would be, it would never be possible to identify a miracle in practice: 'so long as we are unable to say what can and what cannot be the outcome of Nature's unaided performance and original collocations, then though we thus get a means of defining what a miracle *would* be, we are brought no nearer to being able to affirm that *miracula*, as distinguished from *mirabilia*, have ever happened.'[25]

The consequences of this argument on the views of Locke and Mozley are very serious. It renders it impossible to identify in practice a revelation from God. As miracles cannot be identified in practice, the credentials of a genuine revelation cannot be identified in practice. But can Tennant's argument withstand scrutiny? There does seem to be much truth in what he says. Science does revise our conceptions of what is and is not possible in nature so that what one generation sees as a miracle another will take as a purely natural process. The point is colourfully expressed in an inverted way by Rowley: 'If one could have stepped into the medieval world with a gramophone or a radio set, he would have caused greater wonder than these marvels cause us. Had he associated them with religion they would have been classed as miracles, but had he not so associated them, he would have been found guilty of the black arts and would have been put to death.'[26]

It is not at all clear, however, that science undergoes the kind of wholesale, radical revision wherein all its laws are open to change. To be sure, logically, all its laws are open to revision in that the contrary of a law of nature is always imaginable. Laws of nature are expressed in contingent propositions about regularities in nature, therefore there is no logically demonstrable way of guaranteeing their truth. Moreover, there is no logical way of demonstrating that science will not one day deny even its most cherished and hitherto well-established laws. For what scientists state is

a natural law is also a purely contingent matter to be discovered by finding out what they do in fact state. So this too
may logically change. But this does not establish that we
cannot be reasonably sure that certain laws of nature do in
fact hold and that they will hold in the future.

To deny this is to deny that science can provide knowledge.
It is to call in question any realist interpretation of science.
That Tennant comes close to this is amply illustrated by the
stringent condition laid down before claims can be made
about what can and cannot go beyond the powers of nature.

Until we shall have arrived at something like omniscience as to Nature's
constitution and intrinsic capacities, we cannot affirm any marvel to be
beyond them.[27]

We have seen that a miracle, in order to possess the evidential value
which theology used to ascribe to it, must be caused by the immediate
activity of God. Such activity is compatible with science and its reign of
law, and is not antecedently unreasonable from the presuppositions of
theism; but that a given event, however marvellous, unquestionably is so
caused, can never be asserted so long as our scientific knowledge of Nature
is inexhaustive.[28]

The problem with this condition of omniscience is that it sets
impossibly high standards for science, and so long as such
conditions are adhered to, present claims to knowledge on
the part of science must be abandoned. This is surely a drastic
consequence for any theory and enough to cast doubt on its
efficacy.

What is wrong here is that Tennant sets an entirely unreasonable standard of knowledge which can be met, if at all,
only by pure mathematics. What should be said here is that
science can establish that a law is truly a law of nature if it is
established beyond reasonable doubt that such a law will not
be revised. Admittedly this is a rather delicate tool for establishing a law of nature, for the concept of reasonable doubt is
somewhat indeterminate, but surely examples can be furnished
that meet this requirement.[29] Thus it is truly a law of nature
that corpses which have been dead for three days do not come
to life, that water does not turn to wine, that the sun does not
stand still in the sky. To doubt these is logically possible but
not practically possible. Such laws are so well established, so
much part of the body of science, so much taken for granted

in our everyday life, that to refuse to give them the status of knowledge and certainty is to have impossibly high standards in our epistemology.[30]

A similar position to this has recently been advocated by Holland, who imagines the case of a horse that thrives even though it is given no food. Such an occurrence constitutes an instance of what he calls the 'conceptually impossible'.[31] Confronted with this actual phenomenon occurring before his own eyes, Holland is prepared to concede that the conceptually impossible has actually happened rather than scrap or revise his conception of a horse. He will not abandon his conception of a horse because it rests on the experience of generations; because all other horses in the world are continuing to behave as horses have always done; and because our conception of the needs and capacities of horses interlock with conceptions of the needs and capacities of other living things and with a conception of the difference between animate and inanimate behaviour quite generally. He conceded that any number of discoveries remain to be made by zoologists and plenty of scope exists for conceptual revision in biological theory. However, 'it is a confusion to think it follows from this that we are less than well enough acquainted with, and might have serious misconceptions about, what is and is not possible in the behaviour under familiar conditions of common objects with which we have a long history of practical dealings'.[32]

If we can establish certain laws beyond reasonable doubt, then it is clear that the objection raised by Tennant has failed. Events beyond the natural power of nature can be identified, and therefore, if the general logical strategy of Locke and Mozley holds, the case as they present it is not vitiated. But does that general strategy succeed? There are several merits to their enterprise. For one thing they recognize that revelation is necessary if substantial as opposed to extremely modest claims are to be made about God. As has been argued elsewhere,[33] they recognize that some things can only be known about God if God has revealed His will in a manner that is more specific than His revelation in creation. Moreover they are not misled by this claim into arguing that it is logically inappropriate to apply some sort of critical procedure to claims to possess divine revelation.

One can easily be misled at this point, for it is generally accepted, as it was by Locke, that divine revelation should stand in judgement over its recipients.[34] From this it is a smooth path to the claim that no one can stand in judgement on claims to revelation. This move simply fails to recognize the actual object under scrutiny. What is under scrutiny is not divine revelation but a human agent's claim to possess revelation. To examine the latter critically is not to set oneself up as a judge of God.[35]

Furthermore, the general propriety of testing claims to revelation is surely secured by the fact that there are many claims to revelation, not all of which agree, and which call for some kind of assessment.[36] It is because of this conflict that a call for credentials becomes appropriate. It might be useful, therefore, in weighing the strength of miracles to consider a human situation where the call for credentials is appropriate. It is wartime, and Smith, a spy working for Jones, has made contact with a colleague, Brown, in a situation where impostors and counter-spies proliferate. On contact Smith is challenged to show that the message he brings is really from the appropriate authority, Jones. In response he offers his credentials; he repeats a special formula, or he makes a special sign with his fingers. His credentials are accepted without argument by Brown; the message is accepted as coming from Jones.

This illustration helps illuminate the difficulties of the classical argument from miracle. The key problem in the classical account derives from the peculiar circumstances of God. This can be elaborated by noting certain features of the parallel agent in the human situation. Two features about Jones's position mark it off as radically different from God's. First, Jones, Brown, and Smith already belong to a network of interpersonal relationships wherein it is agreed that the performing of certain actions will count as the signs to establish identity and thus to certify the origin of such messages as are delivered. Secondly, it is usually possible to check up, independently of the visible signs, as to whether Smith has been authorized to act as an agent of Jones. Thus Jones can be asked directly about this, or it may be traceable in written documents.

Neither of these conditions can be satisfied in the case of the agents of divine revelation. The latter cannot be, because God is not an embodied agent who can be identified at will and requested to give independent corroboration for his agents. Indeed, if God were like this it is hard to see that there would be any need for agents such as prophets at all. Such agents are needed precisely because God's will is not accessible in this way. It may be that in the after-life such direct access to the mind of God will be available, but such is not the situation now, and it is now that we need the independent supporting evidence. In any case to accept such independent corroboration would be to grant that special revelation can be identified independently of miracle. Moreover, it is true that it is possible to speak of seeking God's will directly, as in prayer, and such seeking presupposes that access to God's will is possible here and now. But it is to be noted that such seeking is set within a theological framework wherein it is already agreed that prophets and Jesus are agents of God, and such a framework will help determine what is to count as the will of God.[37] So the second feature of the human situation cannot be matched in the theological situation. This is enough, on its own, to demolish the claim that miracles constitute infallible proof of revelation. When it is augmented by the fact that the first feature of the human situation is also lacking, the case against the view of Locke and Mozley is very strong.

That this is so is indicated by the fact that there is no agreement between God, His agents, and the recipients of His agents to the effect that when human agents are accompanied by miracles they are then certified as sent by God. In the human situation this is crucial. It is because Smith, Brown, and Jones have established certain conventions that their signs are genuine credentials. Without such conventions they could not thus operate. In the theological situation there are no such conventions, and the only way for this to have been remedied is for God to have told all mankind that His prophets are marked out as genuine by miracles. But the problem with this is that it must now admit to a genuine revelation of a very specific character that is not authenticated by miracle. This is to undermine the whole thrust of Locke and Mozley's view, for it is central to their position that revelation, to be genuine, must be accompanied by miracle.

It follows from this that abandoning miracles cannot involve the abandoning of fool-proof warrants for claims to possess divine revelation, because miracles cannot have this role in any case. It might still be asked, however, if miracles might constitute warrants of a weaker sort for claims to possess divine revelation. Such a revision of Locke and Mozley's account would be in keeping with their view that miracles can be corroborated by other considerations.[38] It would involve accepting that there is no neat, fool-proof test for a genuine revelation, but that the testing procedure must involve the application of several criteria. Such criteria could plausibly involve ascertaining the following: (1) the moral and spiritual character of the putative agent of God; (2) the effect for good that the experience of receiving revelation brings about, e.g. an increase in penitence, peace, humility, spiritual power, and authority; (3) the inner certainty and conviction disclosed by the prophet as to the origin of his message; (4) the inner consistency and overall coherence of the prophet's message; (5) the degree of continuity between what is agreed to be known already about God and the content of the prophet's message; (6) the capacity of the putative revelation to illuminate and deepen what is known of God from elsewhere; (7) the degree of harmony between the content of the message and the course of events that are its context.

If miracles are to operate as warrants, then they do so in virtue of satisfying the final criterion above. In this connection it is interesting that miracles have been said to accompany certain key phases of special revelation in the past. Thus they cluster around Moses, Elijah, and Jesus in the biblical traditions.[39] Miracles will only operate with a high degree of force, however, under rather restricted conditions. They will only thus operate for those who have first-hand experience of their occurrence, or for those who are relatively closely associated with such first-hand experience.

Thus can they operate because they exhibit a design or

purposiveness which will remain enigmatic or unexplained unless they are taken as direct acts of God.[40] In some circumstances, that is, such unparalleled events as miracles are of value in assessing a claim to revelation because they can be accounted for, given that the revelation is true. An analogy will illustrate the logic of this procedure.

Suppose Smith arrives home and finds that a large boulder has been placed in front of his door. He is not unnaturally extremely puzzled by this. Naturalistic explanations, say in terms of the activity of wind, are of no value in explaining the phenomenon. Reflecting further on the matter, he recalls a conversation with a friend in which it was reported that a mutual acquaintance, a champion weight-lifter called Adams, has said that he intended to play a prank on Smith. Smith had rejected this partly because he felt that Adams had not been around of late to reveal this to his friend. But now, however, he sees the whole episode in a different light. It dawns upon him that he should accept his friend's story about being spoken to by Adams, because placing a large boulder in front of his door was just the thing a champion weight-lifter could do, and, moreover, would do, given certain intentions and purposes.

What is important here is not just the logic of the argument but also the way in which the logic can easily be said to be circular. If challenged to give grounds for believing that Adams placed the heavy object in front of his door, Smith can legitimately reply, 'Well, it is supported by the claim that Adams had revealed his intentions to my friend.' On the other hand, if challenged to give grounds for believing that Adams has revealed his intentions to his friend, Smith can also legitimately reply, 'Well, it is backed by the fact that I found this heavy object in front of my door.' This certainly looks circular, but it would be wrong to look on the argument as viciously so. The considerations surely do legitimately lend support to each other, and what matters in the end is the overall coherence of the story, and its capacity to explain the events.[41]

It is surely appropriate to allow miracles to have a positive role in the assessment of claims to possess revelation because the appeal to miracle is analogous to the situation sketched above. The argument is essentially one that centres on the action of a personal agent, and its logic is therefore drawn from the logic of everyday discourse about agents rather than being in any sense scientific or drawn from the order of nature.[42] In essence the argument, that is, is analogous to arguments on the human level that attempt to relate happenings to the action of agents who have brought about these happenings in the fulfilment of certain intentions and purposes.[43] Because the arguments are almost always cumulative, and because the several strands in the evidence lend support and weight to one another, it is easy to castigate such arguments as either weak or circular. But this is an insensitive reading of the situation, for it is clear that we do rely on such arguments in our everyday life, and such circularity as they may possess is not necessarily vicious.

An equally insensitive reading of the argument would be to see it as asserting a strong connection between any extraordinary event in the world and the truth of a theological doctrine. Coleridge seems to have interpreted the classical account of the argument from miracle in this fashion. Thus he severely criticizes Lessing[44] for allowing the orthodox of his day to claim that there was any connection between miracles and revelation.

> He ought to have denied in the first instance and under all circumstances the possible consequences of a speculative conviction from a supposed miracle, having no connection with the doctrine asserted, ex. gr. a man cuts a grindstone in half with his thumb. I saw it with my own eyes. Therefore, there are three and only three self-subsisting Persons in the Unity of the Deity.[45]

This objection simply misreads what is at the heart of the classical view. Trivial events of the kind that Coleridge envisages were expressly rejected by Locke.[46] If the argument is restated in terms of events that exhibit design rather than in terms of events that exhibit mere strangeness or enormity, Coleridge's argument is also wide of the mark.

That miracles do sometimes exhibit purposiveness is acknowledged even in modern times. Thus Nineham concedes that there may be something in the view that 'many of the events described by the biblical writers are of such a remarkable character as almost to demand an interpretation as special divine interventions in history'.[47] That miracles would serve to help establish the truth of claims to revelation has also been acknowledged. Thus Penelhum accepts that 'if the gospel records are true, the events they record are indeed ... both probative and revelatory'.[48] And he further concedes that were there 'signs' today, their presence would rightly strip some people of excuses for disbelieving in certain theistic assertions.[49]

The crucial problem, however, is that few undisputed signs exist in the present. Therefore all that is really available is reports of signs from the past.[50] The implication of this is that miracles will not have the same degree of evidential value for those who have not themselves witnessed them. This follows not from Humean arguments[51] about the general difficulty in believing testimony about miracles, but merely from the fact that we find it much more difficult to doubt the testimony of our own sense than reports of others.

Although this is an important consideration, it should not be allowed to license the conclusion that past miracles can have no force at all in assessing claims to revelation.[52] To establish this, it would have to be shown that all reports of past events were untrustworthy. For if the report is a true report, then its being a report does not rob it of its confirmatory value. If a certain event, E, does confirm to some degree an assertion, A, then a true report of E will also confirm, although to a lesser degree, A. What matters, then is not the fact that there are reports but rather that there are false reports. It is this latter claim that has to be established, and the mere stating that something is a report does not establish that it is a false report. Indeed, any general argument about the untrustworthiness of reports should be regarded with the utmost suspicion for the simple reason that they undermine the possibility of any genuine historical study.

Just how much credence reports of miracles should be given is impossible to specify with any degree of precision in advance of detailed discussion related to specific claims about revelation. Suffice it here to say that they can have some weight in a complex cumulative argument that embraces the considerations already listed. For this reason it is also difficult to specify plainly and unreservedly the consequences of dropping miracle from the overall schema of Christian doctrine. Certainly it does not involve the immediate and drastic consequences implied and/or envisaged by Locke and Mozley. At most it would involve the abandoning of one credential for revelation. As credentials for revelation are by their nature multiple, the loss of one does not immediately entail the loss of revelation. However, to say that it did not involve any loss at all would be an exaggeration as gross as that to be found in Locke and Mozley. It should not surprise us, therefore, if there is among many Christians a stubborn insistence at some point on the retaining of miracle within their theological commitments. If miracle and revelation can legitimately be seen to lend support to one another, then they may well be justified in their resistance to change.

This can be briefly indicated here by reflecting on the manner in which claims about revelation in the life of Jesus might plausibly be defended.[53] Thus, in this instance it is tolerably clear that rejecting a miracle like the resurrection may have serious repercussions on the other warrants to which appeal is made.

That this is so can be ascertained by noting that the kind of considerations brought to bear on his claim to provide unique revelation as expressed by the concept of incarnation involve a high degree of faith in the trustworthiness of those who tell us about him. Without this it would be impossible to know very much about either them or him, and thus it would be impossible to apply any degree of scrutiny to a claim about divine revelation related to him. That the early disciples relied on the resurrection as a strong warrant for claims about his uniquely revelatory role may well have been the case.[54] That is, for them the resurrection was of crucial significance in their theistic convictions about Jesus. If this is so, and if there is a need to rely on them generally for information about Jesus, then abandoning the resurrection may have serious repercussions on one's views about the role of Jesus as revelation from God. This is so because it would be inconsistent to mistrust those whom one considered to be wrong in their views about Jesus on an issue tnat on their account was fundamental to their theistic interpretation of him, while at the same trusting them on most of what else they had to say about him. It is, perhaps, possible that a plausible rendering of this situation could be given, in that reasons might be given for trusting them generally while not trusting them on what is to them a crucial matter. Until such a plausible rendering is forthcoming, it is understandable if there is a certain stubborn adherence to the resurrection, even though prima facie such adherence might seem misplaced. Such tenacity exists because abandoning miracle would undermine in an indirect manner the credentials for revelation in Jesus. Those who believe that reasons must be given for ascribing to Jesus the role demanded by the concept of incarnation will continue to rely on the resurrection in so far as they accept the revised account of the role of miracle developed here from the views of Locke and Mozley.

3

DIVINE REVELATION
AND INCARNATION

In the last chapter I attempted to outline the possible results of removing miracle from the Christian tradition, and found that miracles could legitimately be used as part of a cumulative case for divine revelation.

This account of miracle, as well as the account of divine speaking developed earlier, is undoubtedly very much at variance with much contemporary theological thinking on these matters. To some it will undoubtedly seem to be an attempt to return to the theology of an era whose content simply cannot be reasserted or even revised for today. A judgement like this, however, must be treated with great caution. It would certainly be fair to say that the position adopted here involves the acceptance of beliefs that were more common among Christians, say, in the eighteenth century than in the twentieth. Nevertheless, the discontinuities with earlier eras should also be noted. It does not involve acceptance of any literalist fundamentalism, or any attempt to look upon miracles as being a kind of definitive proof of revelation. More importantly, it should be noted that the conclusions reached were accepted more because of philosophical considerations than because of any inherent desire to hold on to the traditional formulations of the past. Indeed the whole discussion is developed and expressed in a manner that would be almost unintelligible to one who was ignorant of the rise of recent analytical philosophy.

One way in which the latter is reflected is in the use of the idea of polymorphous concepts. This idea has thrown valuable light on the idea of revelation, and enabled a richer account of that notion to emerge than was current in earlier centuries. It allows, that is, the idea that God can reveal Himself other than by speaking. God can reveal Himself in His mighty acts in history, for He is not confined to speaking to this or that prophet. In some contexts this emphasis on revelation in deed rather than word is entirely salutary, for in some quarters there is an exaggerated concern with revelation in word which can obscure other aspects of revelation. Moreover, it is surely appropriate to view miracles as revelation in deed in contrast to revelation in word and therefore as being constitutive of revelation, rather than as independent 'proofs' of revelation. Such an interpretation of miracle would not be at all incompatible with the view of miracle accepted in the last chapter.

The tendency of late, however, has been to swing to the opposite extreme. Most, if not all, revelation has been confined to revelation in deed, without sufficient awareness of the potential emptiness of this doctrine when little is done to specify the deeds that reveal God, and without sufficient awareness of the importance of divine speaking in deciding what deeds God has done in history. As we have seen, deed and word go hand in hand in the human situation, and reports about one will be used to determine the truth of reports about the other.[1] In the case of God this can also apply, although it needs to be emphasized that in both the human and divine situations access to the speech-acts of the agent is of major significance in determining his intentions or purposes.

Classically the recipients of the speech-acts of God have been the prophets. They constitute paradigm cases of men who have been spoken to by God. But divine speaking has by no means been limited to these; in the biblical traditions it embraces figures as far apart as Abraham and Paul, and extends outside that period into the lives of ordinary believers in the present. As regards revelation in deed, there is little doubt as to what constitutes a paradigm instance of this form of revelation. It is the incarnation of God in Jesus. As the writer of Hebrews puts it: 'In many and various ways God spoke of old to our fathers by the prophets; but in these last days he has spoken to us by a Son, whom he appointed the heir of all things, through whom he also created the world.'[2] The contrast drawn here between the revelation through the prophets and revelation through Jesus has been central to Christianity. Jesus has been set apart as being unique in the tradition as a bearer of revelation, and classically this has involved an account of the work of Jesus that posits direct divine action of a unique kind. The term 'incarnation' has been central to the account of divine activity which has captured the mind and imagination of Christendom. In any attempt to determine the significance of divine intervention in Christianity, it would surely be a major lacuna were this act of God to pass unnoticed.

It should be recognized, to be sure, that focusing on the incarnation is no simple exercise, not least because the idea of incarnation has been shrouded in mystery despite the attention it has received in the classical creeds of the early Church and in theology generally. Moreover, it is difficult to determine how far it can be understood independently of its early formulations.[3] To make matters even worse, it is a matter of lasting controversy whether its coherence can ultimately be defended, for at best the idea of God becoming incarnate in Jesus is a paradox. No attempt will be made in this chapter to solve any of these problems: for the most part it will be taken for granted that the idea of incarnation can be understood without a detailed articulation of its expression in the thinking of the early Church, and that it can be defended as a paradox rather than rejected as a contradiction.

It is important to emphasize these well-known difficulties about the incarnation for at least two reasons. First, because there is a recurring temptation to approach the issues related to the idea of divine action in a very general way in the hope that what can be said about the concept of action can be applied to all acts of God. The unexamined assumption behind this type of approach is the conviction that philosophers will be able to provide a general theory of action that can be applied with due qualifications to divine action.[4] The main problem with this approach is that this assumption is a matter of widespread dispute. It is by no means clear that philosophers can give an account of action in the same way that they can give an account, say, of knowledge.[5] Moreover, even if such a general agreed account was available, care would have to be taken not to mask great differences between distinct acts of God. The incarnation illustrates this succinctly. Problems related to this act of God call for extended discussion in their own right.

Secondly, emphasis on the singular position of the incarnation draws attention afresh to the aim of the discussion here. The aim is not to establish the coherence of this notion, nor is it to express it in the kind of detail that would be demanded by one who saw its expression as being best exemplified at Chalcedon; rather the aim is to determine as clearly as possible what is at stake if it is abandoned. Taking for granted that it is a coherent notion, reasons for retaining it will be given, beginning with some general comments about the meaning of the term 'incarnation'.

The English word 'incarnate' functions either as an adjective or a verb. The verb literally means 'to render incarnate' or 'to embody in flesh'. (It also has a transferred or figurative sense but this need not detain us in this chapter.[6]) The verb can take one of two subjects, either deity or soul, although some, for example Söderblom, prefer to use the term 'transmigrate' when soul is the subject.[7] The concept of incarnation thus construed is generally only used in religious contexts, and its usage in this context goes back as far as ancient Egypt and is common in the religious traditions of both East and West.[8] This is reflected clearly in Söderblom's definition: 'The term 'incarnation' is applied to the act of a divine or supernatural being in assuming the form of a man or animal, and continuing to live in that form upon the earth.'[9] Its usage by Christians, however, has so informed our own linguistic heritage that the term is often reserved specifically for the relationship between God and Jesus. In this context it is rare to find it used as a verb. More common is its usage as an adjective, or even as a kind of title applied to Jesus, e.g. when it is said that Jesus is God Incarnate. The absence of the verbal form does not mean, however, that the concept the verb identifies is absent. Other verbs, similar if not the same in meaning, are available. Among the more common are the following locutions: 'become a man', 'take human flesh', 'come down from heaven', 'enter the world', 'visit the world'.

For the subject of these verbs, many are happy to use the term 'God' without undue perplexity. Among the more theologically informed it is more usual to find the term 'eternal Son of God' or 'Word of God' reserved for this role, in order to do justice to the doctrine of the Trinity. This is surely understandable in that the doctrine of the Trinity can be seen as an attempt to render the doctrine of the incarnation intelligible. For present purposes, however, such subtleties will be ignored, because distinguishing between God and Son of God does not affect the main point to be argued.

The verb 'incarnate', however, is not the only one used by Christians to identify the activity of God accomplished in Jesus. Two other families of verbs stand out: the first might be said to be soteriological, in that they focus on God's role in salvation. Examples of such verbs are 'save', 'redeem', 'reconcile', 'deliver', 'restore', 'liberate', 'love'. The second family might be said to be epistemic, in that they focus on God making himself known in Jesus. Examples of such verbs are 'reveal', 'disclose', 'manifest', 'speak', 'make himself known'. The point of obvious connection between all these verbs and 'incarnate' is that these acts are accomplished in, with, and through the incarnation. It is by becoming a man that God both shows His love for us and makes known His true character. It is through the incarnation that He redeems and reveals.

This connection is not, strictly speaking, logical. It does not imply any claim that redemption or revelation involves incarnation as a matter of logical necessity. Redemption and revelation do not entail incarnation in the way in which being a bachelor entails being unmarried. Nor does it imply that the concepts of redemption or revelation were unavailable prior to the incarnation. On the contrary, both were already available in the religious traditions in which the concept of incarnation was developed. Despite this, it would be inappropriate to say that the concept of incarnation did not alter one's understanding of redemption and revelation. They are related in an intimate way to the acts through which God is said to reveal Himself and redeem mankind. Perhaps this is generally true of polymorphous concepts such as redeem, reveal, educate, form, etc. Thus educating in the arts may be radically different from educating in the natural sciences, in that both may involve very different activities, and thus an understanding of one may not necessarily lead to an understanding of the other. In any case, one's specification of the acts in and through which revelation and redemption are believed to have taken place will be reflected in the account of revelation that is propounded. Because of this, revelation and incarnation, as well as redemption and incarnation, will be closely and intimately related.

This connection will now be explored in order to go beyond dictionary definitions of incarnation and explicate its significance in general terms. Thus the loss which would result from abandoning the incarnation will become clear, and our view of the concept of incarnation will be clarified by relation to readily available concepts. This is important, because the concept of incarnation is not drawn from everyday life. By contrast, verbs like 'redeem' and 'reveal' are used in everyday life; so drawing on such concepts to illuminate the concept of incarnation may well prove helpful because we already know what they mean. An extended human analogy will be deployed to throw light on the relation between revelation and incarnation in the Christian tradition.[1f] In so doing, it is hoped that the role of the incarnation in Christian theism can be made reasonably clear.

Consider the following situation. In a moment of generosity a king decides to hand over a part of his kingdom to a destitute people who are to benefit from its fruit and produce. There is one condition: the people are to live together in harmony and justice; if they do not then they will forfeit their share of the kingdom. As time goes by they forget their previous destitution and gradually begin to allow self-centredness and partisanship to erode harmony and justice. When word reaches the king he inquires into the matter, and after due deliberation sends agents with messages about the conditions of their agreement. When these are ignored he sends further agents who warn the people that their injustice will not be tolerated. Rather than fulfil such warnings immediately, the king decides to go among the people himself, to live among them as an ordinary man, sharing in their problems and pleading with them to obey the word of their king. Rather than pay attention to him, however, the people refuse to listen, and eventually kill him. As it happens it is only afterwards that they fully appreciate what has happened. Word is sent from the court that it was the king himself who was in their midst, who had come among them to plead his cause. When this dawns on them they are bitterly sorry for what has happened and forthwith resolve to lead a life of justice and love.

In discussing this situation it is appropriate to speak of revelation in at least three distinct areas. First, there is a general revelation in the kind of relationship that is set up between king and people. The king has established the people in a part of his kingdom to begin with, and the running of the kingdom is left to the people. Such a relationship reveals the generosity of the king as well as his desire to have subjects who are relatively autonomous. Secondly, there is the more special revelation reflected in the activity of the agents who act for the king and deliver his messages to the people. Such action deepens our conception of the generosity of the king as well as informing us of the specific intentions he has for the people. Thirdly, there is the extra-special revelation of the king when he comes among the people himself declaring the king's will and pleading for their allegiance to justice and love. Such action further deepens our conception of his love, in fact so much so that it leads to a radical transformation of the character of the people in the story.

Isolating these three areas or focuses of revelation makes it clear that the analogy presents a human situation where it is coherent to talk of one agent revealing himself to another. It also shows obvious parallels that are present in the Christian story of the incarnation. As an act of God the incarnation does not take place as an isolated event, but is surrounded by other acts that can legitimately be said to reveal God. Two sets of acts stand out clearly: God's revelation of Himself in creation, i.e. what has classically been called general revelation, and God's revelation to prophets, i.e. what has classically been called special revelation. These are paralleled in the story by the background relationship that exists between king and people and by the activity of the agents of the king. The incarnation in turn is matched in the story by the visit of the king to the people as an ordinary man. The story, thus, not only provides an analogy for the incarnation and thus for divine revelation in history; it also sets that revelation in a wider context, thus taking into view revelation in creation and revelation to prophets.

The obvious questions concerning the appropriateness of

the analogy must centre on the legitimacy of the visit of the king as a parallel to the incarnation. The issue can be approached by treating it as a question about identity. Are there any conditions that can be specified as relevant to identifying someone as God incarnate that are analogous to conditions that can be specified as relevant to identifying the man in the story as the king? Surely there are. Let it be noted, however, that in the human story there were no clear-cut criteria of identity for the activity of the king in visiting the people. Indeed during his visit he was not identified as king but was treated as just another agent and eventually killed. It was only after the event that his true identity was recognized, and then only when word had come from the court. But even this message was not foolproof, for there might be no way of convincing the ardent sceptic.

Any criteria for identifying the act of divine incarnation are going to be even more imprecise, but this does not mean, however, that they are non-existent. Bearing in mind the arguments already advanced on the crucial role of God's speech-acts in identifying what God is doing, one factor which has an important role in the decision as to whether a particular human agent is an incarnation of God, will be the availability of divine revelation to particular individuals to that effect. That is to say, if God has told, for example, certain apostles that He has come among us in Jesus, then the fact of that revelation would constitute evidence in support of the claim that Jesus was God incarnate. That such revelation has in fact taken place is an integral part of traditional Christian theism.[11] Whether the bearers of this revelation use the term incarnation is beside the point; what matters is that something to this effect be part of the content of the revelation. Nor does it matter that similar revelation is said to take place outside the circle of apostles, say later in the Church; what matters is that such revelation be available somewhere, and that it be seen to be available by applying the appropriate criteria.[12]

Relying on this alone, however, would be a very hazardous policy. Is there anything else that might support the claim? An obvious candidate would be the post-resurrection appearances of the human agent, who in such appearances would tell others who he was and what God was doing through his life. Such appearances and such assurances would not in themselves furnish foolproof guarantees. One could still accept them as having happened and yet deny that they provide logically compelling reasons for accepting belief in divine incarnation. But that they would lend support to such a claim seems to me obvious. It should be noted that it is not resurrection appearances *per se* that constitute evidence; it is resurrection appearances of a certain kind, namely appearances in which the resurrected human agent tells others who he was. That such appearances have taken place in the case of Jesus seems to be part of the story that Christians have told about Jesus.[13]

This element alerts us to another very important factor, namely the subjective witness of the Holy Spirit in bringing assurance to the believer of the significance of Jesus. It would take us too far afield to explore this in depth, but there is no doubt that the experience of Pentecost was pivotal in the lives of the early disciples. It is commonly thought that this experience simply turned convinced disciples into missionary disciples, but this is inaccurate. Any reading of the New Testament documents must acknowledge the crucial role of experience of the Holy Spirit in coming to faith. As Paul puts it (1 Cor. 12:3): 'no one can say "Jesus is Lord" except by the Holy Spirit'. It seems fair to see the story of Pentecost in Acts as reflecting this important emphasis. Within the classical Christian heritage this has been developed into the doctrine of the internal illumination of the Holy Spirit, which is seen as a vital element in the considerations that lead people to profess the Christian faith.

Doubts could be raised about the cogency of the kind of evidence thus far adduced, and one of these is that although there are no resurrection appearances and no revelations to support the claim that the king has visited his people, there is one important respect in which doubts could have been settled. As there was continuity of body throughout the act, at any particular moment the king *could* have been identified as being in truth the king. In the case of God becoming a man in Jesus, no such procedure is available, for by definition God does not have a body.

Two arguments can be deployed to counter this objection. The first focuses on the way God is identified. One way is to use descriptive phrases that tell what God does.[14] 'Who is God?' one asks the believer, and he replies, 'He is the one who creates and sustains all that is, the one who brought Israel from Egypt, the one who gave the law on Sinai, etc.' The point is well expressed by Rush Rhees: 'Winston Churchill may be Prime Minister and also a company director, but I might come to know him without knowing this. But I could not know God without knowing that he was the Creator and Father of all things. That would be like saying that I might come to know Churchill without knowing that he had a face, hands, body, voice or any of the other attributes of a human being.'[15] Given the fact that God is to be identified by descriptive phrases that specify his activity, it is possible to see how the claim that God is incarnate might be supported by the activity of Jesus. To begin with, the development of the concept of a God within a particular religious tradition will have to happen. Let us assume that such a development has taken place within the Hebraic religious tradition, and that the God of this tradition is to be identified by a network of descriptive phrases such as the following: God, it is said, is the one who creates and sustains the world, the one who brought liberation to Israel, the one who has revealed His purposes to the prophets, the one who alone forgives us our sins, and the one who has promised to intervene dramatically in the future. Let us assume further that Jesus appears in Palestine born into the Hebraic religious tradition. On the one hand it is clear that he is a man. He is born like any other man; he has a human body; he gets tired, hungry, and thirsty like anyone else; he grows up and matures like other men. He is vulnerable to pain and death as men are. These alone are sufficient to warrant the claim that he is a man. On the other hand there are certain respects in which he transcends what is human—his conception is miraculous, and he is raised from the dead.[16]

More importantly he acts in ways which match the acts that are used to identify God. Thus he displays control over nature which points to a knowledge of and relationship to nature that is direct and non-inductive, a relationship such as would be possessed by the one who created the world.[17] Moreover, the healing acts of Jesus wherein he heals by the power of his word point to his participation in the creative power of God who both made and rules the world by the power of his word.[18] In addition he lacks any sense of sin or of the need to repent, reflective of the perfection of God. Further, he claims to forgive the sins that one man has committed against another, a prerogative reserved for God alone. Moreover, he takes it upon himself to develop, qualify, and even correct what God has revealed in the past to prophets, thus suggesting that he associates the intervention of God and His rule with his own life and work in a relationship that is so close as to be identical. Finally he betrays a unique filial relationship to God that suggests a kinship with God not predicated of other men.

Given this situation, it is clear that although God does not have a body, it is still possible to fill the logical space occupied by this in the human situation with alternative data. Because some of the actions predicated of Jesus match the actions of God that are found in the descriptive phrases used to identify God, it is possible to find something remotely analogous in the theistic context to the body of the agent in the human context. Some of the acts of Jesus are precisely those which are relied upon in part to secure reference for the identity of God. Just as God's acts replace man's body in securing identity of reference, so too can the acts of Jesus secure to some degree his identity as uniquely related to God.[19]

The second argument can be stated more summarily. In the human situation sketched, all the evidence is already available.[20] In the nature of the case we know as much as there is to know about the king and his activity, whereas in the case of God this is not so. In the case of what God is doing in Christ, we may then have to wait until an eschatological future to have final confirmation about what it involves. Although we may not now be able to settle all our doubts in a way that exactly matches the human situation, it does not follow that this will always be so. The problem is a contingent one, arising from our present lack of knowledge rather than from logical problems about the criteria for identifying an unembodied agent.

It needs to be emphasized that criteria for identifying revelatory activity are bound to be ill-defined and retrospective.

This is as true of the human situation as it is of the divine. To look for logically compelling evidence in either case is inappropriate. The point is succinctly expressed by T. W. Manson in a comment about the meaning of the word 'revelation'.

Consider what we mean when we use the word in ordinary speech. The most characteristic employment of the word is to describe something that happens between persons. We know someone and think that we thoroughly understand him; and then, one day, he does something which upsets all our previous views. The man we thought to be hard and selfish turns out to be the soul of kindness—or *vice versa*. Some action of his puts him in a new light, and we say 'What a revelation.' What has happened is that some significant act has permitted us to see what was previously hidden. We know our man in a way we did not know him before, and our new knowledge flows directly from something which *he* has said or done. Now revelation in the religious use of the word is something like that.[21]

As Manson rightly implies, in the case of revelation it is implausible to look upon the identification of such activity as a matter of applying clear-cut criteria.[22] We do want to say that we knew the agent prior to this specific revelatory activity, that we knew what were the characteristics of his life and action, and yet we also want to say that we did not fully know what he was like. His true character was hidden from us; we only really know him now that he has revealed himself in certain acts. And given the new revelation, what we knew before is transformed. Enigmatic activity dawns upon us as explained; matters which puzzled and perplexed us are seen in a new light; indeed our very criteria for identifying what the agent is doing may be transformed, thus revealing afresh how imprecise such criteria may have to remain.

This suggestion can be applied without distortion to divine revelation in the incarnation. Prior to the incarnation there is already available revelatory activity that provides knowledge of God. Such revelation is given through the general revelation of creation and through the special revelation transmitted in the history of Israel and by the prophets. With this revelation already within one's conceptual field one is able to see signs of divine incarnation in Jesus' life and work. When this is supplemented by the resurrection appearances and further special revelation to the apostles, the claim that God was incarnate in Jesus comes not as a logically demonstrable conclusion but as a fitting surprise. And once the claim is accepted as true, the incarnation of God in Jesus is allowed to enrich the criteria for divine action already in use. Indeed the former general and special revelation, which in itself was logically necessary if a claim about incarnation was to arise in the first place, may be qualified and corrected in the light of the new revelation. At the very least it will be reinterpreted in the light of the incarnation. To do this is but to treat the new revelation as genuine; it is to ascribe to the incarnation a finality and uniqueness which only such an act as incarnation would merit.

How this operates in the Christian tradition can be seen by noting the role that Jesus is in fact given. Thus the concept of creation is given new dimensions, for the world is viewed not just as the work of the God of Abraham, Isaac, and Jacob but as created in and for Christ, the redeemer and saviour.[23] The creator is now seen as saviour, and thus,

> Heaven above is softer blue
> Earth around is sweeter green,
> Something lives in every hue,
> Christless eyes have never seen.[24]

History as a whole will be seen in a new perspective; it becomes the arena of God's concern and care, and even though what God is doing at any particular moment or even over many centuries may be opaque and unclear, overall its direction is in His hands and sustained by His love. As John McIntyre puts it: 'the manner in which God works and reveals Himself in Jesus Christ *is* the manner in which He works providentially throughout the whole of history'.[25] Moreover, all men will be seen in a new light. They will be seen not just as fellow creatures made by almighty God, but as brothers for whom Christ died. And morality may take on new dimensions. Feeding the poor, clothing the naked, relieving the thirsty, visiting the imprisoned, are now seen as feeding, relieving, clothing, and receiving Christ himself.

The revelation in Christ does not just have a retroactive effect on previous revelation, it also sets logical limits to the content of any other revelation. Thus the approach to putative revelation outside the Christian faith will be marked by a refusal to accept other revelation as equal in status or finality to that of Christ,[26] whilst claims within the Christian tradition to possess revelation that surpasses that of Christ will be treated with equal suspicion. That this is so is reflected in the setting-up of a canon of scripture. It is also reflected in the outright rejection of some claims to possess divine revelation in the present.

Suppose for instance that a rich man after his conversion announces that God has told him to give away his fortune or that God has called him to missionary service. Neither claim will be treated with suspicion by believers. If on the other hand he were to claim that God had told him to commit adultery, his claim would be rejected without further investigation. There is no likelihood of the man being told to engage in religious practices in order to make sure that it was really God he heard. The claim will be ruled out of court from the start; to talk of God telling anyone to commit adultery is to say something that cannot be intelligently predicated of God, and such unintelligibility is not just the result of the action's immorality; it is a result of the concept of God at stake. This concept is part of a complex conceptual apparatus in which Christ has a key role. As McIntyre points out, Christ 'integrates our appreciation of *how* God works'.[27] Thus if God was incarnate in Jesus and if He is the same yesterday, today, and forever, there is no possibility of God telling people to do things which are in sharp contrast with what He has revealed in Christ.

Two further considerations point to the crucial role ascribed to the act of incarnation in Christ, and its revelatory significance. The first is that worship is given to Jesus. It is only because he is accepted as God incarnate that the allegiance given to God can legitimately be given to Christ. Without the incarnation, worship of Christ would have to be seen as idolatry. And given both the claim to incarnation and the fact of worship it is not unnatural for there to develop an interest in stretching the notion of God in the direction of a Trinity to cope intellectually with these phenomena.

The second consideration is the fact that the interest in Jesus on the part of the Christian is as much theological as it is historical. That Jesus existed, that he actually lived, died, and rose again is of course crucial. But what matters as much if not more is the claim that in this man God was among us. This theological interest in Jesus is reflected throughout the New Testament, where neither the epistles nor the gospels make any attempt to write a life of Jesus. Kähler's provocative suggestion that 'one could call the Gospels passion narratives with extended introductions'[28] is accurate enough to illustrate this point without engaging in controversy.[29] The ecumenical creeds are no different in their emphasis. Thus Geza Vermes notes that in the Nicene Creed three-fifths of the content focus on the theological significance of Jesus. 'In formulating her profession of faith, the Church shows passionate interest in Christ's eternal pre-existence and glorious after-life, but of his earthly career the faithful are told next to nothing, save that he was born and died.'[30] In modern times the same theme is tersely expressed by Kierkegaard:

If the contemporary generation had left nothing behind them but these words: 'We have believed that in such a year the God appeared among us in the humble figure of a servant, that he lived and taught in our community, and finally died,' it would be more than enough. The contemporary generation would have done all that was necessary; for this little advertisement, this *nota bene* on a page of universal history, would be sufficient to afford an occasion for a successor, and the most voluminous account can in all eternity do nothing more.[31]

The theological interest in Jesus is reflected equally conspicuously in the attitude which is taken to the suffering of Christ. What matters is not that Christ suffered more than any other man, indeed it is conceivable to think of situations where men have undergone as much if not more suffering than he did, for during most of his life there is no evidence to show that he had anything less than a reasonably happy home and vocational satisfaction. What matters is that in Christ God has shared our life and died for us. It is that God should so love that He gave his only Son that is important. It is because of this that Christians put their faith in him rather than because he embodies human self-giving love. Helen Oppenheimer captures this thus:

It has never been made clear why if human self-giving love is the only ultimate, Jesus Christ should be given such a unique regard for exemplifying it. Other men have lived more obviously for others, and faced even greater sufferings. To put one's faith in him simply as *the* man for others looks like living on theological capital: it is because one is used to thinking of him as God incarnate coming to this world to live and die in it for all men that one is so struck by his self-giving love as to be constrained to call it divine.[32]

It should now be tolerably clear what is at stake if the incarnation has to be abandoned due to pressure from historical science. The loss can be seen in two areas; the first is primarily religious or devotional in character. If the incarnation is abandoned, it would be natural to find a loss in the inspirational value of the story of Jesus. The Christian could no longer listen to this story as the account of what God has done for him and the world's salvation. To do so would be to trade on the resources of the tradition while rejecting their source. It would be to fool oneself about the nature of the world in the interests of piety. There need be no doubt that some theologians will drop talk about incarnation in the name of honesty and clarity. This is altogether a laudable procedure, in that there is a general temptation to smooth over problems in the context, if not the interest, of devotion.

One could of course still hold that God's love is similar to the kind of love exemplified in Jesus' self-sacrificial life and death. Could one not then use the story of Jesus to inspire his own love for God and his fellows? To be sure one could, should one choose. But the loss such a step involves is still conspicuous for two reasons. To begin with such human love is, as has been noted, not the only example of human self-giving, so that focusing on it for inspirational support may be to deprive oneself of greater human resources of inspiration. Indeed to restrict oneself to the story of Jesus would be odd in the extreme.[33] Would it not be better to invent an ideal story to serve the same purpose? Or better still, would it not be more appropriate to focus on someone in the more recent past whose life was less obscure from a purely historical point of view, and who came from a religious and cultural milieu that was not infested with demons, miracles, and apocalyptic riddles?[34]

No doubt some would want to rest content with the story of Jesus. Its hallowed use in the Church, its central role in the eucharist, its influence on the art and literature of the West, its impact on one's own personal life; all these would make many reluctant to abandon it. But would it not be personal preference flaunting itself as scholarship to insist that psychologically and sociologically this was the key story that must be focused on in the Church, not to speak of the world at large? If it is psychological impact or social cement that is needed, then the proper line is to hand the whole affair over to the experts in psychology and sociology and let them determine what is best.[35] To refuse to do this is to act as if the tradition at this point is somehow sacrosanct or to set oneself up as some sort of expert without the appropriate credentials.

The second reason why the loss for devotion is still conspicuous is that the story thus construed is and will remain purely human. It is the story of one man's sacrifice in pursuit of his ideals and love. But the story as traditionally construed in the incarnation is a story about God's searching love. This will stand in judgement over all human stories; indeed it may deepen and enrich our conception of what true love is. So all human stories may have to pale into insignificance in the light of its glory. In short, it is what God has done that secures one's devotion, praise, and love.

The second general area of loss might be designated epistemological. The incarnation if true not only psychologically inspires the believer to trust in God, it also provides a warrant for exercising trust and for believing God to be a God of love. If God has acted as the incarnation specified then it is warranted to believe that God does love us. In so far as this claim is abandoned, alternative warrants will have to be found. Imaginative reflection and meditation on the story of the incarnation in order to fully capture what God's love is like could still be practised by someone who has abandoned the incarnation, but such a person could no longer appeal to the story thus interpreted in order to provide reasons for believing that God is such as the story depicts. The reasons for such descriptions will have to be found elsewhere, for example either in intuition, general revelation, other special revelation, religious experience, or natural theology.

To some extent the traditional believer will want to appeal to some if not all of these kinds of consideration. His beliefs about God comprise a large and sophisticated vision of life and are supported by a tangle of considerations that spread over many fields at once.[36] His conviction about the love of God within this is not tied to one spot in history exclusively but is related to creation as a whole, to his own present religious experience, and to the experience of others through-out the centuries. Thus it would be wrong to conclude that without the incarnation there is no warrant for the claim that God loves us.

Not surprisingly, therefore, some are tempted to argue that, as the concept of God's love is already available in the religious tradition prior to the incarnation, the incarnation can be dispensed with in the interests of economy. According to Wiles, the incarnation 'adds nothing to what is already given in belief in God's creative role and his purpose for the world'.[37] The glory of the created order, the potential for good of the natural setting of our human life, the worth of human relationships; all these can be retained. 'They do not logically require belief in the incarnation.'[38]

Wiles is surely correct to say that none of these logically require incarnation. Indeed it would be plausible to argue that they do not even require theism, for most humanists could with propriety assent to them. His posture, however, ignores two factors that are crucial to this issue. First, the primary significance of the incarnation can be said to lie in the domain of God's love rather in the general areas mentioned.[39] It asserts that God's love has been revealed not just in a general way in creation but very specifically in the life of one man, Jesus of Nazareth. God's love has involved the sharing of the human condition with its suffering and agony here on earth. So to insist on the incarnation involves a change in the quality of love that may rightly be predicated of God. To fall back on the kind of love that is available in creation and God's purpose for the world[40] is to fall back on resources that are meagre in the extreme.

The incarnation may be so central that it constitutes the pivotal divine act that gives content to one's concept of divine love. As Helen Oppenheimer suggests, the incarnationalist is released from the incessant pressure to find peculiar senses for words like 'providence', 'divine intervention', and 'fatherly care', when the facts do not appear to allow their more literal sense.

Maybe he will apply these personal concepts less frequently to the Almighty than some Christians do, but he will be able to apply them less equivocally. His parents have provided, intervened, cared for him by giving him bread not a stone; likewise God has provided, intervened, cared for him by dying on his behalf. If at present he happens to be starving in a garret or suffering from toothache, he must indeed believe that this is within God's ultimate purpose, but he does not have to contort himself to maintain that this is precisely what he means by God's loving concern.[41]

Moreover, once the incarnation has been accepted it may retroactively transform other elements in one's theism in the way which has already been outlined.

Against this Wiles would reply that this may be so for many Christians, but it need not be so. We are being misled by the abstract nature of the concept of suffering as applied to God.

Suffering is not some single entity in which different people share. There is my suffering and your suffering - and they are of many kinds. If the eternal drank of the chalice in the sufferings of the passion, in how direct a sense is that the same chalice as the one drunk by the mother of a brain-damaged child or the chance victim of a psychopathic assault? The suffering in which the eternal Word shares directly can only be a sacramental representation of his self-identification with the sufferings of other individuals. The self-identification itself must be of a different order. It is the truth or otherwise of our speech about that continuing self-identification of God with the sufferings of men and women that is vital to the health of theism. The truth or otherwise of that conviction is not determined by the truth or otherwise of a different order of divine self-identification with suffering in the person of Jesus. There does not seem to be any ground for claiming that the former is either causally dependent on or qualitatively transformed by the latter.[42]

This response puts the emphasis in the wrong place by focusing on the suffering rather than on the love of God. To be sure the two are related, for it is because God has shared our suffering that he is claimed to love us immeasurably. But to suggest that such suffering is not quite adequate unless it is exactly akin to all kinds of suffering is to demand too much. On the other hand, to restrict talk about God's love to the 'continuing self-identification of God with the sufferings of men and women' is too vague and abstract. What matters is that God has come among us in His Son, that He has shared the sufferings of life from within its bounds,[43] and that He has died for us. As Paul put it: 'Why, one will hardly die for a righteous man - though perhaps for a good man one will dare even to die. But God shows his love for us in that while we were yet sinners Christ died for us.'[44]

The second factor that Wiles's general posture ignores is the fact that warrants for the claim that God loves us may arise out of different sources and together support it. One or two of these sources may support the claim, but when they are taken in conjunction with the incarnation then the total support in the mind of the believer may be greatly strengthened. To remove the incarnation, therefore, will be to lessen the support for the claim that God loves us to a greater or lesser degree.

A major problem in expressing this is the great difficulty in agreeing on what precisely the warrants are and how much support they together provide. My own judgement is that the abandonment of divine incarnation does constitute the loss of one very important element in the theist's case for the claim that God loves us. To return to the analogy of the king: from the outset he loved the people. His giving them a place to dwell in, his demand that they should live in harmony and justice, reveal this. So too does his sending of agents to plead with them. But what is especially revelatory of his love is his own visit to them in the form of a servant. For those who doubt that his love is genuine such an act is of major significance in assuring them of his love and in the provision of warrants for such assurance. For those who did not doubt his love, then such an act may bring about a major transformation in their conception of his love; it may greatly enrich the quality of love predicated of God. So central may it be to some Christians in giving content to their conception of God's love that for them it is the very heart of the good news of the gospel. So to give it up may lead to a drastic reassessment of their theistic commitment. How drastic this reassessment will be depends on the extent to which they feel they can find alternative warrants for the conception of love predicated of God.

Another reason why it is difficult to express this in an undisputed way rests on the fact that moral and soteriological considerations can enter into it almost unnoticed. Thus on the moral side the non-incarnationalist may want to know why God, if He intervenes as he does in Christ, does not intervene at other times to alleviate the wanton suffering there is in the world. The non-incarnationalist has at least a kind of moral consistency in the character of the God he worships.

Why God has such a general policy of non-intervention may be a mystery to him, but less of a mystery than a God who intervenes so rarely. On the other side, the incarnationalist may see the incarnation as a fitting and appropriate act of God in that communicating with mankind in this way would seem to be the highest form of revelation possible.[45] Moreover, he may see the incarnation as alleviating to some extent the problem of suffering while admitting that there is an element of mystery about the consistency of God that must remain. In any case, he may rightly insist that the problem of suffering is one that all theists must face, and that this issue cannot decisively resolve the question of the propriety or impropriety of divine intervention in the incarnation.

On the soteriological side, the incarnationalist may want to say that divine intervention in general and divine incarnation in particular are important because of the depth of estrangement there is from God on the human side. Indeed rejection of special revelation is in part not just an intellectual exercise but is part of human rebellion against the creator. Therefore, accepting it will always seem foolish in the eyes of the world and will require divine grace if it is to be fully appropriated. The 'natural man', he may say, thinks he needs no divine intervention because he is blind to the gulf that separates him from God, while the believer has found such new life in the good news of the incarnation that nothing will shake him. Indeed so strong may this conviction be that there may be a rejection of any attempt to argue about the propriety of God's saving acts. Instead what will be urged and proclaimed is an obedient attending to what God has done for us in the incarnation and a call to radical openness to divine grace in the present.

The non-incarnationalist, for his part, may be impatient with what looks like an assault on his soul, and attempt to urge in reply that this analysis of the human condition is too simplistic. It overemphasizes the darker side of life and ignores the extent to which Christians have traditionally attempted to develop the intellectual dimensions of their faith. After all, the doctrine of the incarnation was itself such a development. Moreover, God is a god of truth, so He does not invite us to send our brains on holiday when we respond to the gospel, so the element of intellectual scandal in it should not be identified too abruptly. Above all, we must indeed attend to what God has done in the past, but precisely what this is the point of issue. Whatever our spiritual needs, we must leave it to God to do what he thinks best. As Wiles says: 'God, it is accepted, makes himself known and available to man in the fullest way that is compatible with man's existence as a free being. What that is, is precisely the issue at stake. And that can only be discovered (if it can be discovered at all) by reflection on the world as it impinges on us.'[46]

As with the moral issue already noted, there is no easy way of resolving the issue just outlined. Nor is there an easy way of keeping it from impinging on discussions about the warrants for divine love. Nor perhaps should this perturb us unduly, for the argument is complex and those who crave simplicity or piecemeal deductive strategy will have epistemological nightmares. One can only confess where one's sympathies lie. For my part, although I agree that spiritual judgement must be left to God alone, and that the quest for intellectual rigour must continue unabated, I agree in general drift with the incarnationalist at this point. The incarnation has traditionally been related to a wider vision of life that does lay stress on the sinfulness of man and his rebellion against God. The latter is not only widely supported by experience in general, it also gives point to the incarnation and is in harmony with the emphasis on grace which has been central to discourse about salvation in the Christian tradition.[47] Moreover, Wiles is surely wrong to suggest that what God has done can only be discovered by reflection on the world as it impinges on us. This sets extremely narrow limits to the options that may be open to us, and also sets limits to the freedom of God in acting that are question-begging.

The conclusion to be drawn is that the incarnation does have a very central role in the Christian faith, and those who abandon it must recognize that they must provide adequate alternative warrants for discourse about the love of God for man. They must also give good reasons for maintaining that the story of Jesus should be accorded a privileged position in our account of God's relationship to man, or else be prepared to allow it to recede from the prominent position it has long been given. That the idea of incarnation may strain intelligibility to a breaking point,[48] or that criteria for identifying the incarnate activity of God are imprecise and disputed,[49] must not be allowed to blur these issues. No doubt those who are prepared to abandon the incarnation can be relied on to face them with integrity and equanimity. They have certainly done so in the past, and indeed there is a body of opinion in contemporary English theology currently doing precisely this. The alternative proposal to the traditional understanding of the Christian faith is still in the making. However, it does involve at a minimum an account of divine incarnation which suggests a very different way of construing the incarnation than the one adopted here. As this account of divine incarnation sometimes is related in turn to a general account of divine action it has very serious repercussions for all discourse about direct divine intervention. An examination of this account of divine action should allow us to apply and summarize some of the conclusions reached thus far in this study of special revelation.

4
DIVINE ACTION
AND MYTHOLOGY

In this study so far I have taken it as read that Christians have intended that the doctrine of the incarnation be taken as a real event in history. The case is the same as regards the resurrection of Jesus and God having spoken to prophets and apostles. In other words, these claims have been construed as assertions about the activity of a personal agent. There are two very good reasons for retaining this reading of these central elements in the Christian tradition. First, such an analysis does justice to what Christians over the centuries have intended to impart in these doctrines. Whatever the diversity that may exist, the tradition as a whole has insisted on a factual interpretation; this is a historical fact that cannot be lightly ignored. Secondly, such discourse can, from a conceptual point of view, satisfy the general condition usually associated with such discourse, namely that it be to some extent confirmable or disconfirmable by experience.[1]

This latter claim has not been central to my concern thus far. The major question posed focused on the loss resulting from abandoning claims about direct divine action. But in answering this question I have attempted to make clear how claims about the specified direct divine action were to be understood, and in the course of this I drew attention indirectly to the kinds of consideration that would confirm the claim that God had spoken to someone and that he had become incarnate in Jesus.[2] It is not fatal to the argument that the considerations attended to are broad and somewhat imprecise. All that matters is that they represent considerations that would be relevant to confirming the claims set forth, for they clearly establish the claim that such discourse can be construed as factual.

Nor is it crucial for the correctness of this claim that the doctrines concerned be capable of being worked into a network of scientific theory. To demand this is to demand too much, for it is by no means clear that all factual claims must satisfy this condition.[3] To say that Jones spoke to Smith or that he went to town is not to make scientific statements, but is, surely, to engage in factual discourse about the activity of a personal agent. Likewise to say that God spoke to the prophets, or that He raised Jesus from the dead, or that He became incarnate in Jesus, is not to engage in scientific discourse but it is to engage in factual discourse about the activity of a personal agent.[4] That discourse about divine agency is in some respects mysterious or that it cannot be confirmed as easily as discourse about human agency does not negate this point. All that is required is that there be an element of fundamental similarity between the two kinds of expression, a point that is recognized in that both are accepted as sentences about personal agency, with divine agency seen as analogous to human agency.

Given this, it follows that the discourse about divine agency under review can also be construed as explanatory. Its function in part, that is, is to explain certain happenings in history by relating such happenings to the activity of a transcendent agent. Moreover, the sentences expressing these explanations could also rightly be said to be true or false, known or not known, and if known to be true they would give us information. The explanation provided or the information given would not, of course, be scientific. Not only is it not expressed in the kinds of concept that are part and parcel of standard scientific thought, it is also not expressed in a form that is generally used by scientists. But this is not surprising, for it is not entirely clear that discourse about personal agency fits the kind of explanatory model that is central to most scientific enterprise. All that matters here is that discourse about personal agency can be construed as explanatory and informative.[5]

Now that the logic of the claims about the divine activity under review has been made explicit in that it is classed as factual, explanatory, and informative, we can explore more fully what this involves by contrasting it with a very different way of analysing claims about direct divine action. The heart of this different way is the contention that claims about direct divine action should be analysed as being mythological.[6]

The term 'mythological', as Wiles reminds us, is by no means new to theology.[7] Moreover, it plays a prominent role in a wide range of disciplines outside theology. Its usage, however, is so varied that to appeal to it to analyse claims about divine action does not of itself get us very far. As Baelz points out, 'It is possible to call the language of God's doings mythological but to interpret this language in a number of different ways. It is not immediately clear what the function of such language is.'[8] Furthermore, it is not unknown for the concept of myth to be used in such a way that it masks critical questions.[9] In order to avoid unnecessary interpretative perplexity, therefore, it will be useful to focus on an account of the concept of mythology that has been developed self-consciously and with care. Such an account has been made available by Hick and Wiles.[10] According to Hick, a myth is:

> a story which is told but which is not literally true, or an idea or image which is applied to something or someone but which does not literally apply, but which invites a particular attitude in the hearer. Thus the truth of a myth is a kind of practical truth consisting in the appropriateness of the attitude it evokes - the appropriateness of the attitude to its object which may be an event, a person or a set of ideas.[11]

Such language is to be distinguished from the language of theory or hypothesis. The language of theory begins with some puzzling phenomenon and offers a hypothetical description of a wider situation such that, seen from within this wider context, the phenomenon is no longer puzzling. This type of language is true or false, and must be capable of confirmation or disconfirmation within human experience.

Mythological discourse, on the other hand, cannot literally be true. Taken as it stands, it should not be construed as factual, explanatory, or informative. Although it may indeed capture certain truths about something and thus to some extent be descriptive or informative, its primary function is to evoke certain attitudes in the hearer. To take it as true without some kind of translation would be to misunderstand such discourse and miss its true intention.

The distinction can be further clarified by example. A good example of mythological discourse is to be found in the story of the fall of man. If treated as a theory, the story of the fall of man is false. There is no evidence to support it, and much that conflicts with it. It should not, for this reason, however, be dismissed as of no value. Understood as a myth, the story is still of great value.

So used the story of the fall would seem to be a poetic, picturesque, or parabolic way of saying something that can also be stated in non-mythological language but which is, for most people, conveyed much more effectively, and with much greater power to evoke an appropriate response, by the mythical story. The meaning of the myth may be the way it prompts us to see human wickedness as free and blameworthy, and yet as occurring within a corrupt and corrupting inherited situation for which the individual is not responsible or it may be that it leads us to see that as well as being actually wicked, man has a potentiality for goodness which ought to be actualised. In this way the story of the fall may remind us that there is a sense in which our 'true' nature is good even though our actual state is bad, and may prompt us to realise our 'true' nature. Thus the myth functions in a way close to that of moral exhortation.[12]

Much the same, logically speaking, can be said about the story of God becoming incarnate in Jesus. Traditionally this has been understood as a theological hypothesis. When developed in this direction, however, it has invariably ended in impenetrable mystery with no statable meaning or content. Such a result should not surprise us, however, for such language is not theoretical or literal; it is mythological. What such language aims to do and succeeds in doing is to evoke an appropriate attitude to Jesus as saviour.

This is borne out by what we can legitimately claim about the activity of Jesus. What Jesus did in his lifetime was to bring people into a new relationship with God and with one another. Our historical reconstruction of his life may be scanty and uncertain, but one thing we can know: 'we can know, by looking at those who were directly influenced by Him, through those whom they in turn influenced, that He brought men and women to God with a directness that made all other ways of salvation needless to them. In following Jesus the Messiah they encountered God in a manner that entirely filled their lives.'[13]

Through time this vivid experience of God through Jesus was interpreted or expressed in the language of ultimates. 'Their language was pitched to the level of reality which was to be expressed.'[14] The highest pitch such language can reach is to say that Jesus is God incarnate, and this step his followers took within two generations of his death. Such a step was finally crystallized in the formulations of Chalcedon.

Jesus, however, did not think of himself in such categories. What he did think of himself is a matter of speculative conjecture. All we can say for sure is that he was conscious of being, genuinely and unambiguously, human. He had a special call of God at his baptism, he had religious experiences that left him fully open to the divine Spirit, which provided as a by-product powers of healing and deep human insight. He was intensely conscious of the presence of God, and he must have been aware that God was impinging upon human life more powerfully through his work and ministry than in any other way. In Jesus, then, his followers encountered God. And to be a Christian today is to share the faith of his followers, seeing something of what they saw and feeling something of what they felt. To be a Christian is to encounter God through Jesus. In fact, to say that Jesus is God incarnate, properly understood, means nothing more than that God was encountered in Jesus. 'That *God* has been encountered through Jesus is communicated mythologically by saying that He was God the Son incarnate.'[15]

The truth of this myth consists in its tendency to evoke an attitude which is appropriate to the real character of that which is being identified. As Christians believe that through Jesus God is encountered, and that through him salvation is discovered, the myth of the incarnation is for them obviously true. For them it has evoked an attitude which is appropriate to the real character of that which is being identified.

Such a claim on the part of Christians does not however rule out the possibility that God is encountered every bit as fully in other religious traditions. In the other major religions the human propensity for faith and worship is fully activated, and a total response of devotion takes place. These religions in turn develop their own mythological discourse, whose function is to evoke an appropriate attitude to the sources of salvation within their tradition. The myths thus developed are equally true, in that they all evoke appropriate attitudes. To treat them as competing theories is to misunderstand their mythological character. 'They are more like different art forms, each of which is at home in a different culture, than like rival scientific hypotheses.'[16]

We have now before us a plausible account of what is meant by saying that discourse about divine action is mythological. My argument is that this account of divine action in Christ depends upon dubious arguments about the nature of religious experience, does not do justice to what has been at issue in talk about divine action in the past, and ignores crucial disanalogies between the story of the fall and that of the incarnation.

Let us begin with Hick's claim that what led the early Christians to deify Jesus was the intensity of religious experience initiated by him. As the early Christians encountered God through Jesus, they had to use the language of ultimates to do full justice to him. Parallel to religious experience in this regard are such experiences as falling in love, 'seeing' or being grasped by some important truth, being utterly loyal to a monarch or country. Salvation experiences are a genus of a wider species of experiences that demand expression in the language of ultimates. Hick's account is weak in several important respects.

Firstly, to say that there is a form of discourse that is best described as the language of ultimates does not of itself establish that Christian discourse about divine incarnation in Jesus belongs to that form of discourse. Further arguments will be needed to support this claim if it is to be accepted.

Secondly, that there is no religious necessity to develop a language of ultimates is suggested by the fact that there have been many instances of religious experience that have not led to the kind of discourse exemplified in the incarnation. A telling example is the prophets of Israel. One might well accept that God was encountered in their activity because they had an experience in which God spoke to them and called on them to proclaim His word, but it does not follow that one will ascribe to them the predicates applied to Jesus. The same is true of many of the adherents of the other world religions in their response to the putative sources of divine encounter in their traditions.[17] More generally, many religious believers will claim, on the basis of divine creation, to encounter or experience God through the world of nature. But this does not lead them to develop discourse about divine incarnation to express such experiences or to evoke attitudes in others that would lead to similar experiences.

Thirdly, it is not at all clear how religious experience alone could initiate talk of God being incarnate in Jesus. From a purely logical point of view it is of course conceivable that this was the case. However, it is difficult to claim that it was in fact so. This can be developed by noting briefly the kind of role that religious experience may have had in the development of such discourse. As Wiles has pointed out, experience and other factors are woven together in religion, so that to overemphasize the role of experience is to misdescribe the dynamics of the process of conceptualization. Thus, writes Wiles, 'our experience is moulded by our understanding and our understanding is modified by our experience'.[18] And writing of the early Christians he comments: 'There is no such thing as pure experience; they are only able to experience liberation through Jesus because they already believed Him to be in some form or another a vehicle of God from whom liberation was to be hoped.'[19] This brief but more accurate account of the role of religious experience renders it unlikely that religious experience alone will generate claims about divine incarnation. That this was the case is argued from a historical point of view in Wiles's *The Making of Christian Doctrine*.[20] Early Christian doctrine developed from multiple motives and multiple sources. The interpretative categories used were not just developed because they were peculiarly expressive of religious experience; religious experience was just one among several factors.

In general, this is in keeping with the account of the incarnation developed above.[21] The case for the incarnation, if there is one at all, should take the form of a complex cumulative case in which several considerations come together to license the assertion that God was incarnate in Jesus. Part of this case will, of course, be one's own experience of God as mediated through the proclamation of God's love and grace in the incarnation, but to limit it to that alone would be weak in the extreme. Moreover, it would be to remove this proclamation from its wider context, for the proclamation does not come as an isolated story but is bound up with historical and theological factors that clothe and support it without providing demonstrative proof of its truth.

Whatever account we give of the sources for discourse

about divine incarnation in Jesus, it is tolerably clear that the early Church and tradition until modern times did intend its discourse about divine incarnation as factual rather than mythological.[22] Although the possibility cannot be ruled out completely, it is difficult to construe the explorations of early Christology as myth-making in Hick's sense.[23] Thus the creedal formulations do not seem to have been attempts to induce or evoke appropriate attitudes to Jesus as a centre of divine activity. In so far as the recipients of these creeds were heretics, like Arius, they already possessed such an attitude and were expected to react in a hostile manner to what was said in the doctrinal formulation.[24] In so far as the creeds were meant for the faithful, they already had made an appropriate response to God in Jesus, so any myth-making would have been unnecessary.

It is surely much more plausible to see discourse about divine incarnation as a justification for taking up certain attitudes to Jesus rather than as a way of evoking such attitudes. If Jesus really is God incarnate, then he ought to be obeyed and worshipped as Lord and saviour. Incarnational language is not primarily intended to manoeuvre people psychologically into taking up positive responses to Jesus; it is intended to give adequate backing to the positive response that Christians have made to him, or will make to him.

Hick surely misses this when he attempts to justify worship of Jesus without the kind of backing provided by a factual, as opposed to a mythological, understanding of the incarnation. Hick's defence of worship of Jesus begins with the contention that ultimately only God can be worshipped. In practice, however, we are only able to worship God under approximate and anthropomorphic images. This in itself can be left as uncontroversial, for even to think of God, say as creator, involves the use of language drawn from everyday life. Hick, however, advances from this claim about a recognizably necessary feature of worship, to the more contentious claim that it is proper to consider mediators who bring us into relationship with God as images through whom we can worship God.

Characteristically, in the history of religions, the images through which the divine reality is worshipped have been thought of as beings who are immensely - indeed, for all practical purposes, infinitely - superior to ourselves spiritually, immensely 'nearer' to God but who are nevertheless servants of God rather than the infinite Deity Himself. To worship such a mediator is not to regard Him as the Infinite but to regard Him as so vastly 'higher' than ourselves in the direction of God as to be for us our image through whom the utlimate divine reality can be worshipped.[25]

A monotheist could surely accept that we must worship God as Creator, as Father, as the rock of our salvation, etc. But he would reject wholeheartedly Hick's suggestion that this licenses his worshipping the sources of such images or the human mediator who taught him their propriety. To worship such sources or mediators would simply be idolatry. Christians who worship Jesus have consequently had to face the charge of idolatry, and the doctrine of the incarnation is surely legitimately construed from a logical point of view as one line of defence. It can only function as such a line, however, if it is understood factually rather than mythologically.

Hick might remain unmoved by the arguments deployed thus far. They show that discourse about divine incarnation has been understood factually in the past, but that in the end is beside the point. What is at stake is the critical, second-order suggestion that such discourse, however understood in the past, ought to be understood mythologically in the Church today.

This is indeed an important issue. The answer we give to it may depend on several factors, for example, on the extent to which we are prepared to tolerate paradox in our conceptual scheme. This in turn may depend on the credence we are prepared to give to reports about Jesus or on the role we ascribe to the Holy Spirit in the life of the Church. Further, it may depend on one's response to other world religions; whether one is prepared, for example, to consider them as possessing divine revelation. And this in turn may depend on theological considerations about the nature of revelation. It may also depend on the extent one feels compelled to follow the early Church in its attempt to work out the details of belief in divine incarnation. And this in turn will depend on complex historical reconstruction of early Christian doctrine.

It is not within the capacity of most thinkers to solve many of these problems on their own. Even to become acquainted with the relevant issues is a major exercise in philosophical and theological reflection. What most can hope to do is to work through some of the areas involved, relying for those areas not covered on the work of others. This is not something that should be done with protest or even regret, for in much of our lives we have to rely on the research and genius of others. It is a part of accepting our finitude to accept it with relief. Because of this, it would be futile to argue that Hick's proposal to reinterpret discourse above divine incarnation is obviously wrongheaded. It is in order, however, to challenge it as follows.

As it stands the proposal gives the impression that it is considerations in the theory of meaning that necessitate the reinterpretation of discourse about divine incarnation. This, however, is misleading in the extreme, for it suggests that questions about meaning and questions about justification are unrelated. In actual fact, if the objections against his general or overall position are valid they also undermine his proposal about language. Hick's account of religious experience, his account of what can be known about Jesus, his account of early Christian doctrine, are all central to his position about the meaning of claims about divine incarnation in Jesus. The overall argument and the thesis about meaning stand or fall together, so that to undermine one is to undermine the other.[26]

Just how true this general point is, and just how weak Hick's recommendation is, can be ascertained by following the analogy with the story of the fall of man. What is suggested is that the story of God becoming incarnate in Jesus should be accepted as logically similar to the story of the fall. But this should only be accepted if the proposition 'God is encountered in Jesus' is shown to be true and if crucial disanalogies between the two stories are ignored. Unfortunately for Hick, neither of these conditions is satisfied.

The first condition is necessary because the proposition 'God is encountered in Jesus' is the truth that talk of God being incarnate in Jesus is meant to evoke. The story of the incarnation on the new reading expresses this truth poetically or dramatically and thereby evokes a proper attitude to Jesus. The problem with this is that the claim that God is encountered in Jesus is a particular instance of the general claim we have already seen to be very questionable.[27] It has also been suggested that the idea of divine incarnation is best seen as an attempt to specify what God is doing in Christ. It gives content to the claim that God acted in Christ and thereby to the claim that God is encountered in Christ. Without this content or some other specific divine act in mind, talk of God acting in Jesus is empty, and thereby talk of God being encountered in Jesus is empty. The importance of this cannot be overemphasized, for it is easy to be misled by grand rhetoric. General talk about God acting is like general talk of human agents acting. To say 'Jones acted' is to say next to nothing. Likewise to say 'God acted' is to say next to nothing.

It is true that to say 'God acted in Jesus' is to say more than simply 'God acted', but as soon as we seek to determine what this extra dimension is we are driven to specify what God is doing in Jesus, and are thus led back to the incarnation as one possible answer. It is, therefore, not possible to divorce the concepts of encountering God and God being incarnate in Jesus as easily as might be expected at first sight. Discourse about incarnation gives content to the concept of encounter. Until the latter has been given alternative content, it will not be possible to assent or dissent to the claim that God is encountered in Jesus. As assenting to the truth of this claim is logically prior to acceptance of Hick's recommendation, we are not yet in a position to be able to assess his recommendation. With regard to the story of the fall, we are in the same position, for Hick has given ample content to the underlying assertions about the human condition that the fall is meant to capture.[28]

It is also clear that other disanalogies between the story of the fall and the story of the incarnation are being ignored. Firstly, the story of the fall was given up as a piece of explanatory discourse because of specific scientific theory backed by carefully collected evidence and was thus shown to be false. There are no specifically scientific arguments against the incarnation. Secondly, there are independent considerations concerning the exegesis and critical evaluation of the text in which the story of the fall is embedded that render a non-factual rendering of the material plausible. Prima facie this is not the case with the incarnation. To be sure there is much controversy concerning how much can be known historically about Jesus, and there is also controversy as to how the New Testament confessions of his significance are to be interpreted and related to discourse about divine incarnation. But within this there is room for accepting a position on these matters that would be compatible with a theology that accepts the incarnation. There just is not this kind of room within the consensus that has emerged among Old Testament scholars about the interpretation of the story of the fall.

Thirdly, the truths the story of the fall conveys are truths about the human condition generally, while the truths the incarnation purports to convey are rather about God. The former are about the world in general and therefore may be plausibly read from the world as we know it. The latter are about the character and love of a transcendent agent and cannot be read from the world as we generally know it. Removing the incarnation from the class of the genuine acts of God in the world is therefore a much more momentous undertaking than the appeal to the story of the fall either reveals or warrants.

It is tempting to reply to this that it is at bottom a philosopher's rationalization of a psychological reaction to what at first sight looks like drastic change. After all, most change initially looks momentous. This is especially so in religion, where emotions may become focused on major religious figures of the past. Although this should make us responsive to the sensibilities of the religious believer, it must not halt the attempt to articulate with clarity and rigour that which can be affirmed to be true for faith today. When a mythological reading of the fall was first suggested many felt that this change was so momentous that it would destroy the foundations of Christian belief and practice. We sympathize as best we can with this reaction, but now know it to be unnecessary, for the vast majority of Christian believers outside fundamentalism accept a mythological analysis of the story of the fall.

This reply, however, is far from convincing. Certainly it is entirely proper to draw attention to the strong reaction in many quarters to change in the interpretation of the story of the fall. Against the use of this to make more palatable a reinterpretation of the story of the incarnation, it should be pointed out that a mythological analysis of the incarnation is by no means new. Indeed it has been a motif in modern theology since the work of Strauss.[29] If time for scholarly discussion is in any way a criterion, we are in this case more fortunate than in the case of the story of the fall. Yet many Christian theologians outside fundamentalism have resolutely refused to accept it as satisfactory. This does not establish that incarnation is the only live option for the theologian, but it does suggest that even with regard to the question of reaction to change the analogy with the story of the fall is misleading.

In this care must be taken not to make the presence or absence of consensus in the Church the criterion of truth. That it should be attended to is obvious, but it must not allow crucial questions about the warrants for theological claims about the character of a transcendent agent to pass un-answered. It is here that the analogy between incarnation and fall can easily lead us astray. It is this rather than the psychology of change that should detain us.

A more forceful strategy at this point would be to supple-ment Hick's analysis by recourse to some arguments put forward by Maurice Wiles. This is particularly apposite because his account of divine incarnation is very similar to that of Hick. Thus both propose that the sentence 'God was incarnate in Jesus' should be understood mythologically; both construe the function of mythology to be that of evoking attitudes in the hearer; both are tentatively agnostic about what we can know about Jesus; and both draw attention to analogies between the story of the fall and the incarnation.

It is also apposite because Wiles's approach suggests a plausible counter-attack to my arguments from the dis-analogies between the fall and the incarnation. This begins by appeal to the biblical stories of creation, and develops by focusing on the interrelationship between creation, fall, and redemption. Let me now elaborate.

The story or stories of creation, it might be said, offer a more telling analogy to the incarnation in that the key actor in the story is a god who in creating intervenes at particular moments in the causal operations of nature. For centuries it has been argued that for God to create, He must intervene directly, as suggested by the story, e.g. create Eve out of one of Adam's ribs. Indeed, when the story was first challenged as a factual account of cosmic and human origins, many strongly felt that to give up divine intervention in the causal order was to forfeit divine creation. We now know that this feeling, although understandable, was premature. We can assert divine creation without thereby asserting divine intervention, and we can use the story of divine intervention as a myth to bring home to people more effectively certain truths about God, namely that he is the creator and sustainer of all that is.

These truths about God are grounded in 'man's experiencing the world as a contingent, as in some fundamental sense given, as not self-explanatory'.[30] They are brought home to us, however, by certain features of the world in a way in which they are not brought home by others: 'we are bound to speak of some aspects of the natural order as giving rise more directly to the apprehension of God's creative role than others.'[31] Thus the emergence of the distinctively human in the evolutionary process,[32] and the presence of objects of beauty like the lilies of the field,[33] have a special significance for the doctrine of creation in that they shed light on the significance of the world as a whole and God's purposes for it. Although there is no question of God having actually intervened in the causal order to create either man or lilies directly, it is legitimate to tell a story about God directly making man from the dust of the earth or about God clothing the lilies of the field in order to communicate more dramatically that God is the ultimate source of all existence, and that the emergence of man and beauty are important features in the creative purposes of God for the world as a whole.

Much the same can be said of the incarnation. The general truth underlying such discourse is the truth that God redeems. For a long time it has been assumed that for the concept of redemption to be viable, then God must intervene miraculously in Christ as traditionally understood. In earlier generations, this was understandable because creation, fall, and redemption were knit together so intimately within a complex of beliefs that to assert intervention in one required inter-

vention in the others. Both creation and fall involved intervention—in the former case divine, in the latter human—so
it was natural that redemption would also seem to require
direct intervention. However, we now realize that as we can
assert creation without intervention, so too can we hold to
redemption without intervention.

The story of the incarnation can still be used mythologically. We can talk of God becoming a man to bring home
more effectively the truth that God is redeemer. This truth,
like the truth that God is creator, is grounded in our experience in general. It is backed by 'a fundamental aspect of
human experiencing'.[34] It is 'rooted in the fact that so much
of the most profound personal experience has about it a
quality of response; men have found a sense of purpose,
bigger than their own comparatively narrow concerns, being
elicited as it were by the events of history ...'[35] It is brought
home to us more potently by some events in history as com-
pared to others. Certain events elicit more effectively 'the
sense of response to purpose activity'. 'For the Christian the
life of Christ, and certain other events also within what is
commonly referred to as "salvation history" have an out-
standing potency of this kind and are seen as special divine
actions.'[36] Saying that God became incarnate in Jesus, then,
is one dramatic way of bringing home the truth that God
cares about human suffering and that he elicits from men a
mature response of faith and love in which sin can begin to be
overcome and the goals of human life begin to be realized.

The success of this counter-attack depends on several
factors which I shall now endeavour to undermine. One of
the more salient of these is the claim that there is 'a fundamental aspect of human experiencing' that is sufficient
grounds for the truth of the claim that God is redeemer.
Wiles's account of such experience is so vague that it is virtually impossible to identify or make sense of it. What can
one make of such descriptions as 'profound personal experience that has about it a quality of response' or 'an experience
of receptivity'?[37]

In the light of this vagueness it is not surprising that Wiles
is keen not to press critical questions concerning the appro-

priateness of the descriptions predicated of such general experiencing. Thus he writes:

> What I am trying to describe is not a matter of conscious inference; not a worked out way of explaining experiences to oneself; rather to use a phrase that John Hick has made familiar in relation to the natural world, it is a matter of 'experiencing as', of experiencing what happens to us and what we achieve as being in response to an overall purpose at work in the world. It is the attempt to articulate this way of experiencing life that men have spoken of God as acting in history, a phrase vividly expressing the experience of receptivity which it is intended to express but which can also be dangerously misleading if taken too literally.[38]

This reliance on general human experience to give a basis to talk of divine action in history is surely open to the critique already offered against Hick in relying on religious experience.[39] Thus, as Wiles himself noted, the early Christians were only able to experience liberation through Jesus and thereby relate divine action to such experiences because they already believed him to be in some form or another a vehicle of God from whom liberation is to be hoped. Belief in divine action in history was logically before the experiencing. If this is the case, then it is implausible to see talk of divine redemption as being grounded in a 'fundamental aspect of human experiencing'. That many people sincerely profess to having no such general experience of God as liberator only makes it more implausible.

The same may be said of the attempt to base divine creation in man's experiencing the world as contingent.[40] Many profess to have no such experience; while others who do might only rely on it as grounds for their theism if they believed that God had directly revealed himself more fully elsewhere. Experience of contingency on its own, that is, would be a fragile foundation for the truth of the claim that God created the world.

Given unease about the reliance on human experiencing as a ground for claims about divine creation or redemption, it is inevitable that there will be unease about the related account of special divine actions.[41] Thus if one is sceptical about the difficulty of basing the truth of divine redemption on human experiencing, it is not clear how the 'truth' of this claim can be brought home with special potency by events in history. If no such 'truth' is thus available, then logically it is not available to be brought home no matter what means are specified.

Indeed one wonders whether there is not a measure of inconsistency between the claim that a truth is, on the one hand, based on human experience generally but, on the other hand, brought home very potently by certain events in history. If it is based on human experience why is it not brought home potently by such experience? Conversely, if it is brought home very potently by certain events, might it not be said to be based on these events? Logical inconsistency is too strong a charge to make; there is, at least, something mysterious here.

A factual interpretation of these events as genuinely involving divine incarnation removes this mystery. An agent reveals himself more conspicuously in some acts rather than others.[42] If the incarnation is really a direct act of God, then we have reason to respond differently to Jesus than to other historical events. The incarnation explains why we respond to Jesus as Saviour and Lord. This explanation is epistemic rather than psychological; it gives rational grounds as to why we ought to respond to Jesus, rather than offering a psychological account as to why people have responded positively to Jesus. Interestingly, Wiles is aware of the legitimacy of this type of approach, for he quotes with approval Baelz's suggestion that in the life of Christ the activity of God is 'more fully discerned because more fully expressed, there is a very proper sense in which we may speak of God's *special* activity'.[43] A response to Jesus is discerning, that is, if God is expressing Himself more fully in Jesus than elsewhere. This, surely, is precisely what the incarnation as traditionally understood is meant to capture, for it is a paradigm case of special divine action.

Moreover, it would seem not unnatural to say that the life of Christ brings home the truth that God redeems partly because one actually believes that his life involved a direct act of God in history. That is, these events elicit a religious response to God as redeemer because they are seen as an act of grace on God's part. Belief in divine incarnation in Christ is central to the Christian's experience of God as redeemer, and is instrumental in initiating such experience.

Wiles would no doubt respond that this is the way in which the truth of redemption has come home to many. It was their belief that God was incarnate in Jesus, or something akin to this, that led to their experience of redemption. But this is a contingent matter about their personal pilgrimage to God. What matters is that the underlying truth they have come to see and live by, namely the truth that God is redeemer, does not have to be tied to divine incarnation in Jesus. The latter can be rejected while the former can be retained and grounded elsewhere. To be sure, the life of the historical Jesus will still be important, for his life and death do in themselves give grounds for this claim, so there is no attempt to dispense with Jesus in theology. All that is being abandoned is one particular way of relating Jesus to the Christian's understanding of God, namely the relating of Jesus to God in the fully direct and intimate way that incarnation involves.

We might illustrate the viability of a less direct way of relating Jesus to God by means of example. God creates and sustains snails. He also creates and sustains the saints of the church. But the latter, though part of the created order, provide a better clue to the divine nature than do the former. Similarly with Jesus: although part of the natural created order, he affords the best clue we have as to the nature of God.

If it is now further enquired why Jesus should continue to hold the central place in Christian worship and devotion that he has occupied in the past, then it would be pertinent to point to the role the story of Jesus has had. The story of Jesus is the story 'of that historical happening which did in fact create a new and effective realisation of divine redemption at work in the lives of men and which has remained the inspirational centre of faith to which we belong from that day until now'.[44] Whether Jesus will continue to have an indispensable role for the Church of the future is something that cannot be decided by theologians or philosophers. 'The grounds for such a claim would have to be historical or psychological reflection on the way in which man's spiritual life has been and is formed within Christian faith. Its validity could only be tested by the course of future history.'[45]

If this line of inquiry is pursued in the wider context of inter-religious dialogue, then of course other issues will enter into the discussion. But in the end the discussion about facts and relevant content of assessment must cease. Ultimately the specialness of Jesus can only be commended as a vision for which no further reasons can be given. 'To ask for some further ontological justification of that vision would be to succumb to the category mistake of confusing the human historical story with the divine mythological story.'[46]

In making this response Wiles would be correct to insist that the kind of ultimate breakdown in argument that he indicates may come. As we saw in the last chapter, it is extremely difficult to reach agreement on warrants for divine love. But we do not have to reach agreement on warrants to recognize that some warrants are weak and inadequate. And surely Wiles's warrants are extremely weak. From his revised account we can indeed recognize that he has some warrant for saying that general divine creative activity is more fully revealed in Jesus of Nazareth than in snails or Hitler for some of our activity is indeed more revelatory of our nature than is the rest. But it seems very difficult to see how the umbrella of general creative activity and the religious experience it initiates can bear not only the weight of claims to a general revelation of God, but also of claims about God's forgiveness and His promises, of His redemption and His love, of his commands and His grace in the life of the believer. We can accept that there is revelation generally in creation in both snails and the saints of the Church, but is this all there is? If God has not just acted generally but has also performed certain completed acts in the past of the kind already discussed, then the overall account of revelation available to the theologian is surely enormously enriched. Indeed it is difficult to see how the story of Jesus could be classed as good news unless it did involve going beyond what is available in God's general sustaining activity. As H. H. Price points out, 'News is not something which is logically entailed by what is known already.'[47]

As to the role that Wiles is still willing to give to the person of Jesus, to my mind it would be inappropriate to continue to give him the central role that he has enjoyed at the very heart of Christian worship and discipleship merely on the basis of the Christology suggested by Wiles. Moreover, if it is the judgement of history that is crucial, then my reading of the situation is that we have had the kind of Christology that

Wiles is advocating for a long enough period to know that history has delivered at the very least an open verdict on this issue.[48]

Wiles is also open to censure for the way he has characterized the incarnationalist alternative. It is surely wrong to say that to look for some kind of ontological[49] justification for giving a central role to Jesus in one's theological vision is to succumb to the category mistake of confusing the human historical story with the divine mythological story. Expressed thus, the impression created is that the incarnationalist has made an elementary blunder in his analysis of discourse about divine action.[50] But this charge can only succeed if Wiles's own substantive arguments are sound. The two, as it were, are alternative ways of expressing his position; they are not independent arguments that stand on their own foundation.

One half of his substantive argument is in fact philosophical. It claims, as we have seen, that assertions about divine creation and redemption can be grounded in religious experiences that are elicited by certain events in nature and history. The other half of the argument is essentially historical, focusing partly on considerations about the development of the concept of divine incarnation, and partly on the unavailability of Jesus for an incarnationalist theology. The first half of his substantive argument has already been examined; let me now turn to the second, taking it in the two stages suggested here.

The burden of Wiles's argument as it draws on the history of ideas focused on the interrelationship between creation, fall, and redemption. The early Church, we recall, insisted on the need for specific divine intervention in Jesus because it felt that such intervention was necessary in creation. Once we recognize that there is no need to insist on divine intervention with regard to creation, then the drive to demand divine intervention with regard to redemption has been removed. Incarnation, as classically understood, can be seen as part of the pre-modern or pre-scientific way of viewing the world that was inevitable prior to the rise of modern western thought-forms. If this is the case, it is the contemporary theologian's duty to recognize this for what it is, and develop a Christology that does not involve the kind of divine action expressed by the concept of incarnation.

The motivation that inspires this kind of argument is entirely laudable. The theologian must indeed be prepared to admit that the tradition even in its most central affirmations, including its basic beliefs about God, may have gone astray. Moreover, he must attend to the objections to his beliefs that arise out of his cultural and intellectual milieu. However, there is the constant temptation to think that the innovator in doctrine will have the truth on his side. He is often seen as a courageous and honest figure following gallantly where the argument leads amidst cries of 'heresy' from ecclesiastical authority. This is a much more exciting role than that accorded to the traditionalist, who, as his label suggests, is seen as a kind of reactionary figure clutching desperately to the deposit of the past, nervously shielding it from the winds of the modern world, and creating stumbling-blocks where none ought to exist.[51]

We can be grateful that sensitive theologians eschew the temptation to let this count for much. It is one of the great merits of Wiles's position that, radical though it undoubtedly is, it does not yield at this point but attempts to work through the issues with great care.[52] If anything he is a reluctant innovator, who feels impelled to reinterpret the incarnation because this is where the evidence inevitably leads. All this, however, does not establish that he is right. More especially it does not show that his argument about the interrelationship between creation, fall, and redemption licenses his claim that we can disentangle divine intervention from redemption just as easily as we can disentangle it from creation.[53] As in the case of Hick's use of the fall story as an analogy to the story of incarnation, significant disanalogies are being ignored.

The most significant of these concerns the kinds of truth that the stories of creation and incarnation convey.[54] The former stories convey truths about the world and about God. Concerning the world, they convey the truth that it is a cosmos rather than chaos, that man is of special significance within it, that it is dependent on God for its creation and preservation. In so far as they are truths about God they are of a very general nature, e.g. that He is creator and sustainer of all that is, that He is powerful, that He is wise. To remove divine intervention from the story by treating those parts that speak in this way of God's action as mythological should not make an appreciable difference to one's convictions about God. If there is a god at all he will be identified as creator of all that is, and given this it is obvious that he must be powerful and wise.

However, that God loves us with a love unsearchable, that He has genuinely entered into the miseries of the world, that He can really overcome the evils that afflict us, that He forgives us and restores us to fellowship, that He brings us sinners into the glorious liberty of the children of God—in short that He can and does and will redeem us—are not truths that can be read off the world of nature or of history. It is here that the analogy with creation is positively misleading. That a transcendent agent should be worshipped legitimately as redeemer does seem to involve the kind of divine intervention that Wiles has rejected. That it should require incarnation can never be claimed as any kind of necessity, for it must always be seen as an act of audacious and wondrous grace. But those who accept the kind of divine intervention that incarnation involves should be reluctant to let this inhibit them from relying on such events for their assurance about God's love for them. At a minimum they can confess with some justification that the alternative warrants an offer with a mythological analysis of discourse about direct divine action are inadequate.

At this juncture we arrive back at the point where, as we have seen already, reason-giving may have to come to an end. We have returned, that is, to fundamental disagreements about the warrants that are needed to license claims about divine love. It is in order for Wiles to attempt to take us out of this impasse by drawing on the second part of the historical side to his programme. This strand in the argument involves the contention that theoretical considerations about the relation between God and Jesus in the end leave us on no solid ground. They do not help for the simple reason that the kind of Jesus the incarnationalist needs to give content to his claims about divine incarnation is not available. After drawing attention to the great variety of reconstructions of the story of Jesus made available by historians and insisting that their existence is something the doctrinal theologian must accept, he writes:

It will now I think be clear why I do not consider it necessary to develop in detail my more theoretical affirmation that it is not possible to ascribe an absolute authority to a particular section of experience within the world, such as the life of Jesus. It was unnecessary because no such isolable section is in fact accessible to us. We do not need to discuss whether it would be philosophically and religiously appropriate to ascribe such authority to Jesus, for no such Jesus is available to us or likely to become available to us.[55]

In the same vein he continues:

I want to insist that there is an oddity, which we must not allow our sophistication to obscure from us, in affirming of a particular historical person that he is the embodiment of the divine and at the same time acknowledge that our knowledge about him in himself is at every point tentative and uncertain. Any absoluteness implicit in the concept of an incarnate divine being is necessarily dissipated by the tentativeness of our knowledge of his life and works.[56]

This objection, if it succeeds, really does resolve the impasse for it destroys a major part of the incarnationalist's foundations. The incarnationalist, as I have interpreted him in this study, does need reasonably reliable information of a substantial sort to secure some of the warrants for his claim that God became incarnate in Jesus. Kierkegaard's *nota bene*[57] just is not enough for the person who is interested in warrants for his claims about incarnation and who sees the matter of justification as closely related to the meaning of factual discourse. Moreover, Wiles is correct to point out that this is an objection the philosophers in particular must heed.[58] However, the last word on this should not rest where he has left it.

To begin with, we should distinguish between two quite different claims. On the one hand, there is the claim that the application of historical criticism to the New Testament traditions has produced a large number of alternative reconstructions about what can be responsibly believed about Jesus. Any sensitive and alert theologian must acknowledge this. On the other hand, there is the claim that the presence of major controversy in this field precludes anyone from claiming any measure of confidence in the reconstruction that he might favour. Although these two claims cannot be kept unrelated, they should not be so related that acceptance of the former implies acceptance of the latter.

The former should make us circumspect and sensitive in our judgements about what is historically possible, but it need not make us lose heart or turn agnostic. If this were allowed on the grounds of the general principle that controvery should preclude confidence, then much more is at stake for the theist, for he must acknowledge that his belief in God is and has been a matter of major controversy. But this is a principle that we would reject in most spheres of life, so aside from the warning it gives about the need for caution, it should be ignored.

Wiles himself, in fact, ignores it, for he has enough confidence in his own beliefs about Jesus to claim that we can know enough about his life to continue telling the story of his life and death as a parable of the relation between God and the world. Indeed he is confident enough to claim that 'It is most unlikely that the kind of historical knowledge about Jesus available to us or that may become available to us in the future could ever deform that picture to such a degree as to rule out the appropriateness of linking the incarnation myth in this special way with the person of Jesus.'[59] If it is open to Wiles to be as confident as this in the midst of controversy, then it is open to the incarnationalist to claim the same for his own convictions about what can be said about Jesus. That they disagree on what is available is part of the dispute between them. So long as they have explored the matter with integrity and are prepared to change in the light of evidence, there is no reason why each should not put forward his view with such confidence as he thinks it merits.

The conclusion to be drawn from this is that the second part of Wiles's historical argument does not undermine a central part of the incarnationalist's foundations and thereby resolve the impasse described earlier. What it does do is illustrate afresh just how complex the arguments are. More particularly it bids us be wary of treating provocative suggestions[60] about the mythological character of discourse about divine action as satisfactory. To be sure, there is some discourse in the traditions of Christianity that has been and should be analysed in this way.[61] Indeed, it would be insensitive and unimaginative to think that all its discourse about divine action was factual and explanatory. But to apply this analysis to discourse about divine incarnation and to all discourse about divine speaking and miracles is another matter entirely. To many it may seem to be the more consistent and more rigorous path to take, but this is misleading. It is only more consistent if it is really carried through to the very end, and this Wiles does not do, for it is clear that he only intends to apply it to discourse about direct divine action in the world.[62] Divine creation, divine sustaining of the universe, and even some conception of divine redemption are left intact. And it is only more rigorous if the substantive arguments developed to support this analysis can really bear the weight cast on them, and this is far from established.

This undergirds to some degree the assumption that the traditional believer should not be unduly perturbed if he is accused of offering an outdated analysis of discourse about direct divine action. At a minimum he can claim that the alternative analysis presently available is far from obligatory, and that there is much to support his own factual analysis of the discourse about divine action, as presented here. Moreover, he can justly claim that the abandoning of factual discourse about direct divine action is a momentous step to take. Indeed so momentous that it will destroy the Christian tradition as it is generally known.

We may conclude the first part of this study more generally by noting that the loss of the idea of direct divine intervention from theism is more momentous than one would initially expect. When examining specific examples of direct divine action it was clear that they provide significant warrants for claims about God's acts in history, for his intentions and purposes in acting, and for his love for mankind. It is therefore no trivial matter if they are to be abandoned under pressure from historical criticism.

I have also indicated that claims about divine intervention can legitimately be interpreted as factual, and that they require some support from considerations that are the province of historical science. This brings us to the point where we can naturally change the focus of this study to concentrate on the effect of historical criticism on claims about divine intervention in the world.[63]

5

DIVINE INTERVENTION
AND ANALOGY

Now that an account of the significance and meaning of certain key instances of divine intervention in the Christian tradition is available, we are in a position to embark on the second major phase of this inquiry. It is to be guided by this question: should the traditional claims as set forth in the first four chapters be abandoned because of the character of critical historical investigation? The question as it stands is negative, but this should not be taken to imply that I shall have nothing to say about the positive relation that exists between theological claims about divine intervention and such findings as fall within the domain of history. The question is posed this way simply because it helps focus the issue sharply, and because it suggests a point of entry into a complex discussion.

In this first of a trio of chapters which will examine the thought of three lucid thinkers on the relation between faith and history, I shall draw on and examine the work of Troeltsch to show that the question should be answered in the negative. There are good reasons for focusing on Troeltsch. He has been the inspiration to many who have felt that there is an inevitable and uneasy tension between the historian and the traditional Christian.[1] Furthermore, he has some highly significant things to say about the character of historical inquiry. This is not surprising in that much of his intellectual endeavour was devoted to an analysis of history. To neglect his thought would be to neglect a figure of major importance. Moreover, Troeltsch was convinced that the emergence of history meant the end of traditional Christianity.[2] Exploring his views will therefore pre-empt the charge that an analysis of history that would be congenial to the theological claims set out here has been sought.[3]

It needs to be recognized, to be sure, that Troeltsch must be interpreted with care. This partly stems from the fact that he was something of a polymath: he can rightly claim the titles of theologian, historian, philosopher, and sociologist of religion. It is also owing to the fact that his contribution to an analysis of historical inquiry, although it was expressed in seemingly bare and dogmatic form, was essentially exploratory in character. We are, of course, fortunate in that Troeltsch set out his views succinctly in the essay 'Über historische und dogmatische Methode in der Theologie'.[4] But it would be wrong to say that his views had been made conveniently available in that essay, for 'the fact is that this essay has as its presupposition everything I[he] had written before'.[5] It is worthy of note, however, that there is general agreement among commentators as to what Troeltsch considered to be the central features of historical inquiry, so that there is no need for excessive timidity in interpretation. It is also important to note that it is not crucial for the purposes of this book to give a full and detailed account of Troeltsch's views. What is crucial is that a reasonably lucid account of historical inquiry can be extracted from Troeltsch.

This account will fall into two sections, the first outlining what Troeltsch considered to be the primary aim of historical inquiry, the second describing the central presuppositions of historical inquiry. In this exposition recourse will be made at times to Troeltsch's own terminology, but as he has expressed his views in two distinct sets of categories there is no need to adhere slavishly to his concepts.[6] What matters is the substance of his claims. An attempt will then be made to show that further arguments than those provided by Troeltsch will have to be given in order to license the conclusion that claims about divine action as specified earlier are to be abandoned. Let us begin with Troeltsch's account of the primary aim of historical inquiry.

Attitudes to the past vary from person to person. Some may approach it out of curiosity, others with the hope that it will confirm their prejudices about the ancestors of their political opponents, others with the hope that it will furnish telling illustrations for their next sermon. A distinguishing feature of the historian is that he approaches the past 'scientifically'. He approaches the past with the primary aim of explaining what has happened. According to Troeltsch, such a critical attitude to the past is a relatively recent development, for 'in history as in natural science, systematic thought is the product of a relatively high state of civilisation'.[7] Primitive man did not develop any systematic thought in this area because the scope of his interest was limited, because there was no desire for real knowledge, and because he tended to look at himself as something apart and absolute. The only exception to this in ancient times was the Greeks. They were the first to investigate and reflect historically, in that they wrote untrammelled by the traditions of the temples and the archives of the princes, in that they were impelled by a thirst for knowledge, and in that their travels dissipated limited, insular interests. Thus Herodotus, Thucydides, and Polybius laid the foundations of history by approaching the past with the primary aim of explaining what happened. History for such pioneers was 'an explanation of public events by material and psychological causes, and in particular as a reasoned concatenation of events occurring in the Europaeo-Asiatic arena. Even these early writers took account of analogies and uniformities with a view to reaching general historical conceptions...'[8] These promising beginnings were, however, extinguished by Christianity, which despite incentives to the contrary produced 'not a scientific but a renewed mythological representation of history'.[9] This was so because the scope of its interest was limited, because its account of past events was riddled with speculation, and because it fostered no critical spirit, regarding the desire to explain as a mark of the profane mind. As a result, a mythology of redemption replaced historical reflection.

The rise of humanism and the Renaissance saw the reversal of this process by reverting to the Greek tradition. During this time the foundations of modern historiography were laid. The coming of the Enlightenment and of the Romantic era led in due course to the full flowering of historical studies. Thus there emerged 'the full development of historical reflexion, which notwithstanding all misgivings as to its conclusions, consists, precisely like the modern conception of nature, in a purely scientific attitude to facts'.[10] What Troeltsch meant by a purely scientific attitude can best be illustrated by noting attitudes that stand in a relation of contrast to the scientific attitude. He positively or explicitly characterized this attitude in this way:

In history, as in other things, purely theoretical knowledge is knowledge based upon general conceptions, and that signifies knowledge derived from causal conceptions. The sole task of history in its specifically theoretical aspect is to explain every movement, process, state and nexus of things by reference to the web of its causal relations. That is in a word, the whole function of purely scientific investigation.[11]

To approach the past in this manner is to approach it with an interest of the first degree and such interest is to be distinguished from interest of the second degree.

Generally speaking approaching the past with an interest of the second degree is to approach the past with the aim of establishing the significance of what has happened for human feeling and action. Such interests may be of a varied nature. Troeltsch distinguishes no less than six different interests of the second degree. Thus one could approach the past with an aesthetic attitude, that is, with a desire to achieve 'an artistically rhythmical construction of the course of events'.[12] One could also approach the past just out of mere curiosity and thus with a keenness to focus on the remarkable, the astonishing, and the uncomfortable, ever ready to be excited and moved by graphic descriptions. One could approach the past from a moral point of view, aiming 'to estimate the ethical value of human actions and to derive from history an insight into that which reveals itself everywhere as a moral force'.[13] Or one could approach it from an educational point of view, seeing history as a means of educating national and political opinion, trusting that education is best when it results from the concrete observation of the whole historical process rather than from abstract doctrines. One could approach it out of ideological concern, seeking support in history for the sociological and economic principles which are to be the basis of society. Or one could approach it from a sceptical standpoint, seeking to show that 'history yields but little information, and more than anything else brings home to man the limitations of his knowledge'.[14]

Troeltsch has no desire to deny the propriety of such attitudes; nor for that matter does he desire to exclude them entirely from history. What he is saying is that they do not represent the primary interest of the historian, and that therefore they must be relegated to a position of secondary importance.

So far as historical study is concerned with distinctively theoretical and scientific interests, these other interests as being here of secondary importance must be scrupulously guarded against and excluded. We may grant that, if descriptive historical works were composed upon such rigid lines, they would lack interest and charm for the majority of readers, and the impression they make depends precisely on the combination of purely historical knowledge with the motives and incentives that may be drawn from it. Delineations of this type, however, are necessarily composite, and must be recognised and studied as such. They combine the interest of the first degree, i.e. that of purely historical knowledge, with interests of the second degree, i.e. those relating to the significance of such for human feeling and human action. Such works are accordingly not purely scientific at all, and historical knowledge is to be obtained from them only by a process of elimination.[15]

Troeltsch may have overstated his case somewhat here, but that he is basically correct is borne out by the fact that historians do often make it clear that their primary aim is to find out what has happened in the past, and that it is not their aim to offer, say, moral judgement as to what has happened. A good example in this regard is Bullock's study of Hitler. In the preface to *Hitler, A Study in Tyranny*, Bullock notes that it has not been his purpose 'either to rehabilitate or to indict Adolf Hitler. If I cannot claim the impartiality of a judge I have not cast myself for the role of prosecuting counsel, still less for that of counsel for the defence.'[16] This does not mean, however, that the historian will refrain from moral judgement. Indeed Bullock spares no mercy in his appraisal of Hitler's life. Thus he writes:

The fact that his career ended in failure, and that his defeat was pre-eminently due to his own mistakes, does not of itself detract from Hitler's greatness. The fault lies deeper. For these remarkable powers were combined with an ugly and strident egotism, a moral and intellectual cretinism. The passions which ruled Hitler's mind were ignoble: hatred, resentment, the lust to dominate and where he could not dominate, to destroy. His career did not exalt but debased the human condition and his twelve years' dictatorship was barren of all ideas save one—the further extension of his own power and that of the nation with which he had identified himself.[17]

But such moral appraisal, explicit as it is, must not be taken to be the primary purpose of the historian. His primary purpose is to explain what has happened by offering a critical account of the past that sets out the evidence for the conclusions reached.[18]

It is initially plausible to argue against Troeltsch that his distinction between the interest of the first degree and interests of the second degree is quite irrelevant to a proper account of the nature of history. Thus it might be said that one's motives for doing a particular piece of historical research are irrelevant in that what matters is not why one engages in the research but rather whether the proper canons of evidence have been adhered to in reaching one's conclusions. A historian might, for instance, choose to study the history of the Orange Order in Ireland because of a political commitment about the present troubles in Ireland. But such considerations are irrelevant when he writes the history of the Orange Order, in that his motives do not guarantee the correctness or incorrectness of his account of the history of the Order.

In general, this is surely a proper distinction to make, but it is not clear that Troeltsch need deny it. Indeed to approach the past with the interest of the first degree is but another way of saying that the historian is to be primarily concerned with accurately explaining what has happened, and he can only do this by attending to the canons of evidence that historians rely on. To make this explicit by depicting such an interest as the interest of the first degree may render it more probable that this will in fact occur.

Besides, Troeltsch indicates essential agreement with this distinction between the motives for doing a piece of research and the reasons for the conclusions of research in some remarks about the role of personal experience in historical judgement.

Only in one single point is this simple process of discrimination attended with any real difficulty. One may ask whether, in view of the peculiar nature of psychical causation, or motivation (which will be more fully discussed presently), the insight necessary to determine and appreciate it must not be drawn from personal experience and personal judgment. Such insight, it will be said, is always bound up with subjective estimates of what ought to be. Thus, e.g. only those who feel that certain ethical, political, and artistic excellences ought to exist will seek and discover them as real springs of action, while those who do not so regard them will seldom be able to recognize them as motives, and the less so as historical causes do not lie on the surface or force themselves into notice, but are, as a matter of fact, always brought to light by the sympathetic imagination. Such a view is certainly not wrong. Yet it does not subvert our fundamental principle, since the causes so discovered and realized are, in the sphere of historical study, taken account of as facts only, and not as grounds for the corrections and criticisms of the historian, whose subjective attitude to the facts must, accordingly, be once more discounted. Besides, every supposed and on grounds of analogy, probable cause must be shown to be actually operative in the particular case. Knowledge of the power of motives is thus, as a means of discovery, doubtless bound up with personal judgments, and the knowledge of what should be often serves as a heuristic principle for the understanding of forces actually at work. But the 'ought-to-be' must in turn always be separated from what really is. Historical study is concerned only with the latter, and the personal judgments which have lent keennes to the power of perception must give way before the evidence of the real facts. Historical investigation is, in practice, always subjectively conditioned by the fullness, depth, and range of the personal experience of the investigators themselves, and is thus always marked by irreducible differences in their several starting-points. But the purely scientific aim of historical reflexion is not thereby surrendered.[19]

What has thus far been outlined does not offer any obvious implications for claims about divine action. It might be said that it casts doubt on the capacity of a traditional theologian to engage in historical research in that he may be tempted to allow his religious interest, say, in the unique role he ascribes to Jesus, to diminish the interest of the first degree. This may happen, but it need not happen. On the contrary, his awareness of this interest of the second degree may now act as a spur to guard against such temptation, and for this insight he may be grateful to Troeltsch. Thus he may take steps to ensure that his conclusions are really reached on the basis of evidence rather than being prompted by a desire to satisfy his religious interest. Paying careful attention to the criticisms of fellow historians who do not share his religious interest might be one practical step to take in this process.

If the traditional theologian is to be criticized for making claims about divine action, then it is obvious that the criticism for such claims must arise from other aspects of Troeltsch's account of historical inquiry. To another aspect of Troeltsch's account we now turn, namely to his remarks about the presuppositions of historical inquiry.

By way of introduction it should be noted that the term 'presuppositions' in this context is not an altogether happy one in at least two respects. First, it could be used to cover matters that Troeltsch does not have in mind. Thus it might rightly be said that a historian presupposes a host of things prior to engaging in a particular piece of research. Thus, for example, he presupposes that there is a past, he presupposes the reliability of his eyesight to read the texts before him, he presupposes the laws of logic that enable him to draw inferences from the 'facts' before him, and he presupposes the uniformity of nature in that he takes for granted that the paper he wrote the first draft of his work on will remain essentially the same when he consults it for final writing. Moreover, he may presuppose that the general body of historical conclusions reached in the area of his research are correct, or more specifically, he may presuppose that the controversial thesis he argued in an earlier stage of his career is still correct despite criticisms. Because of this the term 'presuppositions' is too inclusive to capture what Troeltsch has to say.

On the other hand, the term may be too exclusive in that it gives the impression that Troeltsch is dictating rather narrowly in advance the conclusions that the historian may reach in his work. Thus Mackintosh prefaces his exposition of Troeltsch by the remark, 'it is always depressing to be told in advance how much we are going to be permitted to believe.'[20] In one sense this is true of Troeltsch, but what Mackintosh fails to grasp is that in this sense Troeltsch may be quite correct. There may well be certain limits as to what will count as an explanation in history, and if there are such limits then this will to some extent set restrictions as to how much we are going to be permitted to believe *as* historians. Troeltsch, however, did not desire to dictate in advance the specific conclusions historians must reach, for to do that would be to render their efforts redundant; it would be to make historical research unnecessary.

Despite these reservations, the term 'presupposition' will be retained, in that it does capture to some extent what Troeltsch had in mind when he argued that the historian is irrevocably committed to the principles of criticism, analogy, and correlation. As Rand points out, Troeltsch is laying down a set of broad heuristic directives that are to guide the historian in his work. 'They are to influence his aims and goals and help determine what he must look for in his subject matter and what questions to put to that subject matter.'[21] Such directives are presuppositions in that they are taken for granted by the historian throughout his work. Indeed without them he could not practise his art at all. Troeltsch identified three presuppositions: criticism, analogy, and correlation.

Troeltsch's directive that the historian should presuppose the principle of criticism means that the historian is to offer his conclusions in the form of probability judgements of a greater or lesser degree. His conclusions, that is, do not take the form of necessary truths, as in mathematics, but are contingent in character and can be ranged on a scale of truth so that some conclusions may be claimed to be more likely to be true than others. Given this, there will be differences in the inner attitude of the historian to his claims. Concerning some claims he will feel very sure, concerning others less sure, etc. Further, his conclusions will always be open to revision should fresh evidence emerge, and thus they cannot be treated as absolute or final.

Troeltsch's second principle, analogy, is the means whereby the historian grades his judgements. As the historian seeks to determine what happened in the past he guides his work by his convictions about what is taking place in his own time, and uses this as a scale for judging the probability of claims about the past. 'Harmony with the normal, familiar or at least repeatedly witnessed events and conditions as we know them is the distinguishing mark of reality for the events which criticism can recognise as really having happened or leave aside.'[22]

Thus it is by analogy with events that we know take place that we test out the probability of events having taken place in the past. The extent to which we ascribe probability to past phenomena depends upon how far they accord with the normal, usual, or widely attested modes of occurrence that we know. And when we have done this we can go on to observe analogies between past phenomena, so that uncertain features of one may be judged by analogy with the more certain features of another.

As it stands, the exposition of analogy in Troeltsch is far

from precise. In what follows I shall attempt to give further content to this concept by trying out various interpretations. By this process I hope to arrive at an understanding of the notion that is both serviceable in the present and not too far removed from what Troeltsch intended. To begin with, it can be understood in either a narrow or wide sense. On the former reading the historian is restricted to his own personal experience of what is normal, usual, or widely attested. On the latter reading the historian is allowed to appeal to what is normal, usual, or widely attested in the experience of people presently alive.

Both of these are open to objection. The first is surely too restrictive, in that it rules out events that historians fully accept as happening. As Collingwood noted, 'That the Greeks and Romans exposed their new-born children in order to control the numbers of their population is no less true for being unlike anything that happens in the experience of contributors to the Cambridge Ancient History.'[23] Not even if a historian has himself seen someone being murdered or intentionally killed could the aforementioned activity have been allowed, for he still would not have satisfied the restricted conception of analogy. Killing of new-born children would then be analogous to one event in his own experience, but not to that which is normal, usual, or widely attested in his experience.

If the historian had at one time fought in battle or been a member of a band of terrorists that held weekly murder sessions, or if, holding that abortion is a form of child-killing, he has seen abortions performed on a regular basis, then the narrow conception of analogy would be satisfied. But this has only to be stated to be seen to be much too restrictive a foundation for the historian's judgements about the past. Not only is it the case that historians do not operate with such canons of probability, but it is also the case that if they did they would have much less to recount than at present.

The second, less narrow conception of analogy is not obviously vulnerable to the charge of being hyper-restrictive. Certainly it will allow the historian to allow as true a much wider class of statements about the past. On this interpretation of analogy, so long as the event in question is in harmony with the normal, usual, or widely attested event in the experience of people presently alive then it can be accepted as having happened to a greater or lesser degree of probability. What degree of probability is to be predicated I take to be a matter of trained judgement on the part of the historian, as it is difficult to see how any statistical conception of probability could be in use here.

However, there are three distinct objections to be made to this conception of analogy. First, it is quite impossible to put into effect. It would take the historian so long to ascertain what was the normal, usual, or widely attested that it is doubtful whether he would ever find time to do any historical research. We can imagine him going on world tours to find out for himself what were normal, usual, or widely attested events, or we can imagine him consulting specially compiled encyclopaedias that give lists of what is normal etc. for different parts of the world. Moreover, he would need to keep up to date on such matters. Not only do historians fail to engage in such activity with any kind of vigour; it is difficult to see how they could do it and at the same time find time for their specialized activity.

The second objection turns on the fact that it is clear that the historian exercises critical judgement not only with respect to what is claimed to have happened in the past but also with respect to what is claimed to have happened in the present. This is to be expected on the grounds that in one sense there is an identity between past and present. What has been past was at one time the present, and what is the present will at one time be the past. It would therefore be odd to insist that one should have epistemological priority over the other. Rather, one can imagine the historian disputing claims about events in the present by appealing to what he knows has happened in the past just as readily as he disputes claims about the past by appealing to what he knows is happening in the present. This being so, it is misleading to construe his canons of critical judgement as being grounded in the normal, usual, or widely attested occurrences of the present. Such an analysis oversimplifies the character of critical historical judgement.

The third objection appeals to the fact that in some cases historians would be prepared to allow as happening events that are not normal, usual, or widely attested. That Luther nailed his ninety-five theses to the door of the Castle Church in Wittenberg in 1517 is readily accepted as having happened, even though it is not an event that could be classed as usual, normal, or well attested in present experience. To be sure, there have been other dramatic instances of religious protest in the past that are similar to that of Luther, but strictly speaking these are irrelevant in that it is present experience that is said to be the basis for judgements about the past, and in that it would be wrong to class such protests as normal, usual, or widely attested; they are rather not normal, unusual, and rarely attested. More telling counter-examples to this thesis are events of a spectacular character such as the climbing of Mount Everest or the first human landing on the moon, both of which must surely be classed as not being normal, usual, or widely attested.

It is tempting to pause at this point and triumphantly pronounce that the principle of analogy should be rejected outright. To do this, however, would be premature for three reasons. First, the above exposition assumes that Troeltsch was attempting to set out a necessary condition which claims about past events must satisfy. This was not Troeltsch's intention, as I have noted already.[24] Secondly, the above exposition assumes that the principle of analogy operates in independence from the principle of correlation. Neither was this Troeltsch's intention, as we shall see.[25] Thirdly, on purely intuitive grounds there is surely something important enshrined in this principle. What this might be can be explored by recourse to an imaginery piece of historical research.

Suppose a historian is interested in finding out when Plato wrote *The Republic*. Reading through his sources he encounters the suggestion that Plato wrote *The Republic* when he was two years old. There is no doubt as to what the historian would do: he would reject this suggestion immediately. When questioned as to why he rejected this suggestion he would frown, and say something akin to, 'Well, everybody knows that children of two years of age do not write books like *The Republic*.'

In essentials this is surely an appeal to the principle of analogy in that it is an appeal to what everybody knows, an appeal to what is normal, usual, or widely attested. It is because this event would be so disanalogous with the normal that it is rejected immediately. If we challenged the historian to explain why we should accept this principle, he would simply become impatient or annoyed or even question our sanity.

But why, we naturally ask, does he not apply the same reasoning to claims about the first moon landing? Suppose, for instance, he was confronted with a primitive tribe who resolutely refused to believe his story about this marvellous event. They insist that this is so disanalogous to what everybody knows that, precisely for this reason, they will not believe it. Newsreels and newspaper cuttings about the said marvel are rejected for the same reason. Yet the historian persists in attempting to persuade them that it has really occurred.

The subtle role that analogy plays in the foundations of historical judgement can be illustrated by following up this counter-example and asking how the historian is to persuade this tribe. There are three separate fields that the historian will need to work in concurrently. First, he must continue to bear testimony to the event that has happened, and where possible introduce similar testimony to this event from other quarters, e.g. from fellow westerners who are trusted by the tribe.[26] Secondly, he must initiate the members of the tribe into the theories and concepts of natural science, in particular into the theories that make possible space flights and moon landings. Thirdly, he must provide an understanding of the purposes and intentions of those who planned and carried out the moon landings. Given these three considerations, it is probable that the story about the first moon landing will be believed.

It should be noted that it will be believed even if there had only been one single unrepeated moon landing, indeed even if this had been the only one that will take place for centuries. We can envisage this by filling out the story further. Suppose the tribe now refuse to believe by appealing to the fact that this event is not normal, usual, or widely attested even in the west. How will the historian persuade them this time? Surely by pointing out that the human action involved in executing the landing could only happen once because, say, it would cost too much to have more than one, or that the government would not allow it, or that those who landed on the moon caught a fatal disease as soon as they reached their destination and they did not want to waste life like that. This time what is supplied is a variation on the set of beliefs about human agents already given; the act of landing on the moon is fitted into a complex framework of beliefs about people's wants and desires which make a single moon landing intelligible. Once this refinement is grasped and accepted the tribe will be persuaded.

It is clear from this that the principle of analogy is a principle that operates within a wider context. Given an agreed background set of beliefs around the world, it will be used to test out the soundness of testimony to past events. In the cast of the rejection of the claim that Plato wrote *The Republic* when he was two, the background beliefs consist in common-sense generalizations about the behaviour of two-year-olds. The primitive tribe, in rejecting the claim that a man landed on the moon, is also relying on background beliefs about the world and about human agents as they have understood them. In both cases there was an appeal to analogy, while in the latter we can see how this appeal can be challenged by challenging its background beliefs. There is thus an intimate relation between analogy and its context or network of background beliefs. What this context is for the historian, as Troeltsch sees it, is indicated in what he has to say about the principle of correlation. To that we now turn.

The link between analogy and correlation is found by Troeltsch in the fact that analogy presupposes a homogeneity in the activities of mankind from one generation to another. This allows one to posit that change cannot take place at one point in the past without other changes resulting from it. That events are interdependent and interrelated in intimate reciprocity is the essence of correlation: 'all events stand in a relation of interdependence that is correlative and constant and necessarily form a matrix of movement wherein every single thing is interrelated with everything close and each event stands in relation to others'.[27] Harvey infers from this that Troeltsch's principle of correlation implies that historical explanation 'necessarily takes the form of understanding an event in terms of the antecedents and consequences and that no event can be isolated from its historically conditioned time and space'.[28] As it stands this principle is imprecise in two important respects; first, in that there are two distinguishable conceptions of correlation, one strong and one moderate, and secondly in that more needs to be said about the character of historical explanation.

Concerning the former, the strong conception of correlation would consist in the claim that every event that happens is related causally to every other event that happens. This is obviously false. Thus my writing on this paper or the normal events in the day of an Oxford college are not causally related to most events taking place in Australia. It would be facile to read Troeltsch as claiming this. The moderate conception of correlation would consist in the claim that any event that takes place is related causally to some other events that take place. The merit of this interpretation is that it retains what is central to Troeltsch's principle of correlation, i.e. the notion of interrelation or interdependence, but it does not entail a doctrine of all-embracing determinism, a view that Troeltsch rejected.[29] Thus an event such as a military decision to go to war might be partly determined by other events without being fully determined by other events.

Concerning the incompleteness of Troeltsch's account of correlation, it is fruitful to dwell on the sharp contrast he draws between causation in natural science and causation in history. For him there was a radical difference between the two.

In natural science causality implied the absolutely necessary principle that events are bound together by a changeless, all-pervading, and, in all particular cases, identical law of reciprocity. Such laws were established by means of controlled experiment and were the foundations of exact calculation. Expressing this in modern dress, natural science explains an event x by showing that x can be predicted with a greater or lesser degree of certainty by relating x to a set of preceding conditions and laws which together entailed or rendered inductively probable the occurrence of x.[30]

Historical causation is something entirely different. This

is so because it is almost exclusively a matter of psychological motivation.[31] And because of this there is an inevitable degree of unpredictability. This is so, firstly, because in the historical sphere everything passes through the medium of consciousness. This means that there is an element of incalculability or 'irrationality' about human actions and the motives for them, in that it is not possible to know the constant interaction of conscious efforts into which even unconscious elements tend to resolve themselves. Secondly, motives themselves are infinitely complex, so much so that every particular case has its own peculiar and special character and thus defies all calculation and experimental proof. A third reason for this unpredictability or incalculability in history is the fact that in the historical process there ever emerges the new, which constitutes an element of essentially fresh content occasioned by a convergence of historical causes.

Troeltsch's remarks about psychological motivation are far from clear. However, one way of expressing his basic thesis more lucidly at this point is to say that the historian is principally concerned with explanations that make appeal to the choices of a free agent. He explains an event, x, by showing that x is the direct effect of the activity of an agent exercising his free and rational choice. Citing the motives and reasons for the acts of such agents would render such action intelligible but not intelligible in the sense of a causal explanation as used in natural science. Intelligibility would involve placing the actions of the agent in a complex framework of interpretation that is different from and not reducible to the scientific.[32]

This is not to imply that the historian is confined to explanations of this type. As Troeltsch points out, the historian does explain some events by means of natural causation.

Polar limitations, glacial periods, earthquakes, famines, destructive winters, uninhabitable regions, and the like, often play a great part in history, and certainly not always by their purely psychological effects. The destruction of Napoleon's army by the Russians was due only in part to the psychological effects of the cold; and even in cases where geographical and physiological conditions eventually produce psychological results, we have something very different from purely psychological motivation.[33]

Thus far, correlation may be summarized as follows. Historians presuppose an intimate interdependence between events in the past, an interdependence that is reflected in the fact that they offer causal explanations of events. Primarily their concern is to offer causal explanations that involve a complex appeal to the choices of personal agents, but they also make use of the type of causal explanation to be found in natural science.[34]

Reference to personal agents draws attention to one more element of imprecision that needs to be eliminated. Is the principle of correlation operating here either formal or material?[35] A formal conception of correlation would require only that the historian presuppose some relation of dependence between events and that most of his explanations have recourse to the choice of agents. No restriction, that is, would be placed on the type of personal agent that could be appealed to. The agent could be either human or divine. A material conception of correlation would place restrictions on the possible type of agent and thus on the possible type of dependence by allowing only such explanations as have recourse to the activities of natural and human agents. On this view, all past events must be explained in one of two ways by the historian: either by natural causation as found in natural science or by human causation as found in everyday discourse.

It is highly probable that Troeltsch was committed to the latter conception of correlation: 'Once it [the historical-critical method] is admitted, no boundaries can be drawn. It is formed out of the area of natural events and when it is applied to the supernatural it necessarily dissolves the latter into natural categories ...'[36] Given this, it is obvious that serious implications for claims about direct divine action in the past will follow. Of this Troeltsch had no doubts whatever.

Thus far I have sought to outline Troeltsch's account of the nature of historical inquiry. No attempt has been made to challenge the basic correctness of his views. It remains to be asked in this chapter whether commitment to Troeltsch's principles entails or implies that claims about divine action as specified earlier should be abandoned. This same issue can be approached by asking more specifically: could someone assent to the claim that God had spoken to someone, or that God had become incarnate in Christ, or that God had performed a miracle, and at the same time accept the principles of criticism, analogy, and correlation?

If we take these piecemeal, it is plausible to arrive at a response that is partly positive and partly negative. It will quickly become clear, however, that as the principles are so intimately related, a negative judgement on the basis of one principle will entail a negative judgement in relation to all the others. But let us begin with the positive.

Concerning criticism, this is surely something that could be accepted. The claims about divine action cited are certainly not necessary truths, nor need they be absolute in the sense that they are closed to revision in the light of further evidence. They may be accepted, that is, as judgements of probability arrived at after a series of considerations have been weighed together. What some of these considerations are has already been indicated elsewhere in this study.

The situation with respect to analogy is more complicated. On the positive side, an individual might very well accept both that God had spoken to someone and that God had performed a miracle, and not contravene analogy in that he might also believe that such events took place in the present. He might believe for example, that God called people to be missionaries or that God performed miraculous healings. On the negative side, he knows of no events that would be strictly analogous to the incarnation, for this was an event never to be repeated. This, however, need not perturb him unduly, for we have seen that the force of analogy is dependent on the efficacy of its background beliefs. It will depend, that is, on the conception of correlation embraced.

If he is committed to what has been called a formal conception of correlation, there will be no problem for any of the three claims cited. There has been no denial of the claim that events are intimately related to one another and that one should explain events either by showing that they are naturally caused or that they are caused by agents exercising their free and rational choices. To say that God did the acts cited is to imply that there is a relation of dependence between certain states of affairs and God, a relation that is reflected in the fact that to say 'God did it' is to offer an explanation for that state of affairs. Moreover, such an event may be intimately related to other events that are not brought about by God. Thus God's speaking to John Smith may inspire or lead John Smith radically to alter his way of life, and thereby establish a relation of interdependence between a whole series of events. It is difficult to see, therefore, how someone who assented to claims about divine action could avoid being committed to correlation, formally understood.

Given this conception of correlation, he may well be in a position to overrule the absence of analogy. To do this he would have to try in some manner or other to make the incarnation intelligible by relating it to the wider intentions or purposes of God. This in itself would constitute a major exercise in systematic theological reflection. Alternatively, he will offer reasons as to why no such further intelligibility can be supplied, on the grounds, for example, that at present we are not in a position to know why God has become incarnate only once.

It would not be surprising if Troeltsch were to find these positive remarks on the relation between history and divine action perverse. It is bound to appear to many as a sophisticated rearguard action that ignores the fact that Troeltsch was committed to what was called a material conception of correlation; and this of course radically alters the whole picture, for it builds into the concept of correlation the proposition that the historian can only allow natural or human agents as explanatory entities. As this effects analogy it provides different foundations for criticism. It will follow necessarily that someone could not assent to the divine actions specified and at the same time assent to criticism, analogy, and correlation. To put it curtly, everything in the end turns on what one is going to allow as properly explanatory in history. To accept that one can only explain the events of the past either by natural causation or by human psychological causation is to accept at the same time that God does not intervene in the world. And if one is deeply committed to this view, accepting that God has intervened will seem to be the mark of an uncritical and even superstitious mentality. Criticism and correlation are so intimately related as to guarantee this. And this in turn is bound to alter one's views about what it is to have an interest of the first degree. To countenance direct divine activity will be to betray an unscientific attitude to the past no matter what protestations are made to the contrary.

What is wrong with this programme is not that one should be committed in advance. Without commitment to some conception of correlation it is difficult to see how criticism or analogy could operate. Without background beliefs about causes there is only chaos in our assessment of testimony. If events happen as bolts from the blue or at random then there is no way of ascertaining what has happened in the past. The troubles lie elsewhere and are much more subtle in character. Two problems call for mention here.

First, there is a failure to see that discourse about direct divine action is explanatory. Direct actions of God are not bolts from the blue or random events, but are related to a wider conceptual scheme that gives point and intelligibility to their occurrence. As such they provide explanations for events in the world.[37] Moreover, there is no reason why intelligent and critical assessment of claims about direct divine action should not take place. That such claims require careful analysis, or that we are at a loss to know precisely how to exercise critical judgement in their assessment, should not detract from this fact.

No doubt Troeltsch's attitude at this juncture is understandable. He belonged to that tradition in nineteenth-century theology which, in agreement with its founder, Schleiermacher, felt that divine intervention in the world was an unnecessary burden for the religious mind and life.[38] In this he may be correct, but those who regard the instances of such activity at issue here as theologically important and as a gift will take an entirely different view of the matter. That some of those who take this view have in the past been reluctant to scrutinize their claims about direct divine action, or that they have been fearful of the results of historical research on the biblical documents, can be accepted. This does not establish, however, that one can only be critical if one is committed to a material conception of correlation. Failure to see this stems principally from a failure to see that to accept direct divine action is to widen rather than abandon the principle of correlation.

Secondly, there is a constant danger that conceptual points concerning the nature of historical explanation become transformed into debatable metaphysical claims or even into necessary truths. Let us grant, for the moment, that the historian is committed to the material conception of correlation. But this is a logical or conceptual point about the character of historical inquiry. It makes clear what kind of explanation a person, qua historian, can allow. It is not and should not be treated as a substantial claim about the nature of divine activity or about the nature of the world. Nor is this a substantial claim about the all-embracing efficacy of historians in explaining the events of the past. It is precisely this latter claim that the traditional theologian will want to dispute. Both he and his opponent will have to muster arguments of a very different sort than those used to establish a conceptual point about the nature of historical explanation.

An illuminating parallel is the attitude of the natural scientist to acts of God or acts of men. In explaining events the scientist qua scientist does not appeal to either God or man as explanatory entities. He explains events, as I noted, by showing that they can be predicted with a greater or lesser degree of certainty by relating them to a set of preceding conditions and general laws which together entail or render inductively probable their occurrence. But this does not preclude him from believing that either God or man have performed certain acts in the world. Nor does it preclude that God or men have in fact acted in the world. All it precludes is that the natural scientist will believe in such acts qua natural scientist. If he believes that they occur, we might say he believes them qua theologian or qua religious believer or qua ordinary man in the street. And arguments about the rightness or wrongness of these claims will not be resolved by making proper conceptual points about the character of explanation in natural science.

In the case of history, the slide from a conceptual point about explanation to a debatable metaphysical thesis about the world is succinctly expressed by Mitchell.

It is one thing to say that a scientific historian may not offer other than naturalistic explanations—he may not, for example, be other than neutral as to what happened to St. Paul on the road to Damascus. It is another thing to say that he must *qua* scientific historian, provide a complete naturalistic explanation of St. Paul's experience in terms, say, of abnormal psychology. He may, of course, do this if, as it happens, the evidence is clear enough to justify it, but he is not failing in his duty as a scholar if he concludes simply that Paul had an experience of a dramatic kind which altered the whole tenor of his life and which he took to be an encounter with the risen Lord. Similarly with the more problematic case of the Resurrection itself. If there were, as in principle there might be, evidence to justify an entirely straightforward naturalistic explanation of what occurred, the scientific historian must, of course, accept it; but if there is not, he is under no obligation to adopt the most plausible naturalistic explanation on offer in order to leave no gaps in the 'closed web of cause and effect'. Given the controversial nature of religious claims and the known practical difficulties of securing agreement about them, it is a wise policy for the historian not to pronounce upon them; but he is not bound to rule against them. It is another question, and in its own context an entirely proper one, whether in the light of what historical inquiry discovers a religious or a purely naturalistic interpretation of what happened is to be preferred.[39]

Kaufman goes so far as to treat Troeltsch's conception of correlation as a necessary truth, and this leads him to argue that direct acts of God are inconceivable.

An 'event' without finite antecedents is no event at all and cannot be clearly conceived; 'experience' with tears and breaks destroying its continuity and unity could not even be experienced. It is incorrect to suppose, then, that all that is required here is a reformulation of our categories so as to make room for an occasional act of God; the problem is that certain logical preconditions of connection, continuity and unity must obtain if there is to be any experience at all [Kant], and precisely these conditions are contradicted by the notion of particular 'acts of God' being performed from time to time in history and nature. Or, to put the matter in a somewhat different way: it is impossible to conceive such an act either as a natural event or as a historical event, as occurring either within nature or history; in short, it is impossible to conceive it as any kind of event (in the finite order) at all. Our experience if of a unified and orderly world; in such a world acts of God (in the traditional sense) are not merely improbable or difficult to believe: they are literally inconceivable. It is not a question of whether talk about such acts is true or false; it is, in the literal sense, meaningless; one cannot make the concept hang together consistently.[40]

It is to the great credit of Troeltsch that he did not transform a conceptual point about historical explanation into a necessary truth. Indeed, theoretically at least, Troeltsch recognized the need to keep open some crucial questions that the historian may be tempted to foreclose. This emerges in a distinction that he draws between 'empirical historiography' and 'the philosophy of history'. Empirical historiography is concrete historical investigation. Philosophy of history on the other hand designates a kind of catch-all category that embraces a series of issues which fall into two groups. The issues in the first group are 'metaphysical' and focus on the relation of the historical processes in the world to the fundamental forces of the universe. In this group Troeltsch places questions concerning the foundations of the physical world in the 'universal spirit', the connection between the physical and the psychical world, the divine direction and sustaining of the cosmos, and the distinction between the purely natural life of the soul and the spiritual and civilized life that strives to transcend it. The issues in the second group revolve around matters of ethics or value, centring on the significance of the historical process for the living and operative will of each particular age. In this group Troeltsch places questions concerning the teachings of history for the active and constructive will, the inward meaning and significance of that substance of life which takes concrete form in the process of history, the ideal values to be won from that process and to be recognized in it, and, finally, its ultimate meaning and aim.

Troeltsch is insistent that such questions be recognized as lying outside the sphere of history. 'These questions all lie outside the sphere of empirical historiography, and belong in reality to the philosophy of history which explains and estimates metaphysically. Empirical and philosophical history must be clearly distinguished in principle, though in the actual delineation of events they are usually found in some degree of combination.'[41] His most pertinent comment, for present purposes, refers explicitly to questions in the first group and thus to questions about the relation of God to the world. Noting that the metaphysical commitments of the historian are asserted in occasional aphorisms rather than elaborately constructed theories, and that the claim to be free from metaphysical elements on the part of modern historiography is no more than a theoretical emancipation, he continues: 'In the view of the practical importance of the metaphysical presuppositions, their separate consideration and discussion are matters of the highest import to philosophy, and the historian must take care to keep such vital questions open, and not to foreclose them by casual remarks and ostensible truisms.'[42]

To assert that the historian is in practice committed to a material conception of correlation is not to make a casual remark or an ostensible truism. But there is a manifest danger of converting such an assertion into casual remarks about the actual nature of the past that are accepted as ostensible truisms. We may grant that the historian may not, qua historian, write or speak of acts of God,[43] but this does not show that such acts have not taken place. Nor does it show that what a historian might discover could not be part of a cumulative argument in defence of claims about divine action. So those who argue that the claims about divine action cited elsewhere should be abandoned merely on the grounds that they contravene the material principle of correlation are not offering arguments. They are merely restating that principle in different words. Such verbal victories are worthless, and moreover, they do not cease to be verbal when analogy and criticism are interpreted in the light of such a conception of correlation and claims about divine intervention are rejected because they fall foul of these. If claims about divine intervention should be abandoned, considerations of a very different nature from those identified by Troeltsch must be marshalled. That this is so will be borne out in examination of a contemporary restatement of Troeltsch's account of the nature of historical inquiry.

6

DIVINE INTERVENTION AND HISTORICAL WARRANTS

ONE of the major merits of Harvey's discussion of the relation between theology and history is that he offers one way of restating the suggestions of Troeltsch. An exploration and assessment of his views should, therefore, enable fresh stock to be taken of the position adopted in the last chapter as well as further positive remarks to be made about the situation of the traditional Christian with regard to the role of history in his theological commitments.

Troeltsch, as has been seen, insisted that the historian guide his deliberations by the principles of criticism, analogy, and correlation. Although initially it was difficult to accept analogy, it was possible to interpret this in such a manner as to save it from criticism. Examples showed that analogy functioned quite legitimately against a set of background beliefs which, for Troeltsch, were enshrined in the principle of correlation. This principle was thus logically more fundamental than analogy and criticism. Both of these are interpreted in the light of correlation. I also noted that correlation was open to various interpretations, one of which proved relevant in a case against claims about divine action. This was shown, in turn, to be the kind of verbal victory that Troeltsch himself would probably have eschewed.

In structure Harvey's approach is very similar to that of Troeltsch. He too wants to argue that the historian has certain presuppositions or principles that guide his reflection, and that these presuppositions render it extremely difficult, if not impossible, for one to assent to claims about divine intervention in the world.

In my exposition of Harvey's account of history, I have no desire to undervalue the possible independence of his views from those of Troeltsch. That there is indebtedness to Troeltsch is readily confessed by Harvey,[1] but he has imaginatively and creatively developed Troeltsch's views by drawing on the work of others and by adding his own original suggestions. Moreover, he is critical of Troeltsch on at least two counts. First, Troeltsch's analysis 'was formulated in the somewhat ponderous and now unconvincing conceptual framework of German idealism'.[2] Secondly, he considers Troeltsch's formulation of the issues to be somewhat 'heavy-handed' and thus liable to carry the argument too quickly into the never-never land of metaphysical disputes.[3] It is in order to transcend such limitations in Troeltsch, no doubt, that Harvey develops his own formulation of the issues. I shall expound this formulation with enough freedom to bring out its high degree of plausibility as an account of history, but also, I hope, with enough discipline to be a fair and accurate rendering of his views.

As a starting-point it is useful to note that Harvey is distrustful of the term 'presupposition' when applied to history.[4] Such a term is misleading, he believes, for it obscures the plurality of fields implicit in the many types of judgement deployed by historians in their account of the past. Expressed technically, it obscures the fact that history is a field-encompassing field. The idea of a field-encompassing field is central to Harvey's understanding of history. This rests on the recognition of the fact that there is no single identifiable class or field of judgements called historical. Rather, what is available in historical writing and reflection is a diversity of claims. What is given to the audience of the historian is a multiplicity of types of sentence that are brought together into one coherent story of what happened. Thus, a historian may make remarks about people's motives and their money, about their sex-life or their suppers, about their health or their houses. Some of these remarks will be explanatory, some will be purely descriptive, and some will be evaluative or moral. There is no one type of sentence that will be deployed; they will range over a series of fields. By a field Harvey means 'a logical type of assertion that may be delimited from other types, like statements about motives may be distinguished from geometric axioms, or statements about moral guilt may be distinguished from assertions about legal responsibility'.[5] This concept of a field is a logical one in that it rests on the claim that fields are to be identified by noting the logical type of premiss, inference, and conclusion used in argument. To say that two arguments are in the same field is to say that the premisses and the conclusions in the two arguments are of the same logical type.

Once it is granted that the historian makes assertions that range over a variety of fields, it is futile to look for one single way of justifying his assertions. Rather, each assertion will have to be seen in the context of its own field and judged in the light of the standard of justification appropriate in that sphere.

If ... history is not so much a field as a field-encompassing field, which is to say, made up of diverse kinds of arguments making use of correspondingly diverse data and warrants, then the quest for one theory of historical explanation is seen to be fruitless, creating insóluble paradoxes that paralyze thought. It is possible that some explanations will make use of laws; others will employ 'law-like' generalizations; still others will fit neither of these models at all. It follows that there will also be diverse kinds of verification, and no-one can anticipate in advance how one can go about ascertaining their truth. To demand that historians should be able to state in advance and in clear and simple terms the criteria for justifying historical claims is naive, and one can only reply to it in such general terms as 'there should be good data and warrants'. But this tells us nothing until we know what kind of assertions we have on our hands, for there is no one particular kind of assertion peculiar to history. The real issue is not whether history can be objective or a science but whether, in particular cases, diverse kinds of claims can achieve our particular and relevant justification. Just as we do not ask in sweeping fashion whether legal judgments can be objective or not but attend to the more productive task of sorting out those that are adjudicable, so, too, we ought to forsake the wholesale questions about history and attend to the retail standards by which we can realistically hope to measure diverse claims.[6]

In the course of measuring diverse claims, the historian is careful to ensure that his conclusions are qualified to a degree that is commensurate with the evidence available. The historian's assertions, that is, cannot flatly be classed as either true or false. He makes his assertions with varying degrees of force by means of a careful and judicious use of qualifications. 'He indicates what he believes can be affirmed with practical certainty, what can be asserted only with caution or guardedly, and what is to be asserted as possible, given the present state of knowledge. The historian's assent, so to speak, possesses a texture. He does not traffic in mere claims but in qualified claims ranging from tentativity to certitude.'[7]

This reference to the present state of knowledge highlights a further feature that deserves mention, namely the connection that exists between the historian and the common-sense beliefs of his day. He will share the generally accepted beliefs of the time about how the world operates. Doing so, he will presuppose in his deliberations the findings of the sciences, as well as, say, truisms and generalizations about the behaviour of people under stress, the political trends of the period, the institutional capabilities of a nation, the effects of revolution on the rich, etc. etc. In this context I think it is appropriate to contend that the historian does have presuppositions. Indeed, without presuppositions a historian could never arrive at any conclusions about the past at all. As Harvey points out, 'all of our judgments and inferences take place ... against a background of beliefs. We bring to our perceptions and interpretations a world of existing knowledge, categories and judgments. Our inferences are but the visible part of an iceberg lying deep below the surface. Our realities are built up of explicit and hidden inferences.'[8] But the presuppositions that are thus used to determine what has happened in the past form a perspective that is a complex entity embracing a variety of types of assertion. To recognize this is central to any critical and realistic reading of the character of historical inquiry.

It is now clear why Harvey can rightly claim to have offered a reformulation of Troeltsch's 'most important insights'.[9] To be sure there is no explicit reference to the principles of criticism, analogy, and correlation. But as has already been noted[10] such terminological niceties are not of the essence of Troeltsch's views. That the substance of his account is retained is shown by Harvey's insistence that, in history, the past must be ascertained and understood on the basis of the present knowledge available to the historian. The historian arrives at a revisable and qualified judgement concerning what happened in the past by examining the deposits of the past in the light of his present, critically interpreted experience. This fund of critically interpreted experience is constituted by diverse kinds of knowledge and belief; it involves different fields each of which is identified by its unique type of data, warrants, and backings.

The exposition of Harvey's understanding of history is not yet complete, but it furnishes sufficient content to make clear the case he deploys against traditional Christian claims about past divine action. Harvey's discussion is very valuable in this regard because his case is quite explicit.[11] The major proposal he seeks to establish is that the application of historical inquiry to the biblical documents will inevitably undermine the claim that God performed miracles.

A point of entry into the heart of Harvey's attack on miracle is recognition of the fact that miracle automatically calls in question warrants that the historian takes for granted in all his thinking. That this is so can easily be shown by drawing on Harvey's terminology and applying it to the alleged resurrection of Jesus. By resurrection is understood here the bodily return to life of Jesus.[12] We begin with the assertion that Jesus died (datum). Since, on the basis of observed regularity in everyday life and on the basis of well-established laws of science (backing), dead men stay dead (warrant), Jesus was almost certainly not alive on the third day (conclusion), unless, that is, in this particular case the usual warrants can be shown not to apply and thus an exception is created (rebuttal). If this general argument is successful, it is obvious that the claim that God raised Jesus from the dead has been undermined. Just as the claim that Jones raised his arm at time t can be falsified by showing that Jones's arm did not rise at time t, so is the claim that God raised Jesus from the dead falsified showing that Jesus did not rise from the dead.

Harvey's conviction that the case against the resurrection is successful is founded on the claim that a defender of the resurrection cannot make either of the alternative moves that are open to him. He might try to challenge the truth of the warrant applied to the data, or alternatively, he might try to enter a rebuttal. The former is not open to the defender of the resurrection simply because he himself will accept these warrants as true in his everyday life. To reject them now would involve inconsistency or special pleading. The latter is not really open either, because there are two considerations that will tend to render relatively unnecessary any search for a rebuttal.

First there is the fact that the comparative study of religion has revealed that fictitious stories are regularly told about founders of religion by the adherents of that religion. Indeed the historian will expect to find this to be so, for 'if anything has been learned from the comparative study of religion it is that myth and legend are the most natural forms of expression for the veneration of extraordinary founders, teachers and saints of religion'.[13] This provides a generally acceptable account of why the early disciples told the story of the resurrection. Secondly, the accounts of the resurrection of Jesus come from a cultural epoch whose outlook was not informed by the content of science as ours is. As Strauss has pointed out, 'the writers of the New Testament—in fact the people of the entire age—were naïve and mythologically minded folk without any conception of natural law or order. They lived in a mythological time in which unusual events of nature and history were attributed to supernatural beings of all kinds.'[14] This too affords further information on how it occurred that the early disciples told the story of the resurrection. Taken together these considerations do not show that a rebuttal to the warrants of science as applying to Jesus cannot be given. What they do is to show that the search for one is almost certain to be unprofitable.

But even if such a rebuttal could be produced, the defender of the resurrection is still not clear of trouble. Even if he could produce a rebuttal and then could proceed to argue for the assertion that Jesus rose from the dead, there is still room for objection. He would still offend the canons of historical judgement by demanding that 'heavy assent be given to propositions that properly elicit soft assents, that assertions with a low degree of probability be converted into statements possessing a high degree of probability, that mere logical possibilities be confused with likely probabilities. This, in turn, seems to be a function of the fact that the passion of faith is tied indissolubly to certain specific historical assertions of a unique kind.'[15] Because of this failure to take seriously the complex and sensitive texture of historical judgement, Harvey is unreserved and unqualified in his critique of defenders of resurrection.

Thus he shares the general suspicion that traditional belief in the resurrection is obscurantist, for faith is permitted to tip the balance between two possibilities before the historian, a fact that contravenes the principle that faith has no function in the justification of historical arguments respecting fact. In such a situation 'the machinery of rational assessment comes to a shuddering halt'.[16] Furthermore such a belief is internally inconsistent, half modern and half primitive, in that it relies on warrants in normal historical inquiries, but then suspends these when its own most central and treasured content is scrutinized.[17] Moreover the believer in the resurrection is intellectually irresponsible in that he continually enters objections to our normal warrants for no principled reason.[18] Indeed, even talk of a miracle is enough to grind the argument to a halt, for with events which are by definition unique it is impossible even to formulate a standard for estimating what is likely or unlikely. 'Was Jesus born of a virgin? Did he walk on water? Calm the storm? Cast out demons? Talk with Satan? Raise Lazarus from the dead? Turn water into wine? How is it possible even to get into the position of asking whether these are candidates for being historical solutions to historical problems?'[19] The net effect of this is that the traditional believer is not to be trusted. His engagement in historical criticism lacks a certain toughness of mind, and behind this is the falsifying influence of the demand for belief.[20] The best cure for this is a 'revolution in consciousness'.[21] The traditional believer must embrace a new morality of knowledge, he must go back to the Enlightenment and learn afresh with Locke that 'he who would seriously set upon the search of truth ought, in the first place, to prepare his mind with love of it'.[22] Such earnest inquiry will ensure that the proper degree of assent is given to one's assertions.

What is to be said about Harvey's overall case? To begin with, Harvey has combined two very different ways of presenting his case about the character of history, only one of which can be deemed successful. Setting this out with some care will complete the exposition of his view, and prepare the way for a critique of his attack on the resurrection.

His two different strategies that provide the basis for his contention that the historian does and should accept the warrants of science can be identified as follows. On the one hand he supports his contention by noting that the historian inevitably belongs to the culture he inhabits. Let us call this the 'cultural relativist' argument. On this argument the historian should accept the warrants of science because he should accept the prevailing views as to the nature of the world, and for our culture these are partly constituted by the findings of science. On the other hand, he argues that the historian should be committed to the warrants of science because science furnishes knowledge of the world. Let us call this the epistemological argument.

To be sure, Harvey combines both these arguments, presenting them in one breath, as it were, and this is understandable. It is his belief that science, with the increased understanding of the world, has emerged and developed in our culture so that to insist that the historian must share the outlook of this culture is, *ipso facto*, to recognize claims to knowledge on the part of science. But the two arguments are logically distinct, and it would add strength to Harvey's case were they to be kept apart.

The cultural relativist argument appears most clearly in those passages where Harvey writes about 'our modern world-view', 'the historicity of the historian', and 'the common sense view of the world'. Thus he avers that a revolution took place in modern historiography when formal criteria in the critical ideal of historical judgement 'were informed by the new way of looking at the world created by the sciences: when thinking for oneself meant thinking in terms of the new world picture ... Historical thinking only became revolutionary when it was saturated by what we now call the common-sense view of the world, a misnomer in so far as it conceals how much this common-sense view is really the absorption into our natural habits of thought of an earlier and revolutionary thinking.'[23]

Harvey readily identifies with those:

who believe it is impossible to escape from the categories and presuppositions of the intellectual culture of which one is a part, the common sense of one's own time. For what we call common sense really consists of beliefs and knowledge that are the result of long historical development. These necessarily condition the perception and conception of all those who live in a culture. We are ... social and historical beings whose reasons are qualified by our inheritance and history. We are in history as fish are in water, and our ideas of possibility and actuality are relative to our time.[24]

Moreover, Harvey commends H. Richard Niebuhr for seeing that 'the historian includes his history as a member of Western culture who thinks with the warrants and criteria of Western man'.[25] And after approving of Bultmann for seeing the same, he writes:

We *cannot* see the world as the first century saw it. We can, it is true, imaginatively understand how they could have believed what they believed, but these beliefs are no longer practically possible for us. We have, as it were, bitten of the apple, and our eyes have been opened and our memories are indelibly stamped with a new vision of reality ... We have a new consciousness, and although we can transcend it from time to time in an act of historical imagination, we judge what we understand in the light of our present knowledge and interpret it in terms of our existing 'world'.[26]

It is to be noted here that the cultural relativist strand of Harvey's argument, detectable though it is, is not the central foundation for his contention that the historian must pre-suppose science. This is all to the good, for, prima facie, it is vulnerable to criticism. Adequate assessment of it would require much more sensitive treatment than can be afforded here, but two basic points can be made.

First, the presence of this argument can all too quickly lead to a hasty dismissal of Harvey's account on the grounds that all that he has offered is a description of the contemporary historian's historically conditioned mental life.[27] He has not really offered any reasons why the historian's intellectual endeavour *ought* to have the structure that it has. In short, it is more a matter of amateur, armchair sociology than critical philosophy of history. More significantly, it is open to debate whether there are such creatures as 'western man' or such an entity as 'the new world picture'. It might be more realistic to acknowledge that we live in a culture that is pluralistic with respect to world-views, so that atheism, agnosticism, and theism all have a measure of support. And within these world-views the role of science is both complex and disputed. To claim that science of itself constitutes a world-view is not at all clear, while to claim that science gives definite support to one particular world-view is a matter of deep dispute.

Differences in world-view do not, of course, preclude much overlapping and agreement about the nature of the world. Where we find such agreement it might be illuminating to talk of the common sense of that age. And Harvey is correct to insist that the common sense of an age will range over many fields, so that we must beware of 'sweeping appeals'[28] to it in support of an argument. But to accept this is not to accept the cultural relativist argument. We can accept much agreement between world-views, but insist that part of our anguish or joy is the absence rather than the prevalence of any one world-view. Once this is granted, the cultural relativist argument fails to impress, for we can grant that all are tied to their culture, but that in our culture this does not commit us to any particular world-view.

Happily, however, Harvey does not have to rest his case on the cultural relativist argument. Alongside it he has deployed the epistemological argument which argues that it is because science furnishes knowledge that the historian must take account of it in his thinking. When the historian makes assertions that fall within the domain of science, then his reflection must be guided by the relevant findings of science if he is to make claims to knowledge.

This does not mean that the historian must himself become a scientist. What is sufficient is that he rely on the findings of science as generally known. And to the extent that he does so, it must be conceded that there can be no autonomy on the part of the historian.[29] To attempt to arrive at conclusions independently and autonomously would be to risk error. Nor does this mean that science has reached some sort of final truth that cannot be revised, or that the historian must assume this. What is sufficient is that he takes as practically certain such findings as are well attested and form part of the background beliefs of our everyday intercourse with nature and man.

Nor does this mean that the historian presupposes only the findings of science. It is difficult, if not impossible, to put a limit on the number of sciences that history does presuppose, 'but history, like ordinary discourse, presupposes much more than the sciences, for the historian makes judgments about men's motives and values, national character, political trends, institutional capabilities, resolutions—none of which, precisely speaking, can be said to be the subject matter of a science.'[30] Where history does presuppose science, it does so not just because everybody in our culture presupposes it, but because science offers an explanation of nature, because it helps us to understand and make sense of the world, because it enables us to predict and to some extent control the future. Earlier generations were deprived of such understanding even though they did have some understanding of nature. 'Of course, it is true that savages know that a fall from a great physical height can cause death ... But no savage, so far as we are aware, *understands* why bodies fall ...'[31] He does not have a complex set of theories and laws which explain what is going on in nature such as science now provides.

The contention that science has a right to claim knowledge has already been accepted elsewhere in this study.[32] It is further accepted here that the historian should rely on the findings of science if he is to arrive at knowledge of the past. Without science there is inevitably going to be much too great a measure of conjecture or falsehood. The historian, in so far as he proffers knowledge of the past, is committed to any knowledge furnished by science that is relevant thereto. If he offers accounts of the past that include events which challenge the findings of science, he must offer good reasons for their inclusion in any account of what happened. Or, to put it in Harvey's terms, if he challenges the warrants generally accepted in a particular field, he must either show that the warrants are wrong or that in the case at issue rebuttals of a substantial character can be produced. It is one of the most significant and rich aspects of Harvey's account that he has expressed this point so clearly, and he is correct to insist that it must not be obscured or ignored by conjuring up images of positivism.[33]

It follows, moreover, that Harvey is correct to throw down a challenge to any would-be defender of the resurrection. There is a very real issue here that cannot be shirked. I believe Harvey has failed to do justice to the internal and contextual character of the believer's position on the resurrection. We are alerted to Harvey's failure to appreciate the potential strength of a defence of the resurrection by his remarks about miracles. Miracles, according to Harvey, are unique events of a kind that render it impossible even to formulate a standard for what is likely or unlikely. Therefore they cannot even be candidates for solutions to historical problems. It is not so much that miracles are impossible, as '(1) that we do not think miracle is a likely candidate for being an explanation for an event, (2) that we do not know what would constitute data, warrants or conceivable rebuttal to the conclusion that one had occurred. Consequently we do not know how to qualify our conclusions, whether weakly, moderately or strongly. We simply do not know what would "count for an absolutely unique event".'[34]

It is to be conceded that for the traditional Christian, the resurrection of Jesus is in some sense a unique event. At the very least, the resurrection is seen as theologically unique, in that he considers it to be one of those acts of God that reveal His power and love. Being the resurrection of Jesus is enough to guarantee this, for Jesus, as God incarnate, has a unique role in the revelatory activity of God.[35] Moreover, the resurrection has a place in the argument which establishes Jesus in that role.[36] Because of these considerations, the resurrection will be unique in the sense that it will have a status very different from the normal events of his everyday life, or for that matter from any putative miraculous event in his own time, like the resurrection of his next-door neighbour.

This does not entail, however, that the resurrection is unique in the sense that we do not know how to specify tolerably clearly what it involves. The resurrection is a public event in the past involving the return to life of Jesus. To say this much is to avoid the charge of obscurantism, where that is meant to indicate the specifying of an event so indistinct that we do not know enough to say whether it is even conceivable or not. More importantly, to say this is, *ipso facto*, to reveal what data would be relevant to the claim that the resurrection of Jesus occurred. Thus of obvious import would be claims that Jesus had been seen and that the tomb in which he was buried was empty. Both of these considerations have been and still are two of the major considerations that have been the centre of debate about the resurrection. This is surely correct in that they constitute relevant data. Harvey himself virtually concedes this in that he reviews recent influential reconsiderations of these matters.[37] That he can write as follows bears this out.

Terms like 'identification' and 'recognition' and 'flesh' necessarily involve appeal to certain non-unique aspects of human experience. Otherwise, what is the force of the claim that there *must* have been some connection with the flesh since this is the medium of the recognition ... Our naive minds, therefore, naturally reach out for something concrete, such as an empty tomb or the testimony of two men who talked with Jesus on the way to Emmaus or an appearance in which there was eating and drinking. These stories, it could be argued, express not so much the desire for proof, although that is not as unreasonable as we are commonly told, as the need for some specification of what one is being asked to believe. The critical historian can only appeal to the scrutiny of the testimony.[38]

As to the warrants that are relevant to such scrutiny, Harvey has already made it very clear that these will spread over many fields and cannot be furnished in too great a detail in advance of actual consideration of the total data to which appeal is made. The major exception to this has already been made clear, namely that the warrants of science render claims about an event such as a resurrection to be initially highly implausible. Given this the would-be defender of the resurrection must either question the truth of these warrants or offer effective rebuttals as to why they do not apply.

It must be insisted that the former option is not in the least viable. This is not just because he relies on science as a matter of course in his everyday understanding or because science may rightly lay claim to knowledge, but because without accepting the general reliability of science he cannot proceed to identify a miracle with much degree of success. Without reasonably assured knowledge of the laws of nature, there is little hope of distinguishing between the merely marvellous and the miraculous.[39] As Flew has pointed out, 'he needs both the rule and the exception, both the existence of a natural order and the occasional inhibition or transcending of that order'.[40] He cannot, therefore, set aside the warrants of science as false. The only alternative open to him is to attempt to enter an effective rebuttal. Before outlining the sketch of a rebuttal that is potentially relevant, let us note in passing that Harvey has precipitously associated with miracle other events or entities that ought for purposes of discussion be set aside for the moment.

Thus Harvey treats as of equal standing the following beliefs: belief in miracles, belief in a three-storey universe, belief in demons, belief in angels, belief in Satan.[41] For Harvey and for Harvey's paradigm of what it is to be a historian all of these are equally impossible. Thus he identifies with Bultmann's view that 'it is impossible to use electric light and the wireless and to avail ourselves of modern medical and surgical discoveries, and at the same time believe in the New Testament world of spirits and miracles'.[42] Prima facie, this is surely false, in that it is practically conceivable that some of these matters will occasion more controversy than others.[43] Thus we can envisage little or no debate about there being a three-storey universe, but more debate about there being spirits and Satan, as is borne out by the existence of psychical research and recent controversy about occult phenomena and the demonic. We can envisage as much if not more debate about miracles, as is suggested by the continuation of scholarly debate on this issue. Here I shall concentrate on the issue of miracle.

But how can miracles be made potentially possible? How can an effective rebuttal to the warrants of science be procured? It is to be conceded that the twin considerations that can be deployed to make any earnest search look unnecessary do have some force. There does seem to be a marked conjunction of miracle stories with religious heroes, and historical research does suggest that many of these miracles are false. Further, it does seem to be true that before the spread of modern science people were generally more credulous with respect to miracles and at times displayed a distinct craving for the miraculous.[44]

However, it is important not to exaggerate these claims. Such generalizations, as Sider has pointed out,[45] are far weaker than a scientific statement of observed regularity. Thus credulity towards the miraculous is not universal in primitive times, as is intimated by the Fourth Gospel.[46] Nor does conjunction of fictitious reports of miracles with founders of religion or religious heroes guarantee that all reports of miracles associated with such people are fictitious. What such credulity and such a conjunction do is give the historian advance warning to be on the alert for further fictitious stories from primitive sources. They constitute a warning for him to be especially on guard in his testing out the testimony available. Such considerations do not however preclude the need to evaluate instances of miraculous story or cluster of stories in relative independence from false stories. There may well be a genuine exception, and this will only be discovered if the critical work is allowed to proceed uncoerced by these considerations. Indeed, it was only the testing of each instance that allowed the above considerations to be established in the first instance as non-question-begging generalizations. It was by critical scrutiny, that is, that they were established initially.

Harvey might concede this but still maintain that he is unimpressed at two points. Firstly, he will rightly insist that some data for the resurrection must be secured. There must be some reasons for believing the traditions about the appearances and the empty tomb. His own assessment of the reasons marshalled to date is that they are extremely weak. One recalls his stringent remarks about the obscurantism, lack of toughness of mind, inconsistency, and intellectual irresponsibility of defenders of the resurrection. Secondly, he will note that to date all that has been presented is the theoretical possibility of a rebuttal to the warrants of science, rather than the actual provision of such.

Concerning the first of these points, it is noteworthy that Harvey himself admits that his arguments are vague, even *ad hominem* in character.[47] Moreover, there is an implied if not direct attack on the moral integrity of the defender of the resurrection in that he is supposedly not a lover of truth, allows his theological beliefs to corrupt his historical research, and has a faith that looks upon doubt as sin. Furthermore, Harvey is hasty to make appeal to what can only be called ideological factors. This is disclosed in his zealous call for a return to the critical ideals of the Enlightenment and his contrasting of this ideal with 'the ethic of belief that has so long been implicit in Christendom'.[48]

All this may introduce an emotive element into the discussion which is better omitted if good judgement is to prevail. More importantly it may cloud discussion of issues that require detailed historical consideration and are outside the matters to hand. For example, the appeal to the Enlightenment is a two-edged sword. Locke, who is quoted as a spokesman for that era, is not a happy choice to make in seeking someone who exemplified the Enlightenment and thus supposedly believed that it was unreasonable and improper to believe in miracles. Nor is it universally agreed that the Enlightenment really did have the revolutionary effect for good on historical studies that Harvey suggests.[49] It is also important to realize that devout believers were as quick as their unbelieving colleagues to forge the critical tools so indispensable to sound historical scholarship.[50] Moreover, the attempt to write off the historical scholarship of traditional believers as corrupted by the falsifying influence of belief is simplistic. Whatever is to be deplored on this score both now and in the past, it is all too easy to draw up a catalogue of errors by concentrating on a rather narrow selection of material.[51]

Surely the situation is more complex than Harvey would have us believe. It would be more accurate to note that there is wide disagreement within specialist historical scholarship on the reliability of the traditions that tell us of Jesus. Harvey more or less admits this when he notes that the appeal to the Christian perspective and its presuppositions is unconvincing in historical research, 'especially when one is confronted by such diverse New Testament scholarship as is represented by Markus Barth, Rudolph Bultmann, Oscar Cullmann, Floyd Filson, Ernst Fuchs, Robert Grant, Ernst Käsemann, C. H. Dodd, John Knox, Otto Piper, James M. Robinson, to mention only a few'.[52] Yet, contrary to such an admission, Harvey offers his own reconstruction of primitive Christianity in terms of something like a consensus among New Testament critics.[53] Part of the problem is precisely the absence of a consensus among the critics. At best what is available is a number of respectable reconstructions which differ in both substantial content and in the methods used to arrive at that content. Indeed so diverse are the conclusions that some[54] seriously question the adequacy of the sources as they stand to yield answers to our critical questions, while others[55] express fear that the whole critical enterprise may be in danger of sceptical undermining in the mind of the ordinary man in the street because of the experts' failure to reach a reasonable degree of agreement. This situation is indeed a perplexing one, and renders naïve the kind of simplistic appeal to the Bible utilized by even the most candid defenders of miracles in the past. Harvey expresses this when he asks, 'What is the believer to do when faced by widespread disagreements among New Testament historians concerning what can be known about Jesus?'[56] But he has been untrue to his recognition of this when he talks of a consensus among the critics, and when he claims that the falsifying influence of the demand for belief is so clearly behind the New Testament scholarship practised by traditional believers.[57]

Suppose that, despite this diversity, one is partially convinced that the traditions about the appearances and about the empty tomb can withstand a good degree of critical scrutiny.[58] One is assured, that is, that there can be a sensitive openness to these accounts that is not obscurantist, inconsistent, corrupted, irresponsible, or over-exaggerated. The immediate effect of this is not to license the conclusion that the resurrection happened. What such a move will do is to precipitate a conflict between several claims to knowledge which one must now seek to assess and evaluate. The heart of the confict to be resolved is that, on the one hand, there is tested testimony to the effect that Jesus came back from the dead enshrined in the traditions about the appearances and the empty tomb, but, on the other hand, there is common knowledge, backed up by the deserved prestige of science, for the assertion that dead men do not rise from the dead. Harvey rightly feels one must give the common knowledge the greater weight unless good reasons can be marshalled for setting it aside. With that we have arrived once again at the key issue of rebuttal which it was agreed cannot be shirked. How is it to be met?

The clue to possible success is to be found in a feature of miracle that is embedded in the classical concept of miracle in use here. Miracle, in this view, is not just a violation of a law of nature; it is a direct act of God done to further his purposes.[59] What is claimed is not simply that Jesus came back from the dead but rather that God raised him from the dead with certain intentions and purposes. It was an act of God related to His overall purposes for the world. This is often ignored or simply obscured by offering descriptions of miracle which give the impression that such an act of God is artificial and/or arbitrary. Talk of divine intervention, divine interference, or divine fiat[60] can suggest just this, as indeed can the very idea of a violation of a law of nature. When read sensitively, the situation is very different, for the resurrection is one part of a complex and sophisticated story of divine action that stretches from eternity to eternity and involves in a unique way the person of Jesus. As has already been noted,[61] Jesus is not just any old Tom, Dick, or Harry. He is God's unique agent who has come to reveal in a dramatic way at a particular time in history the character and mind of God.[62]

This in itself is sufficient to constitute the kind of substantial rebuttal that Harvey failed to seek. As A. E. Taylor put it, one of the determining factors that leads the believer to agree to events like the resurrection of Jesus is 'his underlying conviction that the plan of the world is dominated by certain absolute values, and that these events are the most striking and transparent examples of the dominance of just these values. They are like the few critical moments in which we find a revelation of the inmost character of a friend and from which we then proceed to interpret the whole of his more ordinary behaviour.'[63] The language here is somewhat dated but the point made is a genuine one. What is offered for belief is not just an anomalous event standing in stark isolation but rather an event embedded in a context that offers an explanation of an occurrence in history. It is an act of God done to further his purposes. It is an event that makes sense given the wider story of God's action and given independent access to that story through his word.

To be sure, this explanation is not a scientific one. We are not, that is, offered a set of natural laws which together with certain propositions about the state of the world would allow us to predict even in retrospect the resurrection of Jesus. But it is almost universally accepted in everyday life, and generally accepted in philosophy, that an explanation does not necessarily have to take this form. Events in the world can be explained when they are attributed to the activity of agents exercising choice, and actions of agents can in turn be explained by relating them to the intentions and purposes of the said agents. Thus the event of blood streaming from A's nose can be explained by saying that B hit A on the nose with his fist and the event of B hitting A with his fist can in turn be explained by disclosing that B hit A, say, to settle an old score, or to coerce A into parting with his money, or to win a bet.

The pattern of explanation appealed to in the case of the resurrection is of this logical type. The event of Jesus returning from the dead is explained by saying that God did it, and this is then explained by relating this action of God to his intentions and purposes, say, that he did this to vindicate Jesus, to save us from our sins, or to reassure his people that he is not defeated by the forces of evil. To develop this in detail is one of the tasks of the preacher and systematic theologian. Suffice it here to note that it sets the resurrection in a class of events very different from many miracle stories of bygone ages. For example, it is radically different from the story of the saint who, after being beheaded, walked a few hundred yards to a cathedral with his head under his arm, entered the sanctuary, and there sang the *Te Deum*.[64] To see the resurrection as an act of God that is intimately related to God's purposes as found in wider theistic vision of life guarantees this.

So satisfactory may this explanation seem that the resurrection may not only seem to be perfectly natural, but, rather, almost inevitable. Perhaps the Lukan Peter reveals this when he says that God raised up Jesus 'having loosed the pangs of death, because it was not possible for him to be held by it'.[65] More recently, D. M. McKay, exploiting the analogy of drama to express God's relation to the world, puts the same point suggestively when he remarks that it would not have made sense for the Creator, when He came into his own drama, to have been destroyed in any ultimate sense by the characters in the drama.[66] Care must be taken not to allow this kind of analogy to mask critical questions about the concept of divine incarnation, but it does help to show how fitting and appropriate the resurrection may come to be seen.

Objection might be made to this strategy to provide an effective rebuttal by insisting that the historian cannot take account of theistic proposals of the kind expressed in traditional Christian theism. Harvey takes this view when he suggests that faith should have no function in the justification of historical arguments respecting fact. But this is precisely the principle that has just been undermined by the argument developed here. Harvey will have to develop a new set of arguments to establish this if it is to be accepted. And in such arguments it will not be sufficient to point out that theological considerations have been illegitimately used to establish, say, the Mosaic authorship of the Pentateuch, or the historicity of Jonah. That some have insensitively and crudely made appeal to theological considerations, about, say, divine inspiration, does not establish the general principle that it is wrong to allow theological considerations to have a role in historical arguments respecting fact. *Abusus non tollit usum.*

Four features of the role of theological considerations demand further clarification at this juncture. First, it would be misleading to describe the appeal as an appeal to perspective or presupposition. One can readily see how such language became fashionable, in that there is in a sense an appeal to the theistic vision of life as a whole and to the idea of God as an agent, and the concept of perspective gets purchase from these. But it is misleading because it masks the specific character of the theological claims that are in operation. What is in mind here is the theological claim that God was doing something quite particular and special in Jesus: He was there incarnate, He was there redeeming and saving us from our sins, He was there revealing Himself in a dramatic and unique fashion. Concepts like perspective and presupposition are too vague and general to capture this element.

Secondly, as has been argued earlier, it is of some importance that adequate independent access to God's mind be available as expressed in His speech-acts, because without it it is going to be difficult to offer any substantial account of the purposes of God accomplished in the act of raising Jesus from the dead and thus making this act intelligible.[67] Without this it will be difficult to say why Jesus rather than someone else should be raised from the dead, and thus give reasons why the warrants normally relied on should be challenged. This is often neglected by those who see miracle as not just a theoretical but a practical possibility. Take, for instance, Merold Westphal, when he writes 'when one speaks of the divine activity no conditions outside of God could be obstacles for the realisation of what is logically possible. If God exists, miracles are not merely logically possible, but really and genuinely possible at every moment. The only condition hindering the actualisation of this possibity lies in the divine will.'[68] This is acceptable as far as it goes. God, being creator and sustainer of all that is, can if He so desires raise anyone from the dead. What evokes unease here, however, is the absence of help on how to determine what is God's will at any particular moment. Clearly, calling what actually happens God's will merely in virtue of it happening is unacceptable. This is so because many things happen which most Christians will clearly say are not God's will, and because some degree of freedom seems necessary on the part of man if a genuine interpersonal relationship between God and man is to be secured. More importantly, it is so because appeal to God's will, in order to render more plausible the occurrence of one event as opposed to another, will have no force if miracle is really and genuinely possible at every moment. If, however, we do have access to God's will for Jesus, if we do know what He sought to accomplish in the life, death, and resurrection of this man because He has told us, then the situation is radically different. Appeal to God's word in such circumstance will give content to the proposed purposes of God that partially make resurrection a plausible occurrence. Such a condition is potentially available in the speech-acts of God related to Paul and the other apostles.

Thirdly, this appeal to theological considerations does not make the scrutiny of the available traditions about Jesus, in general, and about the appearances and the empty tomb in particular, in any way redundant. These still have to be tested as regards their authenticity, integrity, and reliability. Such testing is necessary in order to secure such putative data as the appearances and the empty tomb. It is necessary, that is, to procure certain necessary conditions for the claim that Jesus rose from the dead.[69]

This said, it is difficult to determine the degree to which these traditions will be allowed to carry weight independently of an appreciation of the theological considerations to which they are related. Because the resurrection is such a major deviation from the normal, and because we are as dependent on the early disciples for the data for this as much as for the data for the claim to have witnessed and received divine revelation, there is a certain tendency to accept or reject both of these sets of considerations together. This is partially reflected in Trevor-Roper's suggestion that the New Testament may rightly be rejected as a possible historical source on the grounds that those who believed resurrections would believe anything and therefore, by implication, cannot be accepted as reliable.[70] This may also partially explain the vehemence of Harvey's attack on traditional apologetic for the resurrection. Both Trevor-Roper and Harvey simply ignore the theological context in which the resurrection is situated, so it is not surprising that they consider belief in the resurrection to be the mark of an uncritical mind.[71]

This tendency to accept the whole or reject the whole must be handled with care. Indeed it is tempting to treat this tendency as an attempt to rid us of more subtle historical assessment of the New Testament traditions by presenting us with only two options and forcing us to choose but one. These may be the only options, but any presentation of them must follow rather than precede detailed critical research, which in itself will render them disputed in the present climate of controversy and diversity.

On the other hand, this tendency does highlight the need to bring together a series of diverse considerations which must be taken as a whole in arguments for or against the resurrection. There is a danger that this will be overlooked by treating the arguments as being neatly divisible into fields and then treating the arguments within these fields as being formally schematizable. Such treatment can be immensely illuminating, as has been indicated, and can also bring an element of rigour to the discussion; but it can also lead to insensitivity to both the content and complexity of the arguments that must be developed by both sides in the debate.

It remains to be observed, fourthly, that the appeal to theological considerations to make plausible the resurrection does not involve the abandoning of the principles of analogy, correlation, and criticism as revised and developed by Harvey. There has been no attempt to defend the historicity of any event without taking seriously one's critically interpreted present experience, or to speak of events that are not intimately related to other events and occurrences, or to fail to recognize the need for sensitive critical judgement.

One's critically interpreted present experience has entered dynamically into the matrix of argument in that the normal warrants have been given their full due and only set aside when a potentially effective rebuttal was presented. The same forces that operate in the present have been taken to operate in the past. Thus has the demand for analogy been satisfied. Nor has correlation been set aside. Past events have been seen as embedded in a network of causal relations. There has been no attempt to argue for events that are mere bolts from the blue or isolated units that are not related in the most intimate and complex way with the totality of existence. To be sure, some will claim that one of the key 'forces' alluded to, namely the agency of God, does not really exist at all, or that, if God exists at all, He does not do the kind of action attributed to Him. Atheists, agnostics, and some theologians will do so. However, the point at issue is not the propriety of believing in the kind of God alluded to, but in the more mundane point that commitment to such a belief involves commitment to a pattern of belief whose logic is generally acceptable and whose content asserts rather than denies the reality of causal connections.

Let it also be noted that there has been no surrender of the principle of criticism. There has been no attempt to claim the status of a necessary truth for a statement about the past. Nor has any statement been certified as absolutely certain or immune from revision. What has been potentially said either about the past or about the activity of God is in principle open to revision. If contrary evidence or argument is presented then it cannot be dismissed or ignored. In short there is no holy history that is sealed off in some ghetto or harbour of faith and treated as automatically absolute and authoritative. Moreover, the assertions made call for sensitive judgement that can be graded by means of various modal operators.

Another way to say this would be to note that there is no reliance here on mere authority, in the sense that sources are treated as immune from criticism. There is no returning to the credulity of bygone ages when miracles were accepted uncritically just because they were associated with religious heroes or were recorded in sacred documents. Nor is there any necessity to accept all the miracles of the biblical traditions. Just why some miracles will be accepted and others rejected is a matter that cannot be decided in advance of actual detailed critical research. The advice of H. H. Rowley is apposite at this juncture. 'The miracle stories can neither be uncritically accepted as historical, nor uncritically rejected as fancy. Each example must be examined for itself, in the light of the character of the narrative in which it stands and the purpose for which it appears to have been written.'[72]

It is partly because of the need for this kind of detailed historical research that no attempt will be made in this chapter to decide positively for the resurrection or to suggest what sort of modal qualifier should be applied to this claim. Even though it would be naïve to consider that one's sympathies on this matter had not been disclosed, the argument of the chapter has been deliberately couched in a manner that seeks to avoid any explicit commitments of this nature. This is in keeping with the central purpose of a chapter that has sought to characterize the dynamics of a potential argument for the divine performing of a miracle and to show that such arguments do not contravene the principles and pattern of argument isolated by Harvey. Whether the content of the actual argument should be called historical or not is a matter to be taken up shortly.[73] Suffice it to say that the substantial arguments put forward by Harvey against the claim that God has raised Jesus from the dead have been shown to be open to effective challenge. If claims to divine action should be abandoned, they should not be abandoned because of the character of arguments deployed by historians as articulated by Harvey. In so far as Harvey can claim to present his position as a revised interpretation of Troeltsch in the light of analytical philosophy of history, this confirms the conclusion that was reached in the preceding chapter. Just as Troeltsch, to secure the claim that specific divine actions had not occurred, had to build into his concept of history a material conception of correlation, so too does Harvey have to build into his concept of history the assertion that God is not appealed to by the historian in deciding matters of fact in the past. If such conceptual remarks are to be made, they should not be allowed to foreclose substantial arguments about the reality of past divine activity.

In conclusion, let me emphasize that my central point is a philosophical one. Harvey claims to show that the application of historical criticism to traditional Christian belief renders its commitment to direct acts of God inadmissable in principle. More specifically, belief in the resurrection is not a live option for the modern theologian who would take history seriously. I contest this. Belief in divine intervention and belief in the resurrection are in principle admissable. Whether one should believe in them is a matter that cannot be decided on philosophical grounds alone, and therefore I am not arguing here that this further step should be taken.

7

DIVINE INTERVENTION
AND METAPHYSICS

IN the last two chapters I have taken the most stringent claims about the effect of historical criticism on assertions about divine intervention and shown them to be untenable. Not everyone would accept, however, that the consequences of historical criticism for theology should be characterized as they are by Troeltsch and Harvey. Some traditional theologians, on the one hand, simply ignore the arguments of Troeltsch and the tradition that springs from him, and yet would believe that they take seriously the rise of critical historical investigation. Other theologians, on the other hand, may be uneasy about the position of Troeltsch but would still argue that there is a relation of tension between the historian and the traditional theologian. A good example of the latter is T. A. Roberts. In this chapter I shall examine his position and show that the rival account of history he develops is either incorrect or very similar to that put forward by Troeltsch and Harvey. Because this rival account is accompanied by an exposition of the problem that is supposed to be inherent in claims about divine action, its relevance to the concern of this book is doubly assured.

Roberts has no misgivings about the theological and historical propriety of examining the historical claims embedded in Christian belief. Such an undertaking is legitimate theologically because the Christian religion is a historical religion, not just in the sense that it has a history of its institutions, of its founder, and of its influence on the course of western and world history, 'but also in the more profound sense that its essence lies not in something thought but in something actually achieved by its Founder on the plane of history...'[1] Anyone therefore who takes the Christian faith seriously cannot avoid, from an intellectual point of view, asking historical questions about its founder, for such questions are relevant to some of its central claims. Such questioning may indeed be a risky business, for it may happen that the answering of historical questions may have the negative effect of showing that the supposed historical claims inherent in Christian belief are unsupported by reliable evidence; but such worries ought not to be uppermost in our minds initially. On the contrary, 'the activity of historical criticism must be regarded, in principle, as essentially constructive and creative activity, not negative and destructive.'[2] This is the case because historical criticism, as it has developed over the last two centuries, has so refined and developed its critical techniques and skills as to be in a position to provide reliable knowledge of the past. Therefore, when applied to the relevant sources, it is possible in principle to acquire enough historical knowledge to entitle us to say that 'we know Jesus better than his disciples did'.[3] 'This, in principle, is the constructive and creative task before historical criticism. To those who profess to follow the footsteps of the Master, historical criticism, wisely and reasonably applied, should be their most trusted guide.'[4]

As to the actual character of historical criticism, Roberts recommends that a clear distinction be maintained between historiography and metaphysics. This emerges most clearly in the severely critical remarks he addresses to J. M. Robinson's statement and defence of the philosophy of history deployed in the so-called new quest for the historical Jesus. The details of Roberts's critique need not detain us here; suffice it to note that Roberts faults Robinson on two accounts. First, he had failed to pay enough attention to the actual development of historical criticism in the nineteenth century, and this led to an improper appreciation of what a quest for the historical Jesus involved. Secondly, and more importantly, Robinson had failed to distinguish between history as the process of events in the past and history as a study or narrative of those events. Roberts elaborates as follows:

Historiography is the word used to describe the body of techniques historians have developed to enable them to compile historical narratives. These techniques are mainly concerned with the methods of testing the reliability and authenticity of evidence. In this sense, historiography is not concerned with the process of history in the philosophical sense of determining whether, as Christians or Marxists in their different ways maintain, history has a meaning. Historiography is concerned with the task of answering specific historical questions such as what are the causes of the French Revolution.[5]

It is quite legitimate to make large-scale claims about the meaning inherent in the process of history, e.g. that history reveals the hand of God at work, or that history moves inevitably towards universal progress; but to advance such claims is to advance metaphysical claims about the process of past events rather than write historical narrative. Such claims do not fall within the sphere of historiography in the usual meaning of that word.

This distinction between metaphysics and historiography is illuminated by the explicit application of it to sentences about Jesus. Take, for example, the sentence 'Jesus of Nazareth was crucified.' According to Roberts there is no reason why this could not be asserted by the historian, for it falls naturally within the realm of the historical, i.e. of that which 'can be established by the application of the canons of historical criticism'.[6] Indeed, it is precisely the historian to whom we must turn if we are to receive an assessment of the claim that Jesus of Nazareth was crucified. The question, 'Was Jesus of Nazareth crucified?' must be answered by a rigorous application of historical criticism, complete with its techniques and methods for assessing the reliability of evidence about the past. But when we encounter the sentence, 'In the death of Jesus of Nazareth God was reconciling the world unto himself,' we have a problem for faith rather than for criticism. We have moved from the level of the historical to the level of the religious. To say that God thus acted in the death of Jesus is to go outside the domain of historical inquiry, as that is commonly understood, for 'the historian is not concerned to decide whether God acted or did not act through this event or that'.[7] 'This claim is ultimately a claim to be able to justify, whether on grounds of natural theology, or a concept of Revelation or of an appeal to specific "religious" experiences, the belief in God and the belief, logically dependent upon it, that Jesus is the Son of God.'[8] To look to the historian to evaluate this claim is inappropriate. 'Historical investigation proceeds on the assumption that a study of the past is only possible if the supernatural is shouldered out of the way, for historical study knows no techniques or methods for evaluating the supernatural. ... historical criticism is essentially a secular tool, fashioned to meet secular interests, and thus by its nature useless to evaluate the religious affirmations of Faith.'[9]

If the historian can evaluate the sentence, 'Jesus of Nazareth was crucified,' can he also evaluate the sentence 'Jesus rose from the dead on the third day'? Grammatically these two sentences are the same. Moreover, the latter no more implies a theological sentence about divine activity than does the former. Despite this, Roberts does not believe that historical criticism can be applied to this sentence. His belief rests, at this point, on the claim that such an event as the resurrection of Jesus is so remarkable that the criteria upon which the historian depends for evaluating the probability of an event having occurred can no longer be summoned. The resurrection is so different from the crucifixion that the historian cannot cope with it. There are two quite specific differences. First, the resurrection of Jesus is claimed as a unique and special event in the sense that it is only with Jesus, or through his power, that we have access to such an event. This being so,

there cannot be outside the gospels, or more strictly, outside Christian sources, accounts of resurrection events, in the sense that there may be elsewhere accounts of crucifixion. Therefore one of the historian's main principles of testing the reliability of evidence is in principle, and not merely in practice, incapable of being applied to the accounts of the resurrection. The historian is unable to compare and contrast these accounts with other accounts of resurrection events; such accounts not only do not exist but cannot exist, and this 'cannot' is a logical impossibility on Christian assumptions.[10]

Secondly, the resurrection fails to satisfy a further test which applies to any report of a putative past event; namely, it constitutes a pronounced deviation from the uniformity which the historian assumes society and the world to possess. As regards the crucifixion there is no problem, for everybody knows that men have died by crucifixion. Likewise it is known that when men die they remain dead. The historian assumes that when men die they cease to function as direct causes of further historical events. But an account of a resurrection completely overthrows this assumption, so that, sooner than abandon his assumption that dead men stay dead, he will challenge the claim to resurrection. In such circumstances, 'he must judge that it is improbable that it happened'.[11]

Why is the historian led to make this assumption? Roberts offers two detectably distinct answers to this question. In 1960, his reply seems to have involved positing that this was simply a unique feature of the historian's methodology. Without it 'historical enquiry would be impossible because the possible variations in the interpretation of evidence would be so great that this task would be in practice impossibly difficult'.[12] In 1965 he rejected this, offering instead the reason that this assumption was built into the very language that the historian's techniques embody. As this is one of the distinctive features of Roberts's account of the relation between the historian and believer, he deserves to be quoted in some detail.

If one sees a white, four legged, furry creature one may rightly call it a cat. Had the object been black, but in all other respects similar, it would still have been correct to use the symbol 'cat' to describe it. Yet a black cat is not the same thing as a white cat. This shows us that our use of the word 'cat' allows us to entertain under the notion of a cat a whole range of widely differing phenomena which have many features in common. Thus a Persian and a Manx differ considerably but are both cats, though any four legged creature is clearly not to be described as a cat. The defining characteristics of a cat can be very enumerated as 'a four legged creature with whiskers, a tail, furry coat' and so on. Let us imagine however that we saw an object which in all respects resembled a cat, turned quickly into a dog, and then reverted back to something which in all respects once more resembled a cat. How would we describe such an object? Clearly we have no concept in our language under which such a phenomena could be subsumed. Not only would we, with our present language be unable to talk about it, and thus communicate our thought to others, but *the existence of such phenomena on a large scale would make it impossible for us to use language at all to communicate our thought.* The possibility of using concepts to describe phenomena in the world rests on the assumption, built into the structure of language, that the phenomena to be described by language remain relatively stable, changing only gradually. Since the language of historical writing is mainly that of ordinary discourse, the same assumption underlies the whole of historical methodology.[13]

Apply this general thesis about language to the resurrection of Jesus and the results are obvious. The problem with that event:

is not that the event could not have happened but how if it did happen we are to talk about it ... as Austin Farrer reminded us, we have no recipe for a resurrection. The concept is all but empty. As soon as we ask questions about the resurrected one—does he retain memories of his previous existence and so preserve his self-identity? What kind of body is the resurrected body?—we find ourselves unable to answer such questions. This is not necessarily because there was no resurrection at all, but because, if there was a resurrection, our ordinary language is utterly incapable of communicating what the apostles claim to have seen—the Resurrected Lord.[14]

Given this, it is not surprising to note that Roberts characterizes the crucial problem that overshadows all discussions of gospel historicity as philosophical rather than historical. The crucial question is this: how are we to recognize a historical divine intervention? But to raise this question is to raise an even more difficult question that is logically prior, namely, how are we to talk at all of God fulfilling His will in and through the events of history? 'The problem of the revelation of God in history is ultimately a logical kinsman of the metaphysical problem of how we are to talk in language about God at all.'[15] In the material under review here, Roberts does not offer any thoroughly developed answer to this problem, but an answer can be gleaned from what little he does say. It is given in connection with general remarks about the nature of language already quoted at length, and it can best be introduced by drawing attention to a contrast that he himself puts forward. Roberts draws a contrast between the language of most people (or language as it is used in everyday life) and the language of the poets and of the philosopher in metaphysical moments. Language, generally speaking, is 'an instrument developed to enable man to communicate reasonably effectively about what he takes to be the ordinary relatively stable patterns of his experience in everyday life, experiences of birth, upbringing, marriage, raising a family, building a house, manufacturing articles, sickness and death'.[16] When the poet or philosopher in metaphysical mood uses such language, however, something different happens. His role, it seems, is to convey an unfamiliar vision of the familiar, and to do this he must 'seek to break the stranglehold which language exercises on our thinking by using ordinary language in extraordinary ways'.[17]

It is the same with the religious genius. 'His vision is not a new vision of the familiar, though it may sometimes be this, but a revelation of the extraordinary, of the divine impinging on the finite. To convey this revelation he must fall back on the inadequate language fashioned as a useful tool to communicate thought about the ordinary and the familiar.'[18] The result of this straining of ordinary language is misunderstanding and misrepresentation, a result which is presumably reflected in attempts to evaluate such claims about divine action as have been examined elsewhere in this book.

My assessment of the position of Roberts will begin with his remarks about religious language and gradually work backwards. Concerning his views on the nature of religious discourse, it does not require a treatise to draw attention to their general unhelpfulness. To begin with, reference to the discourse of philosophers in metaphysical moments is significantly unilluminating. Roberts does not tell us how such moments are to be identified. To call in the aid of the poet at this point is unlikely to help either, for there are no clear boundaries between poetical and ordinary language. If there are problems about religious discourse as embodied in religious prose, it is unlikely that these will be resolved merely by saying such prose is a form of poetry. If, for example, there are problems with the discourse of Charles Wesley's sermons, surely these will crop up again even more acutely in his poetry and hymns. Is Roberts not attempting to fill in logical holes with the cement of literary genre?

And what precisely is the problem with religious discourse? That religious discourse involves the stretching of everyday concepts may be accepted, although we must beware of blanket generalizations about it. Moreover, religious discourse itself was once accepted (and in many places still is accepted) as ordinary and everyday, no matter how much the refinement of theologian and philosopher may be deemed necessary. Roberts is, of course, anxious that alien standards of appropriateness of meaning should not be applied to religious discourse. But it seems appropriate to characterize the religious discourse identified by Roberts as factual in the broad sense of that term.[19]

At one point, Roberts characterizes the problem of religious language as being the problem of identifying a historical event as an instance of divine intervention. It is not quite clear what in fact this problem is. It could be a request to specify events that are instances of divine intervention. If it is, then, provided we can talk coherently of the resurrection of Jesus, there is no problem here at all. For this is an event that is an example of divine intervention. On the other hand, it could be a request to provide rules for the identifying of instances of divine intervention in the life, say, of the believer. If so, it is unlikely to be satisfied, since criteria for such divine activity, like criteria for divine revelation,[20] are not easy to formulate with detailed precision. Yet again, it could be a request to justify the claim that we really had identified an event that constituted a divine intervention. If so, even Roberts himself recognizes that such an enterprise will involve an extended discussion of the possibility of natural theology and revelation. Indeed, such a request would require a resolution of some central issues in epistemology.

The conclusion to be drawn from this is that Roberts has not adequately made out his case that the ultimate problem that overshadows discussions of the historicity of the Gospels is a philosophical one about the nature of religious discourse. That there are philosophical disputes about the nature of religious discourse is obvious. That this fact should be taken seriously when attempts are made to separate history from theology will be presently conceded.[21] But, if the analysis of theological claims set forth earlier in this study is correct, it would be wrong to exaggerate the problems that have to be surmounted. Roberts may well be able to make out his case, and it would be premature to claim that he could not succeed, but in the absence of detailed arguments to accomplish this, it must be concluded that his identifying of the crucial problem has been misplaced. A particular analysis of certain theological sentences is very important if an event like the resurrection is to be defended as a past occurrence, but the crucial problem, in so far as there is one at all, lies elsewhere.

Where should the problem be located? Let us pursue this by attending to the assumption of the historian that there is uniformity in society and the world. It can readily be acknowledged that historians do make some such assumption in their work. This can be seen by an example that is not far removed from the historian's workshop. Suppose we are interested in the life, times, and associates of St. Francis. Browsing in our sources of the life of one of his friars, Blessed Gandulf of

Binasco, we come across an episode that runs as follows. When Gandulf died, his body was enshrined, but while this was being done, the swallows he had once scolded for chattering too loudly while he preached flew into the church during the night, then parted into two groups and sang, in alternating choirs, a *Te Deum* of their own.[22] Confronted with such an episode there is little doubt as to what the historian would do. He would immediately reject the story about the swallows as false, albeit touching and charming. And he would do so because it called in question his general assumption about the behaviour of swallows. He has never seen swallows form choirs, nor has it been reported by others known to him. In short, he assumes a uniformity about the nature of swallows that he will use to test out the veracity of testimony. So Roberts is correct to say that historians do assume that the universe, and society within it, possess uniformity. Is he, however, correct to insist, with Bloch and others,[23] that the historian assumes that the universe and society within it possesses sufficient uniformity to exclude the possibility of any pronounced deviations? We can answer this only after examining the reasons that Roberts brings forward to support this more controversial claim.

The heart of Roberts's argument at this point is that it is the nature of language which licenses the conclusion that the historian must exclude any pronounced deviations. But surely this is false. To begin with, there is nothing incoherent in the story of the swallows above. The story is perfectly expressible in our language, and it is only because it is so that it can be seen to conflict with the uniformity associated with the behaviour of swallows. To claim that we have no concept under which to subsume such birds is irrelevant: ordinary discourse can cope with this phenomenon quite adequately, or if it cannot, new concepts can be minted to convey what is meant. Precisely the same can be said about the case of the remarkable cat that Roberts introduces. If it continues to perform the amazing activity described by Roberts, we can quickly give it a new name. These cases provide adequate counter-examples to Roberts's general thesis about language, which claims that for there to be the language we use 'the phenomena to be described must remain relatively stable, changing only gradually'.[24] To be sure, if everything was in a chaotic cacophany of change we could not have language, for in such a situation it would be impossible to identify any particulars and thus impossible to secure identity of reference. But this does not imply that all phenomena we describe have to remain relatively stable, changing only gradually. It is not then because of language that the historian must exclude the story of the swallows or such like as false.

If Roberts's later argument does not succeed, what about his earlier suggestion that he must exclude it because this is simply a unique feature of the historian's methodology? Will this repay reconsideration? Methodology is a rather vague concept, so let us change the question a little and ask, is this assumption a unique feature of historiography? The advantage of this formulation is that we have Roberts's own definition to work with, for historiography, we recall, was defined as 'the body of techniques historians have developed to enable them to complete historical narratives'.[25] Roberts is surely correct to say that historians do have techniques which are taught in the profession. They are taught, for instance, how to make use of bibliographies, read old maps, interpret aerial surveys, ancient coins, medieval charters, foreign date-systems, government statistics, archival catalogues, etc. And historians of the origins of Christianity have developed their own sometimes controversial techniques of analysis. But the point to notice is that it is very odd to include the assumption under discussion in an exhaustive list of such techniques. If one wanted to become a historian one could enroll in a course on interpreting old maps, but what course could one take to learn that society and the world possessed uniformity? More pertinently, what course could one take to learn that they possessed sufficient uniformity to exclude the possibility of any pronounced deviations? Roberts was surely correct to reject historiography as an answer to the question posed.[26]

Is there an alternative answer? Let us take the problem as focusing on the reason why a historian assumes uniformity in society and the world, leaving aside whether under all circumstances he must exclude pronounced deviations. A sensible suggestion at this point is to say that this assumption is derived from what might be called the metaphysics of common sense.

This is a metaphysics that is for the most part unconsciously and uncritically embraced by the historian. It is useful to treat such an assumption as metaphysical for two reasons. First, it is very general in scope, professing to hold anywhere at any time. Secondly, it is for the most part taken for granted, so that we feel at a loss to know what to do when it is called in question and puzzled to know how to justify it to an ardent sceptic.[27] It is useful to call such an assumption part of common sense because it is not peculiar to any one class of people or profession and we rely on it daily whether we be tinkers, tailors, or candlestick-makers, or for that matter whether we be theists, atheists, or agnostics. This assumption is one of those beliefs that is shared by rival world-views rather than contested by them, and might even be considered a necessary feature of any world-view that is to be embraced as true. So to explain it as unique to the historian is out of place; rather we explain the historian's dependence on it in terms of his sharing such common-sense beliefs. That the rise of science has greatly enhanced the role of this assumption and thereby also made historians more aware of it should not be allowed to detract from this conclusion.

If we accept this suggestion, does it follow that this assumption cannot be overruled? Or, to put it in Roberts's phrase, does it mean that we, and the historian with us, must exclude the possibility of any pronounced deviation from it? We can approach this question by looking afresh at the resurrection of Jesus. Must the historian exclude this pronounced deviation? Two preliminary remarks are in order at this juncture. It is exaggerated to say that there are insuperable logical difficulties about finding language to characterize such an event. Contrary to the views of Roberts and Farrer, we do have a 'recipe' for a resurrection, namely that a resurrection is the return to life of a man who has been dead.[28] That there may be an element of irreducible mystery about the resurrected body of Jesus does not preclude our conceptually identifying what a resurrection would be, nor does it hinder a critical scrutiny of the sources in which the resurrection of Jesus is recorded. Roberts has offered no principled reason why the evils of obscurantism cannot be avoided and why the demand for coherence cannot be met in this instance.

In saying this I am not denying that there is widespread discussion as to how belief in the resurrection of Jesus is to be formulated today, and as to how such formulations relate to the New Testament traditions. It is common, for example, to draw a sharp distinction between restoration to life and resurrection to glory. This is wholly acceptable, and helps draw attention to the possibility that religious concepts may be essential to an adequate characterization of the resurrection of Jesus. However, the significance of this in the present context should not be exaggerated. Classically the resurrection has been taken to involve some kind of bodily existence, and if this minimal description of resurrection is accepted then the appearances and the empty tomb are relevant. Such a description will not satisfy everyone, but it is clear enough to make intelligible the charge that the resurrection of Jesus calls in question the warrants of science. That this charge is intelligible casts doubt on the claim that there are insuperable logical difficulties in discourse about the resurrection of Jesus.

Secondly, it is relatively easy to make the claim that Jesus was raised from the dead look ridiculous. All that is required to achieve this effect is to read the last few chapters of the Gospels in isolation, and then compare them with the story of the singing swallows or other such medieval legends. The two cases are initially so similar that rejection of one will prompt rejection of the other. And both will be rejected because they challenge the metaphysics of common sense. Indeed the resurrection constitutes a challenge of major proportions. It is so extraordinary that, were the matter to be left there, it should rightly be rejected as highly improbable, and a search should then be initiated to explain why this story came to be told in the first place.[29]

The suggestion here, however, is that to leave the matter thus is to be expected of a historian with atheistic or agnostic convictions but is by no means demanded by one who is committed to the kind of theological claims discussed earlier. The latter would be well advised to pause and request that his unbelieving colleagues consider the resurrection in the wider context of which it is a part.[30] Two features of this wider context deserve mention here.

On the one hand the resurrection needs to be fitted into its human-historical context. It has to be related to what can be known of the life of Jesus, for example his teaching, his ministry, his relationship to the religious leaders of his day, his trial and crucifixion. In this regard it also has to be related to what we know about the behaviour and assertions of his disciples, to its central role in the preaching and teaching of the early Church, and its relationship, if any, to the rise of the Church and its spread throughout the Roman empire. And all of this will have to be placed against a backcloth of complex linguistic and historical study of the religious, political, and cultural situation of the day.

On the other hand, the resurrection needs to be fitted into its theological-historical context. It has to be read in the light of the wider story of God's acts for the salvation of the world initiated in Israel and brought to a climax in Jesus. This will involve also the further activity of God in the Church, in personal religious experiences, and in providence. All of this in turn will be seen against a backcloth of God's creative activity, including under this the world of man and nature, and against the other anthropological and moral elements of the doctrinal scheme of which it is a part.

It is no objection to this that the whole enterprise is too complex and subtle. Those who crave simplicity can have it if they so desire, but they must then meet the charge of naïvety. It would be wonderful if we could opt for rival historical and theological accounts without the labour of painstaking, sensitive, collaborative research, but such is not to be had by those whose eyes have been opened by the emergence of history as a critical enterprise. Critical historical study has made us too aware of the variety of options about Jesus, about the early Church, and about God to be content with simplistic responses.

Awareness of this does not preclude us from noting that the story of the resurrection of Jesus is, from the point of view of critical scrutiny, in quite a different category from that of the swallows singing the *Te Deum*. Specifically, there is no question of our being asked to abandon our assumption that society and the world possess uniformity. When people bury their dead they are not being asked to expect a miracle or resurrection on the third day. To this extent the assumptions of the historian remain intact, indeed without them it will be quite impossible to tell the kind of human-historical story that will be needed to support the claim that Jesus came back from the dead. Moreover, the story of the resurrection is related to a complex theological system that itself stretches into a subtle and sophisticated vision of life as a whole. It is this that gives point and purpose to what would otherwise be a bare extraordinary occurrence.

Conceding that the resurrection is an extraordinary occurrence will draw fresh attention to a further feature of history that Roberts believes to be impossible to satisfy. One recalls at this point his contrasting of the resurrection with the crucifixion to the effect that there are no recognized instances of resurrection, whereas there are numerous instances of crucifixion which the historian can draw on to test the probability of it having occurred. The crucifixion of Jesus falls in a class of events that include the death by crucifixion of others, so that given information on the latter we can look at the antecedents to the death of Jesus and weigh the probability of his having died by crucifixion. But in the case of his resurrection this condition is not satisfied, and, given Christian assumptions, cannot be satisfied. It can be agreed that as a matter of logic any number of resurrections can be allowed, but as a matter of theology none outside Jesus and his incarnate activity are usually accepted.[31] This being so, the counter-argument deployed thus far has only taken care of half the problem.

As an initial response to this it should be observed that despite what philosophers, theologians, and historians may say, an investigation into the resurrection of Jesus does go on in practice. Between believers and unbelievers and among believers themselves arguments continue as to whether Jesus did in fact rise from the dead and as to the weighting that is to be given to the various data that are utilized. This in itself should make us wary of those who claim that it cannot go on. More specifically, it should make us question any philosophical thesis which insists that no such investigation can be conducted. In this context one of the tasks of sensitive philosophical analysis is to articulate the dynamics of argument in the debate rather than lay down the law as to what can and cannot be investigated by the historian.[32]

Of much greater importance, however, is the fact that the second of Roberts's conditions is no different from the principle or analogy. It would be repetitious to seek to challenge this principle afresh, as its role has already been exposed and qualified. Indeed, the appeal to the uniformity of society and the world is also mirrored in Troeltsch's principle of correlation and in Harvey's contention that the warrants of science are assumed by the historian. That all three of these are variations of one theme is revealed not just by their content but by the fact that they have evoked in each instance an appeal to the theological context of the resurrection.

Roberts has of late overlooked this close similarity with Harvey by casting the debate between historian and believer as a debate between empiricist and idealist understandings of history.[33] Roberts's conviction is that Harvey in developing and applying the concept of warrants has absorbed too much of the metaphysical standpoint of the philosophers who ultimately support him.[34] He does not in fact claim to have established this, but his brief remarks are unconvincing.[35] He is very aware of the need to exercise great care in making appeal to the metaphysics of idealism, for he strongly disassociates himself from those who have seized on idealism and turned it to their own theological advantage.[36] He cannot therefore be accused of heavy-handed appeals to metaphysics and presupposition. Where he can be faulted, however, is in his failure to see that it is with the resurrection rather than the crucifixion that the problem of warrants arises. Harvey is correct to press this issue, and no amount of metaphysics, whether empiricist or idealist, must be allowed to obscure or lessen its impact. Moreover, Roberts himself notes that the historian is likely to pronounce the resurrection as improbable because of his commitment to uniformity in society and the world. This is simply a restatement of the problem that Harvey has highlighted.[37] And both problems can be resolved by entering a rebuttal which shows why the normal warrants can be legitimately set aside.

Roberts might enter a fresh objection to this whole strategy; he might say that appeal to theological assertions to sanction the claim that Jesus rose from the dead is quite out of place. This is so because history is a secular tool unable by its nature to evaluate the affirmations of faith.[38] To bring in theology at this point is, therefore, quite illegitimate.

We can best approach this issue by noting that Roberts has no desire to rule out the legitimacy of making theological claims. Whatever problems he believes such language to exemplify, he does not question the propriety of actually making them.[39] In addition, it is misleading to characterize the theological claims appealed to as metaphysical. To be sure, the wider vision appealed to can with propriety be described as metaphysical because of its extended scope, but to call the theological claims about Jesus relied on 'metaphysical' obscures their specific content about one individual at one time at one place in history, and may beg fundamental questions about their justification. This is essentially a verbal matter, and resolution of this will not bring an end to long-standing battles. If there is to be a fight, however, let it be fought with honourable and clean weapons that do not mask important features of what the believer intends. Moreover, it is misleading to call history a secular tool fashioned to meet secular interests and to assert that 'historical investigation proceeds on the assumption that a study of the past is only possible if the supernatural is shouldered out of the way'.[40] The origins of historical investigation were as much ecclesiastical as they were secular,[41] and we have seen that properly executed the appeal to theology invites us neither to abandon our general assumptions about the world nor to engage in uncritical assertion that has no interest in evidence and discussion.

Strictly speaking, it is even false to claim that history by its nature is useless to evaluate the religious affirmations of faith. As Roberts is himself aware, it could in principle show certain affirmations of faith to be false;[42] alternatively it may show that the historical claims inherent in Christian belief are unsupported by reliable evidence.[43] We can see this in the case of the claim that in the death of Christ God was reconciling the world to himself by reflecting on the effect of historical considerations as follows. Suppose a historian were to show by standard historical practice that in fact Jesus did not die self-sacrificially on the cross, but that he died of measles, or that he was accidentally run down by a Roman chariot.

Would this not put tremendous strain on the theologian's claim about the divine action specified? One could reject the historical proposal out of hand and thus not allow it to falsify one's theological proposal. But to do this would be to reject the propriety of historical study altogether, which is a drastic manoeuvre. For one who could not do this, there is little he could do but give up his theological proposal. The examples of historical possibility are of course unlikely to be secured. But they show that, in principle, historical investigation could undermine theological claims. All that needs to be done is establish that Christ's death was accidental, that it was not something that he freely accepted, that it was something he could not have avoided, or that he did it out of hate rather than love, and it becomes odd to talk of God reconciling himself to the world through the death of Christ. Alternatively, historical research could establish that we are just not in a position to say whether his death was a giving of himself sacrificially, and thereby show that an historical claim implicit in the theological claim under discussion is unsupported by reliable evidence.

What is more likely to be at issue here is whether the historian can positively assert that Jesus rose from the dead or that God raised Jesus from the dead. Both of these stand together at this point because it is the wider theological context implicit in the reference to divine agency that allows one to assert the former without contravening the critical character of historical research. This issue in turn leads into the question of whether one is being a historian or not if one relies on theological considerations to decide matters of fact in the past. Let us take each of these in turn.

The short answer to the first question is that he cannot. As positive commitment to the resurrection involves evaluation of claims about the activity of God, the person who believes in the resurrection must be something of a theologian and not just a historian. To be sure, he will have to exercise historical skills, for some of the data essential to such a claim fall naturally within the province of historical science. But other data falls naturally within the field of theology, and so long as it is possible to distinguish between the field of theology and history, so long will it be essential to stress that history alone cannot establish that God raised Jesus from the dead. The point is well made by Nineham.

An individual historian who is a Christian—or even one who is not—may well lend his support to the theologian in believing that some or all of the events described in the Bible did in fact occur; and what is more, he may well believe that he has full rational justification for doing so. The point is, however, that he will be basing this belief on the whole of his experience—including his religious experience—and going beyond the criteria normally employed in 'scientific' history. Accordingly he cannot expect to carry historical colleagues of other metaphysical persuasions with him and so to provide the theologian with independent support for his contentions; in pronouncing on such matters he will himself have become at least half theologian.[44]

As Nineham rightly recognizes, however, this position raises the second question I posed. Is one being a historian if one relies on theological considerations in deciding matters of fact in the past? It is not as easy to answer this as one might at first expect.

Certainly there is nothing unhistorical in relying on theology, if 'unhistorical' is taken to mean that the presuppositions of historical investigation are being rejected. That this has not been done has been the burden of the argument so far. Moreover, it is difficult to maintain any sharp distinction between history and metaphysics, if by the latter we mean large-scale beliefs about the world. The assumption that society and the world possess uniformity is precisely such a piece of metaphysics, and without it the historian is doomed to failure. In addition, it is not uncommon for historians to engage in quite definite metaphysical assertion of a kind that Roberts would disapprove of. It would be a brave philosopher who would call in question their standing as historians.[45] Furthermore, if the historian discounts theological considerations as irrelevant, he does not entirely cease to be theological. He is simply assuming that the truth of certain negative theological statements, i.e. that God does not exist, or, if He does, He does not do the kind of actions ascribed to Him by Christians. It were odd if the historian could only rely on theological assertions when they are negative rather than positive.

Furthermore, it is possible to speak of theological considerations making a genuine difference to the kind of history a person might produce. Thus whereas a Marxist historian might stress the role of economic factors in the past events, a Christian historian might stress the role of the free choices of human agents, although he would not at all discount the effects of economic factors in life. Both the Marxist and Christian would still be called historians, and this is correct, for both are committed to criticism, analogy, and correlation. Where they differ is in their beliefs about the types of causal agents that operate in the past. They differ, that is, in their assumptions about the principle of correlation. For these reasons we must be wary of hasty judgements as to what is to count as 'scientific' history. We must be even more wary about the kinds of conclusions that can be drawn from a judgement of this sort.

The need for caution is also highlighted by reflection on Harvey's conception of history as a field-encompassing field. Just as the various sciences can be described as fields on which the historian relies, so too can metaphysics or theology. To rule these out in advance is to be heavy-handed and question-begging. If, of course, it can be shown that theological discourse is incoherent, or that it is not of a type that is relevant to the explanation of past events, or, if it is of such a type, that it is false, then of course it should be ignored. But to do any of these is to engage in a field of inquiry potentially related to history. If the arguments to date have been successful it would be inconsistent to ignore the role such beliefs may reasonably play in arguments about the past. If the historian is convinced that theology can be relied on, then the treating of history as a field-encompassing field will encourage rather than preclude his relying on it.

The advantage of using this way of expressing the matter is manifold. It draws attention to the way in which the historian often implicitly relies on authorities for justification for the warrants he appeals to in his recovery of the past. It also recognizes that for the traditional believer the resurrection really is taken as a past public event in time and space that may rightly be termed historical. It recognizes, further, that if the resurrection is to be defended very specific data from the past will need to be secured by means of critical scrutiny of the present sources. There is, that is, a human-historical story as well as a theological-historical story to be examined. Moreover, it openly recognizes that the historian cannot avoid metaphysical commitments. Further, it is suggestive of the need, within history, for careful weighing of considerations of various sorts in making a decision about the probability of an event. Finally, talk of various fields highlights the need to test out the adequacy of the data and warrants in a field or even of the legitimacy of a particular field, and in so doing to exercise the required expertise, for the historian may be quite unskilled to mount such an exercise in that he relies on his fields unconsciously and often uncritically.

However, there are also disadvantages to this way of expressing the matter. For one thing, the metaphor of fields suggests that the kinds of sentence the historian uses can be prized apart and tested in turn for truth by the application of the appropriate data and warrants. This may be possible, but seems impractical. As Berlin points out, even the various facts a historian may mention or use 'criss-cross and penetrate each other at many levels simultaneously and the attempt to prise them apart, as it were, and pin them down, and classify them, and fit them into their specific compartments turns out to be impracticable'.[46] Furthermore, the idea of the historian occupying or relying on many fields all at once gives the impression of a 'jack of all trades' and thus tends to play down both the uniqueness of the critical skills he utilizes and the full intellectual stature of his work. In addition, it suggests an explicit interest in the various fields he occupies that is difficult to detect in the finished products of historical study. Finally, there is little doubt that most historians do in practice ignore theological considerations in their work. Like natural scientists they proceed as if God does not exist. They recognize that theology, like perhaps morality, is a field where dispute seems interminable. Naturally they prefer to steer clear of such disputes, concentrating their primary efforts on what human agents have done and undergone in the past. They do not eschew moral or even theological comment, but, as Troeltsch pointed out,[47] such interests are interests of the second degree.

This is borne out by ordinary usage of the term 'history'. In ordinary usage 'history' can mean either the past or what historians do. It is generally accepted that historians provide accounts of what human agents have done and suffered. This understanding stretches as far back as Aristotle[48] and has been expressed succinctly in modern times by Collingwood.

One science differs from another in that it finds out things of a different kind. What kind of things does history find out? I answer *res gestae*; actions of human beings that have been done in the past. Although this answer raises all kinds of further questions many of which are controversial, still, however, they may be answered, the answers do not discredit the proposition that history is the science of *res gestae*, the attempt to answer questions about human actions done in the past.[49]

Because of this, and because of the disputed character of theological or atheological claims, it is awkward to call arguments about the resurrection of Jesus simply historical. It is more natural to say that they go beyond history to embrace theology. So to answer our original question directly, we say that to rely on theological considerations in deciding matters of fact is to go beyond the ordinary bounds of historical science. There is nothing inherently wrong in going beyond these ordinary bounds, but when we do so we become more than historians.

To ignore theological considerations as a working historian is one thing; to pronounce that they are always irrelevant is another. On the former view, the historian leaves open the possibility of theistic explanation of events, while on the latter he must always remain ill at ease until he has found a naturalistic explanation for every event of the past that is of interest to him. That he should seek naturalistic explanations for events is perfectly acceptable, for the traditional theist will do so as well, even in the case of those events that he explains theistically. But to proceed as if events can *only* be explained naturalistically is to embrace a disputed metaphysical doctrine of a kind that is very different from the metaphysical principle that the world and society possess uniformity. The latter is so firmly embedded in common sense and in rival world-views that its status as knowledge is virtually secure. The former is a matter of widespread dispute and the historian had better avoid it.

The matter in the end calls for a decision about how to demarcate the province of the historian. Concerning this, it avoids confusion if the historian and the theologian are kept apart. The historian does not consider it appropriate to tell us what God has done, and the theologian should not consider it his primary task to satisfy the faculty of history. To give different labels to different professions will release them both to develop their skills with a sense of freedom and independence. It will also highlight the need for detailed analysis and examination of the nature of religious discourse, of its coherence, and of its possible relevance to historical phenomena. But conceptual niceties that decide who should be allowed to say what should not be allowed to obscure or render us insensitive to the possibility of subtle interaction between theologian and historian in the study of the origins of Christianity. Nor should it obscure the need for argument from all sides. It is the cogency of argument rather than the resolution of a demarcation dispute that matters most in the end. This is as true of claims about the resurrection of Jesus as it is about his trial or crucifixion, not to speak of the momentous theological claims that are made concerning him. Let the theologian say what he will, there is no necessity of offending the canons of historical judgement in principle. Or, at least, stronger arguments that those put forward by Roberts will have to be developed and applied if this is to be shown in the instances of divine action under scrutiny. But let this be no cause for complacency when it comes to the actual justification of such claims. The propriety of substantial claims about the past must still rest on tested evidence no matter where such evidence originates and no matter how we label those who provide it.

8

DIVINE INTERVENTION
AND NATURAL SCIENCE

IN the course of the last three chapters I have argued that
commitment to divine intervention does not preclude the
possibility of whole-hearted commitment to critical historical
investigation. On the contrary, it needs such a commitment,
for part of the data that is required to render such claims
acceptable will of necessity be dependent on such investigation. At first sight it would be natural to let the matter rest
there as complete, but on further reflection it becomes clear
that this would be somewhat premature.

The foremost reason why the resurrection is a central topic
in discussions about the relation between theology and history
rests on the fact that it is the kind of event that calls in question
the normal warrants we rely on in our intercourse with nature.
It is because of this that it constitutes a problem for the historian. Indeed it only constitutes a problem for the historian
because he is committed, and quite rightly committed, to the
metaphysics of common sense, and this in turn involves
commitment to the data and warrants of science.

By way of response to this problem I have sought to show
how one might legitimately claim that there are features of
this event, in particular its theological character, that allow
one to waive the warrants that we normally accept. If these
features are relevant to such a move, if they can in virtue of
their logic perform such a role, and if they can honestly be
believed, there is no reason why a historian should object. If
he is to object, he must acknowledge that he is making claims
that are far from being a central part of his competence and
expertise, or he must concede that he is relying on philosophical authority to make good his claims.

One way that this might be developed would focus on the
relationship between history and science. As we have seen,
history and the metaphysics of common sense are closely

intertwined. The metaphysics of common sense is in turn closely intertwined with the data and warrants of natural science. So, if claims about divine intervention are hostile to the aims and practice of natural science, they will *ipso facto* be hostile to the aims and practice of history. It is important therefore that a development as important as this be given consideration.

In this chapter I shall explore this objection with reference to the resurrection. It will be suggested that this is an event that is, practically speaking, scientifically inexplicable. This however is not something that renders it embarrassing from the point of view of natural science. In its character as a direct act of God, it is in fact in harmony rather than hostile to the demands of science. I shall begin by noting briefly some possible logical connections between different kinds of explanation.

Generally speaking it is not appropriate to appeal to the direct activity of personal agents to explain an event if that event can be adequately accounted for in terms of its preceding natural conditions. Thus if Jones arrives at his office to find that his private papers are strewn all over the floor, it would be inappropriate to explain this event by relating it to the criminal activity of burglars if he knows that it was caused by the gale that blew up during the night.

It is likewise inappropriate to explain an event as the direct activity of God if that event can also be explained as the result of natural forces or as the result of human agents acting on their own initiative. Thus it would be inappropriate to claim that God overturned Smith's car on the road from Oxford to Abingdon if Smith's car was overturned by the wind or as a consequence of the activity of certain enemies of Smith.

In this example we can recognize a paradigm case where there is incompatibility between a theological description or explanation of an event and a naturalistic explanation of an event. Moreover, this relation holds independently of any account of a distinction between types of explanation. It would hold, that is, even if one believed that in the end explanations in terms of actions can be replaced by explanations in terms of preceding physical conditions. It is secured more by the specificity than by the type, by the content rather than by the form. Thus it is as clear as the incompatibility between explaining the condition of Jones's office by referring to the activity of burglars acting on their own intiative in contrast to the activity of his wife acting on her own initiative; or it is as clear as the incompatibility between explaining Smith's car overturning by referring to the wind in contrast to referring to a mechanical failure in the braking-system.

To claim that there may thus be a relationship of incompatibility between a theological and a naturalistic explanation of an event does not imply that there will always be a relation of incompatibility between a theological and a naturalistic explanation. This can be shown by reflection on other examples.

Suppose Smith after being cured by medical treatment goes to church to thank God for having healed him. In attributing the healing to God, Smith is partly explaining the event of his healing by referring it to the activity of God. Initially it might seem that there was incompatibility between attributing this event both to the activity of God and to the activity of the doctors who performed the necessary operation or prescribed the necessary drugs. But this is not so for two reasons. First, the theological explanation used may be very general. There may, that is, be no appeal to the direct intervention of God, as would be the case if Smith looked on his cure as an instance of a miracle. Secondly, what Smith is doing is selecting one very general condition, which as a theist he believes in, and claiming this to be the most significant cause of his healing in the context of worship. The reference to divine action is reference to God's creating and sustaining the world. As a full explanation of his healing this would be inadequate because it would not explain why he was cured in this instance rather than, say, a week later. To procure an adequate explanation reference to the activity of doctors and the properties of certain drugs will be essential. But there is nothing improper, generally speaking, in focusing on the general activity of God to explain the healing in that it is common in many explanations to select that which is most significant in the total set of conditions that have brought about an event and ignore for the moment all the standing or negative conditions that are also required if the event is to be fully explained.[1]

Another situation where there is no incompatibility between a theological and a naturalistic explanation is the case where God appoints chosen human agents to perform certain acts on His behalf. Suppose God appoints a prophet to deliver His word to a certain group of people. It is legitimate in such circumstances to say both that the prophet speaks to the people and that God speaks to the people. In this example there is a relation of strict liability between the events initiated by the prophet on God's behalf and God. There is nothing surprising in this in that it is common to hold that there is a relation of strict liability between an agent and certain events in the world even though those events were not directly brought about by that agent. Thus in certain commercial, legal, and diplomatic situations it is possible for persons to be held responsible for what is done by their agents; and reference to the persons who appointed the agents will be essential if a full explanation of the events the agents initiate is to be secured.

Yet another example where the activity of God can be appealed to to explain an event is the case where the event in question can be subdivided into other events, one of which is brought about by God directly and is of crucial significance in the total nexus of causes. Thus if one of the crucial events in the exodus from Egypt is the event of God speaking to Moses, it is natural to speak of God bringing the Israelites out of Egypt even though God may not have performed any other direct acts in the exodus.[2] As in the healing example, this is warranted by the general custom of picking out one cause as the real explanation even though as a full explanation it would be inadequate.

Despite the compatibility between theological and naturalistic explanations exhibited in these examples, it is important to abstain from broad generalizations such as that an event can be explained both theologically and naturalistically at the same time. In the absence of detailed specification of the precise explanations in mind such a generalization is too ambiguous and vague to be informative. In fact three key concepts in this generalization are ambiguous.

The term 'explain' is ambiguous because it is not clear whether this means an explanation in terms of the activity of personal agents or in terms of general laws and antecedent conditions. The term 'naturalistically' is ambiguous in that it is not clear whether this involves reference to human personal agency alone, to human personal agency together with non-personal agency, or to non-personal agency alone. The term 'theologically' is ambiguous in that it is not clear whether this refers to general divine activity in creation, to direct divine activity focused on because of its cruciality rather than its total sufficiency, or to direct divine activity alone. Given such complexity and ambiguity it is advisable to proceed piecemeal, and specify the type and content of theological and naturalistic explanations in mind, and thus examine the possibility of compatibility or incompatibility in each case. In this chapter I shall attend to the relation between the resurrection of Jesus understood as brought about by a direct act of God and putative scientific explanations. A point of entry into this issue is the fact that it is not at all peculiar to claim that there are events that are not scientifically explicable. Thus it has been central to classical libertarian traditions to claim that human actions are scientifically inexplicable. This position has been lucidly stated by Swinburne in a passage that does not conceal the controversial status of his book.

When a man marries Jane rather than Anne, becomes a solicitor rather than a barrister, kills rather than shows mercy after considering arguments in favour of each course, he brings about a state of the world by his free and rational choice. To all appearances this is an entirely different way whereby states of the world may come about than through the operation of laws of nature on preceding states. Someone may object that it is necessary that physiological or other scientific laws operate in order for the agent to bring about effects. My answer is that certainly it is necessary that such laws operate in order for effects brought about directly by the agent to have ulterior consequences. But unless there are some effects which the agent brings about directly without the operation of scientific laws acting on preceding physical states bringing them about, then these laws and states could fully explain the effects and there would be no need to refer in explaining them to the rational choice of an agent. True, the apparent freedom and rationality of the human will *may* prove an illusion. Men may have no more option what to do than a machine and be guided by an argument no more than a piece of iron. But this has not yet been shown and, in the absence of good philosophical and scientific argument to show it, I assume, what is apparent, that when a man acts by free and rational choice, his agency is the operation of a different kind of causality from that of scientific laws. The free choice of a rational agent is the only way of accounting for natural phenomena other than the way of normal scientific explanation, which is recognised as such by all men and has not been reduced to normal scientific explanation.[3]

It is less controversial to claim that some events cannot be explained scientifically because of our ignorance. They are not in practice open to scientific explanation. Such would be the case with regard to the shape of the birthmark on a nineteenth-century slum child or the early unremarked death of an ice-age mammoth. These are inexplicable because we do not have enough information to hand to develop a standard scientific explanation.

Other events are in practice inexplicable from a scientific point of view because, unless we stop the search for explanation somewhere, it will go on for ever.[4] Thus, that the fundamental laws of science operate as they do cannot be given a scientific explanation, simply because citing these fundamental laws is involved in giving a complete scientific explanation of any event. Logically, of course, one could seek an explanation of the present fundamental laws of science by appeal to yet more general laws that together with a set of preceding conditions would explain their existing. But then this set of general laws could not be scientifically explained unless another set of yet more general laws were postulated, and so on *ad infinitum*. Clearly the explanation must stop somewhere, and the event that constitutes the stopping-point will be scientifically inexplicable.

The resurrection of Jesus falls very definitely into that class of events that is inexplicable not as a matter of principle but of practice. Logically it is the kind of event that could fall within the range of standard scientific explanation. It is logically possible, that is, to conceive of a scientist positing a law of nature to the effect that under certain conditions men rise from the dead. However, there are two fatal objections to the view that the resurrection of Jesus will as a matter of fact be explained in this way.

First, the resurrection of Jesus does not fall within a general class of resurrections, and thus one condition for the development of a law of nature is lacking. The resurrection would be treated as a freak result or a misobservation to be forgotten rather than as an anomaly to be absorbed into current scientific theory. This can be shown as follows.

It is a commonplace that scientists encounter events or reports of events that call in question their current theories. And the history of science might well be seen in large measure as the endless attempt to revise and refine current theory in the light of inexplicable events. However, not every inexplicable event is allowed to call in question current theory. What is needed as a minimum is that the event in question constitute an anomaly, that is, an event that has been repeated under similar conditions to that on which it was first noted. To be sure, even an anomaly may not lead to an immediate revision of current theory. Thus the anomaly might be noted by a scientist, but he might feel that current scientific theory could cope with it, given minor revisions. In other circumstances he might be less open-minded on the question of the capacity of current theory in coping with this anomaly. He might feel, that is, that current theory will have to be given up one day, but for the present he is content to leave it as it stands in that it enables him to predict and control those events which are his present concern.

We can contrast this with a situation where we have, not an anomaly, but a freak result, that is, an event which is not repeated in similar circumstances.[5] What is reported or observed is a totally isolated phenomenon, an unrepeated occurrence concerning which there is not even the beginning of a theory. What happens in such a case is generally unproblematic. Either the event is simply forgotten and no more is ever heard of it, or it is classed as a misobservation of something else. An example of the latter would be the Russian claim to have observed volcanic activity on the moon. This claim was made once at one observatory, and it called in question for a time the generally accepted view that the moon was volcanically inert. When this observation was not repeated by other observers elsewhere, majority opinion was that this was an instance of misobservation. Something else, it was said, had been misdescribed or misinterpreted.

When looked at from the point of view of science alone, it is highly probable that the resurrection of Jesus would be treated as a freak result rather than as an anomaly. It is true, of course, that claims have been made concerning other resurrections than that of Jesus, e.g. the case of Lazarus. However, such claims are either highly disputed or are generally associated with Jesus in such a way that they are not believed unless the resurrection of Jesus is itself already accepted. In other words there are no undisputed occurrences of resurrection which would allow the resurrection of Jesus to be accepted as a genuine anomaly that would call for the revision of current scientific theory.

This is borne out by the standard types of response to the resurrection of Jesus. Those who believe in it believe in it partly because they are convinved that it is a paradigm instance of a direct act of God in the world. Classically they have accepted it as a miracle, i.e. as a basic act of God. They do not in such circumstances seek a scientific explanation for it, nor do they seriously request scientists to set about revising current scientific theory in order to accommodate it. Indeed the provision of an adequate scientific explanation would be incompatible with their belief that it is a direct act of God. To explain it naturalistically, say by the findings of psychical research, would be to render redundant talk of the direct activity of God. It would also make inappropriate any appeal to the resurrection as a sign of the unique significance of Jesus in the purposes of God for the world. So in traditional accounts of the resurrection there is no attempt to seek seriously a scientific explanation. Nor are any scientists likely to seek it either, as we shall see.

On the other hand, those who reject the traditional account can be seen generally to adopt one of two strategies. Those who take a hostile attitude to the Christian faith either reject the resurrection as a fraud or lie, or argue that it is the product of the fertile imagination of the early Christians, or claim that it is a collective hallucination. In each case they look upon it as unworthy of serious consideration. Those who are more sympathetic to the early traditions of the Christian faith and thus seek to appropriate something of their significance for today treat the resurrection not as a statement about events in the post-mortem existence of Jesus, but as a statement about the rise of faith in the disciples or a statement about the theological significance of the life and death of Jesus. This is a sophisticated version of the view that the traditional descriptions of the resurrection should be classed as misobservations, though highly significant misobservations that can be accounted for by the cultural context of the writers.

There is then, practically speaking, little possibility of the resurrection of Jesus being looked upon as an event that calls for scientific explantion. Because it does not fall within a class of repeated anomalies it will, from a purely scientific point of view, be rejected altogether or explained away as the product of imagination or misobservation. From the point of view of logic this situation could change, for it is possible for judgements of misobservation to be revised. Thus there is little or no tendency nowadays to class reports of the healing activity of Jesus as misobservation or fraud. But the reason for this is that many of them can be fitted into a class of anomalies that is too well supported by contemporary observation to be ignored by science. If theories to explain such phenomena are not currently available they will be sought in due course. But with the resurrection of Jesus this is not the case, and no one is seriously going to contend that it will be fitted into a class of genuine anomalies. We have no undisputed reports of resurrection to look to, and those who suggest that one day we shall have such a class will be treated as sceptically as those who claim that the sun will not rise tomorrow or that heavy objects near the surface of the earth will cease to fall next week. Logically such events are possible, but neither science nor common sense will take them seriously.

It was precisely because of this that Harvey was correct to press the point that the key problem with the resurrection is its calling in question the warrants of science. What I want to suggest is that it is in the best interests of science to accept the kind of rebuttal proposed earlier. To accept the resurrection as an act of God relieves science of the burden of altering its present, highly successful theories. In essence this is the substance of the second reason why it is unlikely that the resurrection of Jesus will be given a scientific explanation.

Suppose that one is seriously prepared to countenance the resurrection as an explanation for certain events in history. One is prepared to accept this event as happening rather than accept the various naturalistic attempts to explain away such data as the appearances of Jesus to the disciples, the empty tomb, etc. Nor is one prepared to leave the data as a mystery that defies explanation, or radically reinterpret the resurrection as, say, the rise of faith in the disciples, or as an event described in so Pickwickian a manner that one merits the charge of being obscurantist. Suppose further that one now goes in search of an explanation for the resurrection. The issue that arises is this: is it more worthwhile to accept the explanation that God brought it about directly, or should one go in search of a scientific explanation? The whole situation is, of course, artificial, for it suggests an all too atomistic method of going in search of explanation as if one generally divides and conquers the data to be explained piece by piece. Moreover, it ignores the fact that it is unlikely that resurrection will be accepted as a datum that requires explanation unless one is committed to the availability of a theological explanation, for theory and data interact on each other. But the issue as it stands is clear and suits our purpose satisfactorily.

That it is in the interests of science to take the former choice is suggested by two considerations. First, in accepting a theological explanation one is not contravening the types of explanation that the scientist himself accepts in his everyday life. Explaining events in terms of personal agency is a well established and universally understood convention to which no exception can be taken as a matter of logic. Moreover, a scientist will not consider it his duty to explain those events that are the direct results of personal agents. Thus, for example, he will consider it redundant to seek to explain scientifically the removal of his car from his garage if he can explain it by appealing to the activity of his wife. If he is a psychologist who is attracted to the materialist theory of the mind he may, of course, go further, and say that he thinks it possible to give a scientific explanation of the activity of his wife. But in taking this further step he need not deny the general logical adequacy of personal-type explanations, and he will have to confess that he is embracing a philosophical theory that is still a matter of major dispute. Above all, he will have to accept that in the case of an explanation that refers to the personal agency of God no further scientific investigation is logically possible, for God is not an embodied agent. Nor need this be a matter of embarrassment to his philosophical leanings, so long as he holds that the identity between mind and brain is not a matter of logical necessity but of contingent fact.

Secondly, in seeking to find any scientific explanation for

the resurrection it is likely that the price to be paid for success is much too high.[6] Let us call the event of the resurrection of Jesus R and total set of physical laws that govern the bodily processes that follow death L. In order to modify L to account for R we would then need a new set of laws, L^1, which to be acceptable to the general scientific community would have to satisfy several stringent conditions. This new set of laws, L^1, would have to be relatively simple relative to all the data to be explained, would have to be able to predict all the tested predictions of L, would have to be able to predict R, and would have to be more successful in predicting future data than L. If these are the conditions that have to be satisfied, it is on reflection beyond the bounds of responsible optimism to hold that such a law will be formulated. It might satisfy the second and third conditions, but its chances of satisfying the first and last conditions are slim. In such circumstances it would be better to accept an alternative explanation that relieves one of the burden of interfering with a body of laws whose reliability has been so widely established. Precisely this is provided by a theological explanation of the resurrection that sees it as a direct act of God done to fulfil certain intentions and purposes.

I must emphasize here that there is no suggestion that a theological explanation be accepted uncritically at this point. This too should be tested for adequacy, even though our criteria for such testing may as yet remain much less clear than our criteria for testing the adequacy of scientific explanations.[7] Nor is this a resort to a kind of *deus ex machina* brought in at the last minute to fill in the gaps left by science. The artificiality of our supposing a scientist to look for a scientific explanation of the resurrection precludes this interpretation. Nor in fact do arguments for the resurrection proceed in this kind of way, for there is generally an interaction of theology and data at once, the theology or atheology partially determining what is to count as needing explanation.

The implication of these considerations is that there is relation of mutual harmony between the traditional theologian and the scientist. The theologian has no need to call in question the content of science. The theologian for his part looks to science with the kind of respect that allows and even relies on its claim to knowledge. Moreover, in positing the resurrection he does not arbitrarily set aside the warrants of science, nor does he require the scientist to alter his well-established theories regarding the natural processes that follow death. In not requiring the latter he relieves the scientist of a burden that would be difficult to bear. The scientist on his part cannot call in question the logical propriety of accepting a theological explanation of the resurrection, for this is a special case of personal explanation, and is thus already firmly established in his everyday life. If, in fact, he does challenge it, say by arguing that the notion of an incorporeal agent is incoherent, he will be taking sides on a philosophical issue that lies outside his authority. Alternatively, if he challenges it by arguing that God does not exist or that, if He does, He does not intervene in the world, he will be taking sides on complex philosophical and theological issues that are not open to scientific investigation and that therefore also lie outside his authority.

This whole strategy might be challenged, however, by arguing that the resurrection can be fitted into the type of law-like generalization developed by scientists. Such a generalization could be briefly expressed as follows. (A) Whenever God comes to earth incarnate in a man, then that man in whom God is incarnate comes back from the dead. (B) Jesus is God incarnate. Therefore, (C) Jesus will come back from the dead. Sentence (A) is equivalent to a statement about there being a law that holds when certain conditions in the universe hold; sentence (B) provides information about conditions in the universe which together with (A) allow us to make predictions about further states of the universe as expressed in (C).

Such an attempt to challenge the claim that the resurrection is scientifically inexplicable is suggested by H. H. Rowley in some remarks directed to the healing miracles of Jesus.

The greatest discoveries that await us in the world of personality are the discoveries of the possibilities of the life that is linked with the power of God, the capacities of the personality that is enriched by the indwelling Spirit of God; and the greatest achievements that are open to us are the achievements of God through us. The uniqueness of Jesus lay precisely there, in His oneness with the Spirit of God and in His being the perfect vehicle of God's will. In His activity God was active, initiating succour for needy sufferers through the powers of personality and Spirit just as truly as He initiated succour for Israel by making the winds His messengers and the storms the instrument of His will.[8]

Rowley concedes that this reading of the situation does not solve immediately problems related to such phenomena as restoration of the dead or nature miracles. However, secrets of life and death not open to people generally may be open to Jesus. Because of his unique relation to God, he can do marvellous things that involve a higher knowledge of nature than we at present possess. Thus there is no need to posit any violation of a law of nature and thereby to speak of an event that is scientifically inexplicable. Just as by utilizing the laws of magnetism human agents can overcome the laws of gravity, so by laws as yet unknown to us may God overcome the laws of nature related to death. 'It may be possible for God, as well as for man, to employ one natural power to overcome another. But to suppose that in order to achieve His will, God was reduced to the necessity of "breaking the rules" from time to time, would be less honouring to His wisdom and power than to suppose that His works were the agents, and not the embarrassments of His purpose.'[9] From this it is not difficult to extrapolate to the view that even the resurrection will one day be open to scientific explanation. God in raising Jesus from the dead was using laws that will one day be discovered. In the meantime we can rest content with the law-like generalization that when God becomes incarnate in a man, that man rises from the dead. How God does it will be known more precisely when we can specify the laws he is utilizing.

This kind of strategy is plausible but unacceptable. First, it just does not make sense to ask how God raised Jesus from the dead if the divine action at issue is a miracle. A miracle is, by definition, a basic act of God that is done straight off without recourse to any causal chain that would bring about a desired effect.[10] As there are no causal chains that can be described by law-like generalizations, there cannot, as a matter of logic, be higher laws as yet undiscovered to account for the resurrection.

Secondly, even if this objection is rejected as question-begging, this strategy involves a major act of faith for the future in that it looks to prospective developments in science to furnish the higher laws not known at present. The analogy with the laws of magnetism and gravity as at this point is seriously misleading, as is the reference to the healing activity of Jesus. With the former we do have laws to hand, while with the latter there is enough well-attested testimony to similar contemporary events to render a search for possible laws worthwhile. But there does not seem to be any practical assurance that laws will be formulated to cover resurrections, for, as was argued above,[11] no such testimony for resurrections exists.

Thirdly, any attempt to treat the formulated generalization as a potential candidate of proper law-like generalization while the search for higher laws is conducted is vitiated by the fact that it fails to satisfy two conditions which must be met if the scientific community is to find it acceptable. Such conditions are, first, that proposed generalizations be couched in terms of naturalistic concepts, and, secondly, that they be either universal or statistical in form.

It would, no doubt, be rash and quite unacceptable for anyone to lay down stringent limits to the concepts that scientists may one day have to use in their explanation. However, it is not rash to set one limit, namely that God will not function as a key concept in their explanations. But the strategy sketched above depends on the reverse of this, namely that such concepts as 'God' or 'God's Spirit' will one day be welcomed by scientists when they formulate laws of nature.

As to the failure to satisfy the second condition, the situation can be shown as follows. From the point of view of grammar, the generalization cited is indeed similar to a law-like generalization. To say 'When God becomes incarnate in X, X rises from the dead,' is grammatically akin to saying 'When water is heated to 100 degrees centigrade, it turns to steam.' Both exhibit the form 'if A then B', but beyond that the analogy ends. The former is surely more akin to the sentence 'If the Americans visit the moon, they will place a flag on its surface.' In the latter case there is no guarantee that a flag will be thus located. There is always room for a free decision to refrain from such activity. It is likewise with God, for His acts are a matter of grace. There is no law which specifies that under certain conditions He will universally do x, or that under certain conditions it is, say, 75 per cent statistically probable that He will do x. Scientific laws are generally susceptible to such formulation. If water is heated to 100 degrees centigrade, it will turn to steam, other things being equal. Given the prior conditions, the outcome is predictable.

Furthermore, because divine activity is a matter of grace, the theological objection raised by Rowley against direct divine action is misplaced. Thus it is surely odd to speak of a miracle being an embarrassment to the purposes of God. On the contrary, it is possible to conceive of a miracle as being an expression of divine wisdom and power in that God achieves His purposes through a direct act like raising a man from the dead rather than taking a more circuitous route. Moreover, it is inappropriate to speak of God being reduced to the necessity of breaking the rules. It is part of human finitude to leave God to achieve His purposes in whatever way He deems necessary. In attempting to describe what He is said to have done in the resurrection of Jesus, it seems altogether less complicated and less mysterious to regard it as a direct act done immediately.

A more recent set of arguments that would challenge the harmony between theology and science suggested in this chapter has been developed by Diamond.[12] The first part of his discussion is devoted to showing that miraculous occurrences cannot be ruled out by definition or by dogmas concerning what can or cannot happen in nature. Miracles cannot be ruled out by definition because the operation of natural forces is not inexorable and because predictions based on scientific laws are not infallible. They cannot be ruled out by dogmas concerning what can or cannot happen in nature, because scientific results are always provisional, and 'The cumulative impact of successful scientific work cannot, logically cannot, preclude the possibility that dramatic exceptions to the most well established laws of nature will be observed and validated even in a very secular culture and by scientifically sophisticated thinkers.'[13]

Both these points are now widely agreed as acceptable. There is nothing self-contradictory in affirming that a miracle has occurred, and science cannot prove that its laws are not violated. Attack on miracle, therefore, must be made on other grounds. Diamond develops his attack by drawing a distinction between occurrence and interpretation and then arguing that the cost of affirming a theological interpretation that involves reference to the direct activity of God is too high.[14] In his view, the record shows that in the long run scientists come up with explanations of events that initially defy naturalistic explanation. Moreover, to accept a theological interpretation of events that can be naturally observed would impede the work of scientists at the operative level by forcing them to sacrifice their autonomy. Furthermore, naturalistic interpretations of observable events do not require a sacrifice of any concepts that are important or integral to religion.

That there is a clear distinction between occurrence and interpretation is brought out by reflection on an imagined instantaneous cure at Lourdes. A totally withered leg of a two-year-old child is restored to full normal functioning after immersion in the waters. There are absolutely no known medical theories to account for this healing, yet a crack team of scientists all agree that it has occurred. The authorities of the Roman Catholic Church say it was something done by God through the instrumentality of the Virgin Mary. The scientists say they do not know why it occurred. At best they can announce that they will start a search. It is their hope that they will fit this event into such a generalization as: 'If physiological type y (with certain kinds of affliction) comes together with the same person with psychological type x and is immersed in chemical waters type z, then instantaneous healing will result.'[15]

Both the theologian and the scientist can offer support for their respective interpretations. Thus the theologian can say that he does at least provide an explanation, i.e. God brought about the cure. Such an act poses no problem to God, because with Him all things are possible. And, although it cannot be asserted that He will always act to cure the sick directly, it is an act that fits in with the picture of God as a loving father. Moreover, the theological explanation is of benefit to science in that it allows the scientist to preserve the adequacy of his present theoretical commitments. In a situation where we have an unrepeated extraordinary occurrence that shatters the fabric of contemporary scientific understanding of nature, it is better to see such events as caused by God, because incorporating them into present theory would involve too radical a revision of extremely useful, relatively simple, fundamental principles.

The scientist, however, should not be beguiled by such friendly overtures from the theologian. To begin with, he should remember that his explanation, when he finds it, will be of much greater predictive value. The action of God through the action of the Virgin Mary is quite unpredictable; indeed, any 'laws' governing God's grace would be quite inaccessible to our limited intellects. Moreover, the scientist should recall how successful he has been in the past, and this would provide warrant for the claim that, given time, he will develop theories of the requisite simplicity. It must be conceded that this does involve an element of faith that is dogmatic, even messianic. But it would be better to have that kind of faith than to sacrifice his autonomy as a scientist. This contention that the scientist is surrendering his autonomy is central to Diamond's discussion, so I shall set it out in some detail.

Diamond invites us to consider a scenario where a group of leading scientists are baffled by the failure of a 1,000 megaton bomb to pollute the atmosphere even though it has been exploded. The bomb, that is, explodes, but it has no visible effects. On investigation the scientists discover that a well known pacifist priest has been mounting a prayer vigil in which he requested God to keep the explosion from polluting the atmosphere. Assume, continues Diamond, that the scientists are prepared to allow for the possibilty of 'supernatural' exceptions to the status quo, and at once it will be seen that they have opted right out of the scientific enterprise. This is so because 'in a situation of this kind, these scientists would not be able to determine whether the exception was supernatural. Therefore the head of the investigating team would have to phone the Pope to ask him to send one of his investigating teams ... to the area.'[16] In other words they could not begin their scientific work until they were sure that they had natural exceptions rather than 'supernatural' exceptions. The former are exceptions that will be repeated whenever the same circumstances occur. The latter are exceptions that will be repeated only if God, in His grace, wills them to be repeated. To decide this issue, it seems, the Pope will have to send a team to check out the claim that God was answering the priest's prayers.

This, however, would be unacceptable. 'Scientists cannot function as scientists if they have to appeal to leading figures in some enterprise to tell them what to do. Scientists, as scientists, must operate with autonomy, that is, they must set their own rules and referee their own games.'[17] Reflection on the case of the withered leg is said to bear this out.

The views of the Church authorities would even interfere with scientific research, for example, a scientist might want to examine the waters to determine whether there was a special chemical ingredient that helped with the cures. The Church authorities would, presumably, assure him that just as a chemical analysis in desecration of the consecrated host would not reveal anything that differentiated the consecrated host from the non-consecrated waters [*sic*], so too the waters of Lourdes would not turn out to be chemically distinctive.[18]

In such circumstances it is not possible to reach a kind of compromise where one tries to have it both ways, i.e. continue the search for chemical ingredients in the water, and thus grant science its autonomy, while holding that the Church's theological interpretation is the correct one. This is revealed, according to Diamond, when we imagine that one of the scientists is a Southern Baptist who has been raised in a theological tradition that is hostile to the Roman Catholic Church. 'He is open to the intervention of God in earthly affairs, and especially to the possibility of divinely caused healings, but *not* under the auspices of the Roman Catholic Church.'[19] Confronted with the healing, there are only two options open to him. Either he can, qua Southern Baptist and qua scientist, look on this event as an instance of the normal kinds of unusual event that scientists study; or he can accept the Catholic interpretation and convert to Rome. In short, he cannot have both the theological interpretation and the autonomy of science at the same time.

Nor, says Diamond, should this worry the religious believer. There are alternative theological traditions that can be embraced. Thus liberal and existentialist theories have shown that a reactionary espousal of divine intervention, as illustrated by Austin Farrer, is to be resisted.

> They have insisted that we can understand God's relation to men on the model of freedom. Free decisions cannot be made a matter of public observation or scientific predictability. Nevertheless, in making them, human beings operate within the fabric of natural regularity. Freedom does not enable a human being to jump out of a twelfth storey window and fly up instead of falling down. So too, God's revelatory activity must be understood within the framework of scientific understanding.[20]

Construing God's activity in this manner avoids any sacrifice of the scientist's autonomy. Moreover, it encourages religion to break with the tendency to focus on observables and thus misunderstand its own character. On this analysis, 'faith involves an element of trust that persists in spite of the way things go in the observable order'.[21]

If these arguments succeed, they represent a serious challenge to the position developed in this chapter. Of particular importance is Diamond's claim that there must be a relation of hostility between a traditional theologian and science. But his arguments go further afield than this, so I shall clear the ground by examining the other claims he has made.

Let it be noted as a preliminary that there is nothing reactionary in the overall strategy to establish a relation of harmony between theology and science.[22] Thus there has been no attempt to cash in on the decreasing prestige of science, or on recent developments that have sought to undermine the inexorable deterministic character of scientific laws.[23] On the contrary, the position advocated here involves the view that scientific conclusions should be given the status of knowledge, that the warrants of science be relied on unless reasons to the contrary be available, and that the simplicity of scientific theory be preserved.

Nor does the stance adopted involve any surrender of the idea of faith construed as a trust that persists in spite of the way things go. The believer trusts in God for many reasons, but above all because of what God has done for him in redemption in Christ. He loves because he has first been loved. But this does not imply that his trust may not be tested to the limit by troubles without and trials within. He may face persecution from a hostile society, for example, or he may face personal suffering. In neither case will he give up his trust automatically. So it is true to say that in a very real sense his trust will continue despite the way things go in the world. The liberal, existentialist, and traditional theologians all share this view of faith, so it is inaccurate of Diamond to exhibit it as a monopoly of the former two traditions alone.

However, the traditional theologian will acknowledge and even insist that this element of trust should not be exaggerated. If trust in God, for the Christian, does in part depend upon God's saving activity in Christ, and if such claims can be rendered implausible or false by historical investigation, it is clear that such trust will be dependent on the way things go in the world. In this sense it is not true to say that faith will or should continue no matter how things go in the world. The only way to avoid this is either to deny the historical character of revelation or to find adequate alternative warrants for one's trust in God, or to make trust in God a sheer leap of faith that has no warrants at all.[24]

It is also to be noted that Diamond has committed himself to a very anthropomorphic conception of the limits of divine activity. That there must be some element of anthropomorphism in our understanding of divine action is necessary if intelligibility is to be secured and discourse thereon made possible.[25] But it is surely inconsistent for a theist to insist, as Diamond does, that the limitations of man's free actions be predicated of the free actions of a god who is Father Almighty. Further, there is no logical or theological necessity in the claim that God's revelatory activity be understood within the fabric of scientific understanding. On the contrary, if some measure of divine intervention is essential to revelation, then in virtue of that alone there must be some events that are scientifically inexplicable. Whether such intervention shatters the fabric of scientific understanding will depend on the instance of divine intervention specified. That it does so in the case of the resurrection of Jesus would seem to be the case. But such an act will still be a free action of God understood in very general terms as analogous to the free action of men.

Moreover, it is not at all clear how Diamond intends to reconcile his belief in free human action with his view that all events will one day be given scientific explanation. This is a problem that continues to be a matter of dispute, and theists in the past have been committed to both sides in the controversy about freedom, but if the incompatiblists are correct, then Diamond can rightly be accused of possessing an inconsistent body of beliefs. Indeed, he has explicitly committed himself to the position that free decisions cannot be made a matter of public observation or scientific predictability.[26]

By clearing most of the foreground we are now in a position to examine Diamond's contention that a traditional theologian merely by asserting direct divine intervention is interfering with the autonomy of science. Autonomy means here that scientists must be free to set their own rules and referee their own games. It is this that rules out the possibility of their making a request to Rome to help them decide whether the bomb that exploded without the usual effects is a natural or 'supernatural' exception. The reasoning throughout this discussion is confused.

To begin with, let us agree that the scientists do send for help to Rome. It is exaggerated to claim that this involves any sacrifice of autonomy. It is the scientists themselves, not the Pope or the pacifist priest, who initiate such overtures. Therefore, in a very real sense it is the scientists who are deciding what is to be done, and presumably when a reply has been made they can make a further decision as to its value.

In any case, it is not clear how sending a request to Rome is going to settle the question as to whether the exception is natural or 'supernatural'. This is so because no religious community has any formal criterion or specialized expertise for identifying direct divine action. If and when a judgement is made it will probably involve a complex of considerations that embraces both theology and science.

Further, it is just false to claim that there will be interference. To be sure, it is true that if the Church believes that God prevented the bomb having effects by directly intervening and that God cured the withered leg through the agency of the Virgin Mary, it will assure the scientists that they will find no natural cause for these events. But this follows from their beliefs about God and His activity, and does not at all entail that they will interfere in the work of the scientists. The scientists can still conduct all the necessary experiments, and will be encouraged to do so, as Diamond himself concedes.[27]

Moreover, there is no reason why a scientist cannot accept provisionally the theolgoical interpretation while still seeking a purely naturalistic explanation. In fact, he might consider his failure to find in practice a naturalistic explanation as evidence of a sort for the theological explanation. Thus he might argue that although he could never establish conclusively that an event is not caused naturally, failure to find a naturalistic explanation does render more plausible alternative explanations in so far as these can be independently supported. In accepting a theological explanation he is not, of course, accepting an explanation that will have the same predictive value as a scientific explanation. But this is largely irrelevant, in that part of the uniqueness of scientific explanation is its predictive value, and there is no logical necessity for all explanations to have the same degree of predictive value.[28] In any case, to engage in the search for naturalistic explanation it is, strictly speaking, not necessary for the scientist to believe his search will be successful. He can provisionally accept one explanation for an event, while testing out the possibility of another. Thus, a detective may accept that A murdered B while testing out the rival claim that B's death was due to purely natural causes. Because of this there is no need to read the situation as one where there is a forced option between believing the theological interpretation and refusing to engage in the search for a scientific explanation.

In one sense there is a forced option. It is not possible on pain of inconsistency to believe in the theological explanation and also in the future availability of a scientific explanation. But this is a matter of definition. To claim that God did x directly means that x was not caused naturally. But this analytic truth does not rule out the empirical possibility of an individual accepting a theological explanation for x while investigating x as a scientist and thus playing the scientific 'game'.

Nor does accepting a theological explanation for the cure of the withered leg entail any necessity of converting to Rome if one is to be honest. Diamond can only claim this because he has cooked his definitions to entail this consequence. Thus, he introduces a Southern Baptist who is defined as one who cannot countenance divine intervention under the auspices of

Rome. It is no surprise that he cannot accept a theological interpretation of the cure, for this follows as a matter of definition. An Anglican scientist, in contrast, might accept the theological interpretation while aiding his humanist colleagues in the search for a naturalistic explanation.

Diamond is, of course, correct to say that science does have rules. And one fundamental rule of science is that one must search for naturalistic explanations. But it is not a rule of science that all events, given time, will be given a naturalistic explanation. The latter is a metaphysical claim that is false. As we have seen, some events are scientifically inexplicable because they involve an infinite regress of explanation that must be stopped somewhere as brute unexplained fact. Others are in this position because they can be adequately accounted for by the activity of personal agents. Because of this it would be better to describe the kind of faith exhibited by Diamond not just as dogmatic and messianic but as doomed to failure.

To express objection in such terms is to express it in as strong a manner as is perhaps possible. As a minimum, however, it is in order to emphasize that commitment to science does not entail commitment to the metaphysical thesis that all events will be given a scientific explanation. Nor does it entail commitment to the view that the events under scrutiny will be given a scientific explanation. All that is necessary is that one should believe that they can, in principle, be given a scientific explanation. This renders largely irrelevant Diamond's appeal to the past success of science.[29]

Finally, it is important to note that the examples of putative divine intervention furnished by Diamond are drawn from the present. In this there is both advantage and disadvantage. The advantages are that it allows him to make available a clear distinction between occurrence and interpretation and to make vivid the relation between the theologian and the scientist. The disadvantages are also twofold. First, it leads him to turn aside from the issue of the relation of theology to science by changing to a quite separate problem, namely the problem of evil.[30] But this is a problem that faces any theist, and the extent to which it is either relieved or compounded by belief in divine intervention would require extended independent consideration. Secondly, it is highly unlikely that scientists would seek a naturalistic explanation for the resurrection of Jesus as keenly as they would seek an explanation for the events specified by Diamond. As has been argued, it is unlikely that anyone will believe in this event if it is not also taken to have been an act of God. Focus on putative contemporary instances of divine intervention, therefore, obscures the extremely messianic and dogmatic faith that will be needed if one is to believe that this event will be explained by the future theoretical resources of science.

Diamond will not need such a faith, to be sure, for he does not believe in the resurrection of Jesus as traditionally understood. But this is because he relies on the kind of arguments deployed by Harvey rather than because he has argued anything new concerning supposed hostility between a traditional theologian and science. It is perhaps also because he does not consider the abandoning of the resurrection as involving the sacrifice of a concept that is central to religion. At this point a fresh controversy will arise, but whatever is to be said in it, it is clear that this is an issue that stands independently from the issue that has concerned us in this chapter. A theologian can take no comfort from Diamond's arguments in order to undermine the position that has been espoused in this study.

9

CONCLUSION

THE purpose of this study has been modest. It has attempted
to show that belief in divine intervention is a permissible
option for the modern theologian, while eschewing any
attempt to show that such a belief is obligatory. To do so
would require the examination of a mass of data and argument that cannot be done here. Moreover, it would require
the detailed defence of assumptions that had to be made in
the body of this study in order that the overall structure might
be exposed to view. In addition, it would be insensitive to
claim that any attempt to map the relation of theology to
history was final or complete. The riches and genius of both
are too generous and diffuse to be amenable to neat schema-
tization. Further discussion and refinement will be needed so
long as both are with us.

Within such a framework, it has been argued that belief in
divine intervention is not something that should be cast aside
as of no importance. On the contrary, divine intervention is
a central element in the Christian tradition that is still very
much with us. To continue to believe in it for this reason
would, of course, be odd, even reactionary; too many theologians have felt it to be a burden to the mind for it to be
retained merely for tradition's sake. But retained it should
be, for it is at the foundation of claims about God's purposes
and God's love that are unlikely to retain either their credibility or their inspiration if they are abandoned.

However, even this, important though it is, would not be
sufficient to warrant adherence to divine intervention if it
involved a *sacrificium intellectus*. If it involved a rejection of
the genius of the modern era then there is little doubt as to
where the commitment to truth should lead us. Unfortunately, there is no quick way of deciding what the genius
of the modern era involves. But, as a minimum, being modern involves commitment to the achievements of Western

civilization, particularly its intellectual achievements. There are two fronts where modern intellectual achievements impinge acutely on theology, the philosophical front and the historical front. The tradition must flow between these two disciplines if it is to go forward into the future.

The importance of history is obvious. For one thing, it contains within itself the development of all the sciences, for it draws on all of these as ancillary disciplines for its data and warrants. So, hidden within it are the total reserves of knowledge that the modern world has furnished. On the other hand, it is indispensable to the recovery of the riches of the Christian tradition. Its contribution to the interpretation of scripture, of theology, and of church history is surely magnificent and measureless. The theologian who would turn his back on this is a fool, however much he may feel that his work has been in bondage to a discipline whose experts threaten to swallow up the riches of faith.

It is at this point that the services of the philosopher are essential. His expertise is needed to sort out the tangled relationship that exists in practice between theology and history. If the arguments of this study are correct, the theologian need have no fears that the historian must pronounce his commitment to divine intervention as hostile to the critical canons of the historian's trade. Those who have argued thus have been premature in their claims that this is the case. Moreover, the theologian can also be grateful to the philosopher for reassurance that his commitment to divine intervention is not an arbitrary commitment. Not only are claims about divine intervention part of the foundation of a comprehensive and coherent theistic vision of life, they are also of a kind that permit in broad terms the application of critical scrutiny, for in logic they are analogous to claims we can readily recognize and assess. That much work remains to be done on the logic of explanations that have recourse to personal agents, and that such a logic will require appropriate qualification when applied to God, should inspire neither panic nor diffidence. On the contrary, they should inspire patient, diligent, and imaginative reflection.

In the course of the interaction between the tradition, history, and philosophy much will, of course, change. There is no way in which we can ensure that this or that element will be preserved. Moreover, the three may combine in ways that may alternatively perplex or amaze us. Because of this, there will be many ways of developing a Christian view of the world that will lay claim to do justice to all three at once. Within this, it would be a great loss should either lack of intellectual vigour or lack of sensitive religious faith prevent the renewal and development of those elements in the tradition that have absorbed us in this study.

I hope that this book will encourage historians of the Christian scriptures to develop an understanding of the biblical material which will capture the great riches of that material without surrendering their critical acumen. One of the difficulties that face us is that there is a tendency to narrow the range of options. Somehow we have to swallow the material whole, just as it is on the surface, or we appropriate only that data that can be fitted into a naturalistic metaphysics. There is a telling simplicity and even consistency about both these options, but in my view the reality of God and what He has done for our salvation cannot be fitted into either scheme without distortion. What is needed is a fresh and holy readiness to make critical and sensitive judgements about God's activity in the world that call on both theological and historical skills and stretch these to their limits. At present it is not easy to achieve this in practice. For that we need a body of theologians and historians who share an openness to divine intervention in the world, who share an intuitive grasp of the radical significance of the great classical heritage in theology, and who are fully aware of the rigours of historical study. These must work with patience on the interpretation and appropriation of the tradition, and so participate in a continued conversation about what is most true in the faith of our Fathers. This is one area where those contemporary evangelical theologians who have broken with the fundamentalist orthodoxy of the recent past might make a lasting contribution to the Church in our day. Were they to heed those historians who have been forced of late to reconsider the significance of canonicity, revelation, inspiration, and even miracle in their critical scrutiny of the Bible, then the future would almost certainly be bright. At the very least, it will not be boring.

NOTES

INTRODUCTION

1. For a spirited attack on fundamentalism see James Barr, *Fundamentalism* (London: SCM, 1977).
2. See, e.g., John Hick, 'Revelation', *The Encyclopedia of Philosophy*, ed. Paul Edwards (New York: Columbia University Press, 1967), pp. 189-91.
3. Oxford University Press, 1981.
4. See especially his *Introduction to the Old Testament as Scripture* (London: SCM, 1979).
5. See, e.g., Walter Wink, *The Bible in Human Transformation* (Philadelphia: Fortress, 1973).
6. The work of Richard S. Swinburne is especially significant; see, e.g., *The Existence of God* (Oxford: Clarendon Press, 1979).

CHAPTER 1

1. *The Catholic Encyclopedia* (New York: Robert Appleton Co., 1912), xiii. 1.
2. See John Baillie, *The Idea of Revelation in Recent Thought* (New York: Columbia University Press, 1956).
3. *The Religious Experience of Mankind* (London: Fontana, 1971), p. 26.
4. Waco: Word, 1980.
5. I develop these points in *The Divine Inspiration of Holy Scripture*.
6. Ibid., ch. 4.
7. *The Concept of Mind* (London: Penguin, 1963), pp. 143-44.
8. *Education as Initiation* (London: University of London, 1964), p. 15.
9. For an excellent review see Avery Dulles, *Revelation Theology* (New York: Seabury, 1969).
10. *Theology of Revelation* (London: Search Press, 1973).
11. 'Does Christianity need a Revelation? A Discussion', *Theology*, lxxxiii (1980), 108-9.
12. Eph. 2: 20.
13. For a helpful historical treatment of Paul's call see Johannes Munck, *Paul and the Salvation of Mankind* (Atlanta: John Knox, 1957). See also Jacob M. Myers and Edwin D. Freed, 'Is Paul Also Among the Prophets?', *Interpretation*, xx (1966), 40-53.
14. 'Does Christianity Need a Revelation?', p. 112.
15. Plato discusses this briefly in the *Phædo*.
16. N. W. Porteous, 'The Limits of Old Testament Interpretation', in *Proclamation and Presence*, ed. John I. Durham and J. R. Porter (London: SCM, 1970), p. 12.
17. John Hick, *Philosophy of Religion* (Englewood Cliffs: Prentice-Hall, 1963), p. 72.

18. Alan Richardson, 'Revelation', in *A Dictionary of Christian Theology*, ed. Alan Richardson (London: SCM, 1969), pp. 294-5.
19. G. Ernest Wright, *The Old Testament and Theology* (New York: Harper and Row, 1969), p. 44.
20. Baillie, *The Idea of Revelation*, p. 28.
21. This general point has been missed mainly because the debate has been cast in the past as a debate about whether revelation is propositional or not. When the debate is changed to focus on the role of divine speaking, which is really the point of divergence, then this can emerge more clearly. Commands and promises are not, strictly speaking, propositions, for they cannot be true or false. But commands and promises are surely utterances and would therefore be verbal revelation.
22. See, e.g., William P. Alston, 'Religious Language', *The Encyclopedia of Philosophy*, ed. Paul Edwards (New York: Macmillan, 1967), pp. 169-70. Gilkey suggests such a univocal understanding of speaking as predicated of God was central to the pre-critical or prehistorical era of theology. See Langdon B. Gilkey, 'Cosmology, Ontology and the Travail of Biblical Language', in the *Journal of Religion*, xli (1961), 196. This is surely a very insensitive interpretation of the tradition.
23. Clark H. Pinnock. *A Defense of Biblical Infallibility* (Philadelphia: Presbyterian and Reformed Publishing Co., 1967), p. 4, n. 15. Pinnock has moved from a strict fundamentalist position in recent times, but it is still far from clear that he has discarded the theoretical framework of fundamentalism.
24. Strictly speaking it does not follow from the fact that God says something that the content of what God says is true. Suppose God dictated the story of Jonah to someone. It would not follow that it was a historical truth that Jonah lived or that he was swallowed by a big fish. In order to license that conclusion, additional premises about what God intended in the story would have to be supplied. Fundamentalism, however, is generally taken to involve some sort of literal interpretation of scripture as well as involving an account of the origin of scripture, so the point made here still stands.
25. See, e.g., Clark H. Pinnock, *Defense of Biblical Infallibility*, pp. 29-31.
26. See, for example, Kenneth S. Kantzer, 'The Christ-Revelation as Act and Interpretation', in *Jesus of Nazareth Saviour and Lord*, ed. Carl F. H. Henry (Grand Rapids: Eerdmans, 1966), pp. 243-64.
27. Consider the remarks of Troeltsch about the thoughtless manner in which some theologians of his day rejected the positions of previous generations of Christians, in this case the orthodox appeal to direct divine activity in the world and the Hegelian appeal to historical development. 'The popular disdain in which many theologians today hold these theories is superficial and thoughtless. These theories take their revenge though, in that they continually lend themselves to these theologians in piecemeal and inconsistent forms. Orthodoxy

and Hegelian speculation have often been pronounced dead with profound feelings of superiority, but just as often their funeral orators have themselves made use of the forms that had been declared defunct, though in their use the foundation and inner spirit are lost.' Ernest Troeltsch, *The Absoluteness of Christianity* (London: SCM, 1972), p. 56; cf. John Locke, *The Reasonableness of Christianity*, ed. I. T. Ramsey (London: Black, 1958), pp. 66-7.

CHAPTER 2

1. 'Signs and Wonders', in *The Interpreter's Dictionary of the Bible*, ed. George A. Buttrick *et al.* (New York: Abingdon, 1962), p. 348; cf. S. V. McCasland, for whom miracle is 'an event, whether natural or supernatural, in which one sees an act or revelation of God'. See 'Miracle', in *The Interpreter's Dictionary*, p. 392.
2. B. W. Anderson, 'Signs and Wonders', p. 348.
3. Ibid., p. 348-9.
4. I would be content to define a miracle as an event that is scientifically inexplicable and brought about by a god. I see no reason why a miracle cannot in principle be repeated. This way of rendering the older view of miracle is not obviously open to Chryssides's charge of incoherence on the ground that the attribution of agency presumes the possibility that an event brought about by a rational agent is in principle repeatable. See George D. Chryssides, 'Miracles and Agents', in *Religious Studies*, xi (1975), 319-27. A miracle by this description will have antecedent conditions and is likely to be repeated when these conditions are repeated, but as the conditions concern the will of a god they are not of the kind considered by science. The relation between theological and scientific explanations of events is considered in Chapter 8.
5. See, e.g., Arthur C. Headlam, *The Miracles of the New Testament* (London: John Murray, 1915), p. 350; cf. Joseph Butler, *The Analogy of Religion* (New York: Ungar, 1961), p. 145.
6. The invisible direct acts of God could of course have obvious effects in the external world. But it is the event itself and not just its sheer miraculous character that is invisible.
7. Locke's account is most clearly set forth in *The Reasonableness of Christianity*, ed. I. T. Ramsey (London: Black, 1958). It is also briefly sketched in *An Essay Concerning Human Understanding* (London: Ward, 1968), Bk. IV, ch. 19.
8. J. B. Mozley, *Eight Lectures on Miracles* (London: Rivington, 1865).
9. Both Locke and Mozley believed that there were truths about God that were undiscoverable by human reason. It is not wholly clear what the content of such revelation involved. Locke seems more intent on distinguishing the provinces of faith and reason by contrasting their grounds than by contrasting their content. See especially *Essay*, Bk. IV, ch. 18; cf. *The Reasonableness*, pp. 57-9.
10. *The Reasonableness*, p. 82.
11. Ibid., pp. 83-4.

12. F. R. Tennant suggests that such qualifications are fatal to the argument as a whole in that they point to a vicious circle in the reasoning. See his *Miracle and its Philosophical Presuppositions* (Cambridge: Cambridge University Press, 1925), p. 86. But this is surely not so. All that such qualifications do is make clear that miracles are not any sort of demonstrative or absolute proof of revelation.

13. See, e.g., Locke, *Essay*, Bk. IV, ch. 10; Mozley, *On Miracles*, pp. 70, 80, 120.

14. See Locke, *Essay*, Bk. IV, ch. 18, sections 3, 8; id., *The Reasonableness*, pp. 84-5. Mozley, *On Miracles*, pp. 25, 213.

15. See Locke, *The Reasonableness*, p. 37; id., *Essay*, Bk. IV, ch. 10; Mozley, *On Miracles*, pp. 18-19.

16. Locke suggests that doubt is to be removed by attention to the number, variety, and greatness of the miracles. See *The Reasonableness*, p. 83.

17. 'The Apologetic Defence of Christianity', in *Science and Religious Belief*, ed. C. A. Russell (London: University of London, 1973), pp. 181-2. Cf. Chadwick's comment on Mozley's *On Miracles*: 'The book is the last statement, by a great English Protestant theologian, of a world of divinity which henceforth vanished except in the scholastic manuals.' 'Evolution and the Churches', in *Science and Religious Belief*, p. 289.

18. *Faith and History* (London: Nisbet, 1949), p. 167.

19. The conceptions of faith embraced by Locke and Mozley are almost identical. Both see faith as assent to propositions, but Mozley insists that there is an irreducible element of trust even in the assenting to propositions; this is not present in Locke. For Mozley this trust is needed because of the astonishing or amazing content of the propositions to which one assents. See *On Miracles*, p. 100; cf. Locke, *Essay*, Bk. IV, ch. 18, section 2.

20. It is probable that both Locke and Mozley were motivated by such a consideration.

21. Obviously the idea of faith is not limited to these uses but they are probably the most significant uses.

22. This is one of Kierkegaard's central themes in *Philosophical Fragments* (Princeton: Princeton University Press, 1962). See, e.g., pp. 125-6: 'Now just as the historical gives occasion for the contemporary to become a disciple but only it must be noted through receiving the condition from the God himself, since otherwise we speak Socratically, so the testimony of contemporaries gives occasion for each successor to become a disciple, but only it must be noted through receiving the condition from the God himself.' Neibuhr also stresses this witness of the Spirit, see *Faith and History*, p. 165.

23. It was partly because of this that Locke felt it important to discuss 'enthusiasm'. Appeal to immediate revelation could only be allowed against a background of agreed revelation: 'it is not the strength of our private persuasion within ourselves that can warrant it to be light or motion from heaven, nothing can do that but the written word of

God without us, or that standard of reason which is common to us with all men'. *Essay*, Bk. IV, ch. 19, section 16.

24. Tennant, *Miracle*, p. 32.
25. Ibid., p. 49.
26. H. H. Rowley, *The Relevance of the Bible* (London: James Clarke, 1941), p. 114.
27. *Miracle*, p. 33.
28. Ibid., p. 67.
29. Both Locke and Mozley were aware of the difficulty of specifying for certain what is a law of nature. Locke just leaves the difficulty unsolved. See *The Reasonableness*, p. 86. Mozley adopts a solution similar to that developed here. See *On Miracles*, pp. 146-7.
30. Cf. Freud's judgement: 'There are various fields where we have not yet surmounted a phase of research in which we make trial with hypothesis that soon have to be rejected as inadequate; but in other fields we already possess an assured and almost unalterable core of knowledge.' Sigmund Freud, *The Future of an Illusion* (London: Hogarth, 1973), p. 51.
31. By this phrase Holland does not mean an occurrence the description of which involves a self-contradiction. For Holland, x is conceptually impossible if x is ruled out by our ordinary understanding of the way objects behave.
32. R. F. Holland. 'The Miraculous', in *American Philosophical Quarterly*, ii (1965), 48-9.
33. Ch. 1 above.
34. The relation between revelation and morality in Locke is too complex to be pursued here, but see especially *The Reasonableness*, pp. 60-7.
35. This point has been well illustrated by Donovan: 'Human judgment, opinion and consensus can enter in without its following that what can be learned from scripture will be limited to human ideas about God. Suppose I receive what seems to be a message from an important Government official, giving me information and instructions highly relevant to my future well-being. And suppose the message is brought to me by word of mouth, by a rather puzzling intermediary from a different culture, speaking a foreign language, and by no means as well informed about current affairs as I am. The fact that I think it proper to make some checks on whether the message is what it seems, whether the intermediary is likely to have got it right, and so on, does not mean that I am pitting my reason against the authority of the official. Nor does it follow that I can never have good grounds for taking from the message any information which I could not equally well have thought up for myself.' Peter Donovan, *Religious Language* (London: Sheldon Press, 1976), p. 75.
36. Both Locke and Mozley mention the claim of Islam, albeit briefly and very insensitively. See Locke, *The Reasonableness*, p. 81; Mozley, *On Miracles*, pp. 30-2.
37. Locke was very aware of this. See above, n. 13.
38. See above, n. 15.

39. See Anderson, 'Signs and Wonders', p. 249; cf. Edmond Jacob, *Theology of the Old Testament* (London: Hodder and Stoughton, 1958) p. 244; also Headlam, *The Miracles of the New Testament*, p. 341. There is a tendency, however, to ignore here other clusters of miracle stories, e.g. in the early Church.

40. Mozley astutely recognized that the argument, even in its stronger form, is really an argument from 'design'. See *On Miracles*, pp. 73, 129.

41. In Mozley's presentation of the argument it certainly does look circular. Miracles 'prove' that the revelation comes from God, but the revelation is in turn used to support the claim that a miracle has occurred.

42. For this reason the remarks of Dillenberger (above, p. 30) must be read with caution. As Dillenberger himself acknowledges, the argument from miracle was not confined to the eighteenth century. Indeed it was common in the early Church, and goes right back to the Exodus and the Elijah traditions. Its appeal, therefore, does not rest on its 'scientific' character, as its prevalence in the era of Newton might suggest. As I have noted already (above, n. 40), Mozley clearly saw that the argument was in form similar to the argument from design. That the logic of the argument from design centres on personal agency has been made clear recently by Swinburne, in 'The Argument from Design', *Philosophy*, xlii (1968), 199-212.

43. That arguments in the case of divine agency are more complex and more self-involving and hence much disputed does not negate this point.

44. Lessing may have granted this not because he actually believed in the argument from miracle but because he was convinced that the crucial attack should be mounted elsewhere. For Lessing there was an ugly, broad ditch between historical truths and theological truths which could not as a matter of logic be bridged. As he put it in his famous dictum, 'accidental truths of history can never become the proof of necessary truths of reasons'. See 'On the Proof of the Spirit and of Power', in G. E. Lessing, *Theological Writings*, tr. Henry Chadwick (London: Black, 1956), p. 53. As theological claims about divine action are not necessary truths of reason, Lessing's argument at this point is quite irrelevant to the position adopted here. Moreover no attempt is being made to *prove* any particular assertion about divine action. The importance of Lessing's views for a proper analysis of the relation between history and theology is, in my judgement, greatly exaggerated. See, for example, David A. Pailin, 'Lessing's Ditch Revisited - The Problem of Faith and History' in *Theology and Change*, ed. Ronald H. Preston (London: SCM, 1975), pp. 78-103.

45. Quoted in Lessing, *Theological Writings*, p. 32.

46. 'It cannot be expected that God should send anyone into the world on purpose to inform men of things indifferent, and of small moment, or that are knowable by the use of their natural faculties. This would be to lessen the dignity of his majesty in favor of our sloth and in prejudice to our reason.' *The Reasonableness*, p. 84.

47. D. E. Nineham, 'The Lessons of the Past for the Present', *The Church's Use of the Bible Past and Present*, (London: SPCK, 1963) p. 154.
48. Terence Penelhum, *Problems of Religious Knowledge* (London: Macmillan, 1971), p. 110.
49. Ibid., pp. 110-11.
50. Lessing, of course, made much of this point long ago. 'Miracles, which I see with my own eyes, and which I have the opportunity to verify for myself, are one thing: miracles, of which I know only from history that others say they have seen them and verified them, are another.' *Theological Writings*, p. 51.
51. Arguments similar to Hume's will be considered in chs. 5 and 6.
52. Cf. Coleridge on Lessing 'It is absurd to affirm that the most unquestioned and unquestionable historic evidence ... is in no degree a substitute for the evidence of my own senses—that the conviction produced by such *best possible* confluences of Testimony bears *no* proportion to the conviction produced in me by the recollection (i.e. testimony of my memory) of my own experience'. Quoted in Lessing, *Theological Writings*, p. 32.
53. This matter will be discussed more fully in the next chapter.
54. This would seem to be generally accepted by New Testament scholars. See for example 1 Cor. 15; Rom. 1: 4.

CHAPTER 3

1. See above, ch. 2.
2. Heb. 1: 1-2.
3. For a very suggestive article that argues that the story of the incarnation not only can, but should be, understood as logically independent of the early formulations, see Stephen Sykes, 'The Incarnation as the Foundation of the Church', in *Incarnation and Myth: The Debate Continued*, ed. Michael Goulder (Grand Rapids: Eerdmans, 1979), pp. 115-27.
4. See, e.g., Schubert Ogden's 'What Sense Does It Make to Say, "God Acts in History"?', in his *The Reality of God* (London: SCM, 1967), esp. pp. 174-9. A similar strategy has been adopted by James A. Keller in his 'The Concept of Divine Action' (unpublished doctoral dissertation, Yale University, 1970).
5. Although there is a wealth of material on action in recent analytical philosophy (see, e.g., Alan R. White (ed.), *The Philosophy of Action*, (Oxford: Oxford University Press, 1968); Norman Scare and Charles Landesman (eds.), *Readings in the Theory of Action* (Bloomington: Indiana University Press, 1968)), no agreed theory of action has developed. Indeed much of the work is of a piecemeal character focusing on aspects of actions. I am in sympathy with those philosophers who hold that the term 'action' has so many diverse uses that any single theory will tend to be stipulative in the end. A healthy protest against the temptation to opt for a simple account of action is to be found in J. L. Austin's 'A Plea for Excuses', in *Philosophical Papers* (Oxford: Clarendon Press, 1961), esp. pp. 126-7. That philosophical study related to action points to dimensions that may

help to clarify the notion of an 'act of God', is clearly grasped by Gordon D. Kaufman in his 'On the Meaning of "Act of God"', in his *God the Problem* (Cambridge: Harvard University Press, 1972), p. 126, n. 7.

6. A mythological understanding of the concept is considered in ch. 4.

7. N. Söderblom, 'Incarnation', in *Encylcopaedia of Religion and Ethics*, ed. James Hastings (Edinburgh: T. and T. Clark, 1914), vii 183.

8. For this reason I am reluctant to link the term indissolubly with early Christological formulation. Moreover, it has been used by theologians who are more at home with the Reformers than with the Fathers.

9. Söderblom, 'Incarnation', p. 183.

10. In evaluating the appropriateness of any analogy for divine activity, it is useful to bear in mind three general conditions of success: (1) the analogy must represent a human situation in which it is in order to speak of the human agent performing the action specified; (2) it must represent to a reasonable degree the claims about the divine action specified; (3) it must not be so heavily qualified that it whittles away the action as it is found in the human situation. How far these conditions are satisfied is a matter of sensitive judgement.

11. It is assumed at this point that revelation has been imparted to Paul and others in their attempt to interpret what God was doing in the life, death, and resurrection of Jesus. What the content of this revelation is and even whether revelation has in fact been given is and will remain a matter of controversy.

12. See above, ch. 1.

13. See, e.g., Luke 24: 25-7.

14. This point is generally overlooked by those who insist that agents cannot be identified as they do not have a body. I am indebted to Alston for this suggestion. See William P. Alston, 'Religious Language', *The Encyclopedia of Philosophy*, ed. Paul Edwards (New York: Macmillan, 1967), p. 169.

15. 'Religion and Language', in his *Without Answers* (London: Routledge and Kegan Paul, 1969), p. 131.

16. It is often felt that the virginal conception of Jesus is incompatible with any doctrine of the genuine humanity of Jesus. This seems to me to be wrong. Compare a trivial example. Suppose a friend visits one's house with a cat, at least one takes it to be a cat. It looks like a cat, and does the normal things that cats do: it 'mews' when hungry, purrs when stroked, drinks milk for breakfast, is chased by the dog from next door, etc. Surely, one would still consider this to be a cat even if one were to discover that it had been created *ex nihilo* by God? The concept of a cat, that is, does not entail any necessary causal conditions concerning its origin. The concept of a man is likewise loose and unspecified.

17. This could also be expressed as involving revelation in deed rather than in word.

18. On this see Alan Richardson, *The Miracle Stories of the Gospels* (London: SCM, 1941), p. 53.

19.   This suggestion about securing reference for the incarnate activity of God is offered very tentatively. It depends on the possibility of securing reference for disembodied agents as outlined above. This whole question requires much more attention than can be given here, but I simply want to indicate that I do not consider the logical problems insuperable.

20.   This need not always be so in the human situation. Some take their secrets with them to the grave. Others, for security reasons, may have their secrets kept hidden in government files for years after they are dead.

21.   'The Nature and Authority of Canonical Scriptures', *A Companion to the Bible* (Edinburgh: T. and T. Clark, 1939), p. 5.

22.   Compare the remarks of Austin Farrer: 'In most fields of enquiry it is possible to set up models of argument and canons of proof. The usefulness of such aids varies greatly from one field to another. In the matter of revelation it must surely reach a vanishing point. If there is no *a priori* model for the form of God's self-disclosure, how can there be *a priori* canons for the marks of its authenticity? There is no major premise which lays it down that every child virginally born, or every good man making divine claims, or every crucified man raised from the dead, is a Person of the Godhead. There existed in the minds of Christ's contemporaries certain premises about the supreme human instrument of divine intervention. The Gospels devote a surprising amount of space to the demolition of them.' 'Revelation', in *Faith and Logic*, ed. Basil Mitchell (London: Allen and Unwin, 1957), p. 101.

23.   Col. 1: 16.

24.   From a hymn by George Wade Robinson, *The Methodist Hymn Book* (London: The Methodist Publishing House, 1933), no. 443.

25.   *The Christian Doctrine of History* (Edinburgh: Oliver and Boyd, 1957), p. 36.

26.   The connection between belief in direct divine activity as specified in the incarnation and the 'absoluteness' of Christianity was recognized astutely by Troeltsch. See his *The Absoluteness of Christianity* (London: SCM, 1972), pp. 52-61. Troeltsch objected to this connection on the grounds that the 'form' in which religious truths arise was distinct from their 'normative value'. In other words an account of the causal origin of an idea was irrelevant to its value as a bearer of religious truth. What Troeltsch failed to see was that there may well be such a logical connection. As agents are known by what they do, the causal origins of certain events, i.e. that they were brought about by x, will be crucial in our appeal to these events as a bearer of revelation. Thus if x has written a diary, believing that x has written a diary may radically alter its status in relation to other books if we are interested in knowing something about x. Its origin, therefore, may be crucial in the evaluation of other material. What is lacking in Troeltsch's own account of the relation between the world religions is any adequate attempt to explore the concept of revelation in

general, and divine revelation in Christianity in particular. The whole area of 'comparative religion' requires, of course, extended discussion in its own right.

27. *The Christian Doctrine of History*, p. 37.
28. *The So-Called Historical Jesus and the Historic, Biblical Christ* (Philadelphia: Fortress Press, 1964), p. 80, n. 11.
29. Schweitzer's well-known conclusions in his *The Quest of the Historical Jesus* (New York: Macmilla, 1968) bear this out.
30. *Jesus the Jew* (London: Collins, 1973), p. 15.
31. *Philosopical Fragments* (Princeton: Princeton University Press, 1962) pp. 130-1. Cf. the following remarks of Martin Kähler: 'Do I really need to know more of him than what Paul "delivered to the (Corinthians) as of first importance, what (he) also received, that Christ died for our sins in accordance with the scriptures, and that he appeared" (1 Cor. 15: 3 f.)? This is the good news brought in the name of God (1 Cor. 15: 12 f.; Rom. 1: 1 f.; 11 Cor. 5: 18 f.; Gal. 1: 6 f.). This is the witness and confession of faith which has overcome the world (1 John 5: 4). If I have all this I do not need additional information on the precise details of Jesus' life and death.' *The So-Called Historical Jesus*, p. 60.
32. *Incarnation and Immanence* (London: Hodder and Stoughton, 1973), p. 61.
33. Christians have, of course, drawn inspiration from the stories of saints and martyrs, and also from fictitious stories; but the emphasis given to Jesus by Christians in the past is surely staggering in its proportions if taken as a human story alone. Imagine what it would be like to give similar attention to a first-century monk from Ceylon.
34. The question of historicity must not be exaggerated at this point by the traditional Christian, for he too needs an accurate sketch of the life and death of Jesus. Indeed he needs more, for he also stresses the importance of the resurrection. It is, however, a pressing issue for those who emphasize that conclusions about Jesus' life must be tentative in the extreme.
35. This whole issue was grasped in a typically forthright manner by Troeltsch in 'The Significance of the Historical Existence of Jesus for faith', in *Ernst Troeltsch, Writings on Theology and Religion*, transl. and ed. by Robert Morgan and Michael Pye (London: Duckworth, 1976). For Troeltsch it was a law of social psychology that Jesus was indispensable for the community and cult of Christendom. At best this is an imaginative suggestion for further research; at worst it is armchair sociology.
36. This account of the justification of religious belief is a matter of controversy. It is the one, however, that seems to do most justice to the kind of disputes that take place between theists and atheists. It certainly matches the religious experience of many. It is by no means original, but has been lucidly expounded recently by Basil Mitchell in *The Justification of Religious Belief* (London: Macmillan, 1973). See also Richard Swinburne, *The Existence of God* (Oxford: Clarendon Press, 1978).

37. Maurice Wiles, *The Remaking of Christian Doctrine* (London: SCM, 1974), p. 119.
38. Ibid.
39. This is not to deny that the incarnation may not have significance in many other domains of one's life and beliefs. It is part of the task of the preacher and systematic theologian to explore this to the full.
40. Wiles has a general account of divine action which precludes any instance of divine intervention. If the arguments developed in ch. 1 are correct, it is not at all clear that Wiles has any warrant of substance for his talk about God's purpose. His general position is examined in ch. 4.
41. *Incarnation and Immanence*, p. 67.
42. *The Remaking of Christian Doctrine*, p. 72.
43. To this extent Jesus did share the agony of the kind of random, 'natural' suffering that Wiles rightly brings to our attention.
44. Rom. 5: 7-8. cf. John 15: 13, 'Greater love has no man than this, that a man lay down his life for his friends.' The matter has been well expressed by John Baker. 'It has, however, been argued that even if God did share our life this would change nothing. Each man's pain is different, and God cannot share them all. But we do not need that he should. All we need is that he pass through our Valley of the Shadow, not trace its every path. To have been *one* "man of sorrows and acquainted with grief", to have died once in pain, alone and frustrated, in doubt and darkness, that is enough. After all, he does not ask any of us to do it more than once.' In 'The joy beyond our night of sorrow', *The Times*, 18 December 1976, p. 14.
45. The matter is well expressed by Aquinas: 'Now the nature of God is the essence of goodness ... and hence whatever pertains to the principle of good befits God. It pertains to the principle of the highest good that it should communicate itself to creation in the highest way; and this communication reaches its highest when "he so joins created nature to himself that one person comes into being from three constituents, the Word, the Spirit and the flesh" (Augustine, *De Trinitate*, xiii. 17). Hence it is manifest that it was fitting that God should be made flesh ...' *Summa Theologiae*, iii. i. 1.
46. *The Remaking of Christian Doctrine*, pp. 118-19.
47. Compare Kierkegaard: 'all talk of God's earthly beauty, when he was after all only in the form of a servant, an individual human being like one of us, the cause of offense; all talk of his immediately manifest divinity is not an immediate characteristic ... and the Teacher must first develop in the learner the most profound self-reflection, the sense of sin, as a condition for the understanding... *Philosophical Fragments*, p. 116.
48. If the idea of divine incarnation is incoherent, then of course there is no point in asking what is at stake if it is abandoned. Moreover, to look for criteria to identify such divine activity would be meaningless. Whether it is incoherent is, let it be emphasized again, a matter of dispute that cannot be resolved here.

49. In one sense it would be fair to say that question about criteria for identifying the incarnate activity of God is quite distinct from the issue of the loss of the incarnation for Christian theology. However, it is important to give some sketch as to the conception of incarnation in mind before discussing the loss involved. Also, to a large extent the question of the meaning cannot be divorced from the question about how such a claim might be justified. Recourse to the human analogy reveals how the two are in fact interrelated. The appropriateness of the analogy, as we saw, can be challenged by claiming that the type of evidence availabale to justify the claim that the king visited the people could not be available in the case of the claim that God had become incarnate in Jesus. Whether evidence of the kind specified is historically available is another question quite distinct from the issue of the loss involved in the abandoning of the incarnation. Although I think such evidence is available, it is not crucial in the present context that I be correct in this. In chs. 5 to 7 I am at pains to argue that the historian is not bound to rule that such historical evidence as is needed could not be available. This, to my mind, is the more crucial issue for it radically affects the question of what historical evidence actually is available.

CHAPTER 4

1. I am not wholly convinced that all factual discourse must satisfy this condition. I am treating it here as a sufficient but not a necessary condition of factual discourse.

2. See above, ch. 3. Considerations that would tend to confirm the resurrection of Jesus will be discussed below, esp. chs. 6 and 7.

3. It was the error of logical positivism to insist on this condition. The matter is discussed with reference to claims about divine activity in the Christian life by Basil Mitchell in 'The Grace of God', *Faith and Love* ed. Basil Mitchell (London: Allen & Unwin, 1957) esp. part 1.

4. Cf. Ninian Smart's comment: 'It seems possible to say then that a kind of explanation is being offered when we say that such-and-such an event is due to God's direct action. It links up the present event in an intimate way with the creator, with religious experience elsewhere and outside this particular context, with much else that is, supposedly at least, known about God's actions in history. In short, the explanation attaches the event to a whole nexus of facts.' *Philosophers and Religious Truth* (London: SCM, 1969), pp. 34-40.

5. It is generally agreed in philosophy that this is the case. It is a matter of major controversy, however, as to whether explanations in terms of personal agency are logically distinct from explanations in terms of laws and preceding conditions. My sympathies are firmly on the side of those who think that they are logically distinct. See below, p. 107. Even if they are not distinct, it would still be fair to characterize discourse about divine agency as different from scientific discourse, in that the latter self-consciously limits itself to non-divine or natural agents.

6. An explanatory versus mythological analysis is not the only possible
    option. Recent analytical philosophy of religion is rich in attempts to
    construe religious discourse in general and therefore religious dis-
    course about divine action in particular as non-factual. I have chosen
    to discuss the mythological analysis because of (i) its prevalence
    among theologians, and (ii) its specific application, as developed by
    its proponents, to a particular divine act, the incarnation.
7. Maurice Wiles, '"Myth" in Theology', *Bulletin of the John Rylands
    Library*, lviii (1976), 226.
8. Peter Baelz, 'A Deliberate Mistake?', in *Christ, Faith and History*,
    ed. S. W. Sykes and J. P. Clayton (Cambridge: Cambridge University
    Press, 1972), p. 25; cf. Wiles: 'If the theologian is to make use of it
    [myth] in his work he needs to recognise the loose and elusive character
    of the terminology he is adopting: it is not something to be taken in
    hand lightly, unadvisedly or wantonly.' '"Myth" in Theology',
    p. 226. Cf. Schubert Ogden in 'Myth and Truth', in his *The Reality
    of God* (London: SCM, 1967), p. 101.
9. This is cogently illustrated in R. W. Hepburn's much neglected essay,
    'Demythologizing and the Problem of Validity', in *New Essays in
    Philosophical Theology*, ed. Antony Flew and Alasdair MacIntyre
    (London: SCM, 1955), pp. 227-42.
10. Hick and Wiles initially made their proposals in independence of one
    another.
11. *God and the Universe of Faiths* (London: Macmillan, 1973),
    pp. 166-7. The use of the adverb 'literally' here is not altogether
    satisfactory, especially when it is applied to discourse about divine
    action. But the general sense at issue is clear enough for us to allow
    it as it stands. It is not altogether easy to find a set of concepts that
    express the contrast at issue; participants in the discussion tend to
    develop their own terminology as they proceed.
12. Ibid., p. 168.
13. Hick, *God and the Universe of Faiths*, p. 113.
14. Ibid., p. 116.
15. Hick, *God and the Universe of Faiths*, p. 172.
16. Ibid., p. 176.
17. The major exception to this is Buddhism, but it is an open question
    whether incarnation in Buddhism is exactly the same as incarnation
    in Christianity.
18. Maurice Wiles, *The Remaking of Christian Doctrine* (London:
    SCM, 1974), p. 57.
19. Ibid., p. 53.
20. Cambridge: Cambridge University Press, 1967.
21. See above, ch. 2. Wiles, as will be indicated, would not accept that
    the relevant evidence sketched there is very cogent. See below, p. 89.
    Nor, of course, would Hick, as his remarks about what can be known
    about Jesus make clear. He would probably also reject any attempt
    to develop a cumulative argument for any theological assertion. See
    his *Faith and Knowledge* (Glasgow: Collins, 1974), ch. 7.

22. It is not implied here that pre-modern thinkers unacquainted with recent developments in philosophy about meaning would have expressed their intentions in this manner. What matters here is not their theory about discourse but their practice and usage.

23. Hick is equivocal on the intention of the early Church. Most of his exposition suggests that they intended their discourse as factual. But the following statement is difficult to harmonize with this: 'in retrospect we can see that the fundamental heresy which the church has rejected in all the many forms which human ingenuity has devised is that of treating the myth as an hypothesis.' God and the Universe of Faiths, p. 171. Hick may be saying that it is difficult at this point to know what the early Church intended.

24. Wiles points out that the Fathers chose the term *homoousios* because they knew it would be opposed. See *The Making of Christian Doctrine*, p. 36.

25. *God and the Universe of Faiths*, p. 178.

26. I recognize that this claim challenges the attempt to make philosophy of religion a second-order study that is distinct from religion and theology. On the other hand my argument is itself in keeping with the usage of religious discourse as actually found among religious believers.

27. See above, ch. 1. See also my *The Divine Inspiration of Holy Scripture*, ch. 4.

28. The assertions that Hick considers the fall to express are not the only ones that have been suggested. Cf. Wiles, '"Myth" in Theology', p. 240, where he points out that for him the fall expresses the truth that men fall below the highest that they see and that they could achieve.

29. The importance of Strauss's *Life of Jesus*, published as long ago as 1835, is noted by Wiles as follows: 'Undoubtedly the ensuing discussion of Strauss' thesis did much to establish the word more firmly in the English language but also the concept at the heart of theological study and debate.' '"Myth" in Theology', p. 227.

30. Maurice Wiles, 'Religious Authority and Divine Action', *Religious Studies*, viii (March 1971), 5.

31. Ibid., p. 6.

32. Maurice Wiles, 'Does Christology rest on a mistake?', in *Christ, Faith and History*, p. 9.

33. Wiles, *The Remaking of Christian Doctrine*, p. 37.

34. Wiles, 'Religious Authority and Divine Action', p. 5.

35. Ibid.

36. Ibid., p. 6.

37. The appearance of *The Remaking of Christian Doctrine* does not alleviate the vagueness of his earlier publications. Wiles speaks there of a 'sense of purposiveness' (p. 35) which is somehow incorporated in the traditional teleological argument. This is still very unclear. Contrast the lucidity of R. G. Swinburne's attempt to restate the teleological argument in 'The Argument from Design', *Philosophy*, xliii (1968), 199-212.

38. 'Religious Authority and Divine Action', p. 5.
39. See above pp. 72-3.
40. In *The Remaking of Christian Doctrine* Wiles seems to want to relate this experience of contingency to 'a basic insight embodied in the traditional cosmological argument for the existence of God' (p. 34). The relation, however, is obscure, so that it is difficult to assess the support that may come from the cosmological argument at this point.
41. Wiles seems to be working, at this point, on the assumption that it is legitimate to apply the concept of myth to all instances of divine action. Thus for him 'the concept of myth impinges most vitally on theology not in relation to particular miracle stories but rather in relation to the whole structure of belief in divine action and divine incarnation'. See '"Myth" in Theology', p. 230. If this is the case there is a radical inconsistency in his proposal, for *his* assertions about divine creation and redemption ought to have been translated or expressed in other terms before they were grounded in experience. His own discourse, that is, would still be mythological, for it involves discourse about divine action. I do not, however, believe that Wiles is open to this charge. What he is opposed to is divine action involving direct intervention in the world, and it is examples of these to which he wants to apply the concept of myth.
42. See above, p. 55.
43. 'Religious Authority and Divine Action', p. 8. The emphasis is as in the original.
44. 'Does Christology rest on a mistake?', p. 10.
45. '"Myth" in Theology', p. 244.
46. 'Does Christology rest on a mistake?', p. 11.
47. H. H. Price, 'Religious Experience and its Problems', in *Faith and the Philosophers*, ed. John Hick (London: Macmillan, 1966), p. 36.
48. Wiles can describe his theology as 'deistic insofar as it refrains from claiming any effective causation on the part of God in relation to particular occurrences', *The Remaking of Christian Doctrine*, p. 38. For this reason I cannot regard Wiles's theology as radically new.
49. Wiles prefers to call the traditional account of the incarnation 'ontological' or 'metaphysical' rather than factual or explanatory.
50. Wiles has made it clear that he is not accusing the incarnationalist of nonsense or incoherence at this point. Restating the main thrust of his argument, he writes: 'The traditional Christological statements are logically very odd. They relate God and man in a way which certainly appears at first sight to offend against the grammar of our normal speech about both God and man. But that does not mean that they can be declared nonsensical *a priori*. The logic of relating language about God and language about man is far too unclear and mysterious a thing for so high-handed a judgment to be justified.' 'A Reply to Mr. Baelz', in *Christ, Faith and History*, p. 35. The appearance of *The Remaking of Christian Doctrine* has not altered this judgement. Thus he writes: 'I am calling into question the church's traditional belief in Christ as both God and man only in the

sense that I am insisting that it cannot properly be taken as the starting point of our enquiry; we have no right to treat it as an unquestionable axiom. I am not calling it into question in the sense of denying that it could conceivably be the conclusion of our enquiry; I do not intend to say that it is an impossible or absurd belief.' *The Remaking of Christian Doctrine*, p. 43. This is a very different way of stating the issue. Category mistakes, such as 'Friday is in bed', surely are nonsense.

51. Whether divine intervention is hostile to the demands of science is discussed in ch. 8.

52. His article on myth in theology is an excellent example of his concern to make clear his position by relating it to a wider historical and theological context.

53. I take it for granted here that Wiles does not want to say that the early Church believed in intervention *solely* because of the inter-relationship between creation, fall, and redemption, for he has himself drawn attention to the multiple sources of early Christian doctrine. I also take it for granted that Wiles is relying on the second phase of his historical argument to rebut any charge that he is begging the question. The latter could arise in that we normally look for psychological reasons as to why people believed a proposition, p, only after it has been shown already that p is false. If divine intervention did take place in the incarnation, then the early Church would have been correct to believe this whatever the psychological inspiration they may have had from other elements in their theism.

54. The other two disanalogies referred to above (pp. 77-8) apply with the same force as they did in the case of the fall.

55. *The Remaking of Christian Doctrine*, p. 48.

56. Ibid., p. 49.

57. See above, p. 58.

58. He writes: 'It certainly seems to be true in my experience that many of those Christian philosophers who are most acutely aware of the intellectual difficulties inherent in the basic affirmations of theism are almost naively credulous in their handling of the historical tradi-tions about Jesus, while many of those who are most scrupulously critical in their assessment of those historical traditions seem un-warrantably easy-going in the confidence with which they continue to affirm their basic theistic convictions.' *The Remaking of Christian Doctrine*, p. 111.

59. '"Myth' in Theology', p. 244.

60. Wiles writes of his first article in this field, 'Does Christology rest on a mistake?', that 'It was intended to be the starting point for further discussion ...' See 'A reply to Mr. Baelz', p. 35.

61. For various reasons, however, one may not be altogether happy with characterizing such discourse as mythological. Wiles himself feels that the term 'myth' may be unusable in the general life of the Church. See '"Myth" in Theology', p. 246.

62. See above, n. 41.

63. Unfortunately many who discuss this issue rarely take the time to claify what claims about divine action involve. The general strategy is to focus on the nature of historical criticism, and then to turn rather abruptly to its implications for theology. By reversing the order I hope to achieve a greater balance in the discussion.

CHAPTER 5

1. Perhaps the most lucid is Van A. Harvey, whose work is examined in ch. 6. It is well known that this was the position adopted by Rudolf Bultmann (see his *Existence and Faith* (New York: Meridian Books, 1960), pp. 289-96). It is also of interest that Wolfhart Pannenberg holds that divine intervention is incompatible with critical historical study (see his *Basic Questions in Theology* (London: SCM, 1970) i. 76).

2. Thus James Luther Adams writes of Troeltsch's claims: 'Of special significance is the fact that the findings and presuppositions of the historical method have given a body-blow to traditional Christianity.' See his introduction to *The Absoluteness of Christianity* by Ernst Troeltsch (London: SCM, 1972), p. 8.

3. Cf. A. O. Dyson's comment: 'It is not difficult to get the impression that where philosophy of history has been used by the theologians, it has been used selectively in ways which confirm positions about history already reached on theological grounds.' 'History in the Philosophy and Theology of Ernst Troeltsch' (University of Oxford D. Phil. thesis, 1968), p. 15.

4. In Ernst Troeltsch, *Gesammelte Schriften* (Tübingen: J. C. B. Mohr, 1913), ii. 729-53.

5. *The Absoluteness of Christianity*, p. 36.

6. Troeltsch set out his views in a different format from that adopted in *Gesammelte Schriften* ii. 729-53, in his article 'Historiography', in *Encyclopaedia of Religion and Ethics*, ed. James Hastings (Edinburgh: T. and T. Clark, 1914) vi. 716-23.

7. 'Historiography', p. 716.

8. Ibid., p. 717.

9. Ibid.

10. Ibid., p. 718.

11. Ibid.

12. Ibid.

13. Ibid.

14. Ibid.

15. Ibid.

16. Alan Bullock, *Hitler, A Study in Tyranny* (London: Penguin, 1962), p. 14.

17. Ibid., p. 804.

18. That this is the case has been argued cogently in recent analytical philosophy of history by Danto. See Arthur C. Danto, *Analytical Philosophy of History* (Cambridge: Cambridge University Press, 1968), pp. 136-7.

19. 'Historiography', pp. 718-19.
20. H. R. Mackintosh, *Types of Modern Theology* (London: James Nisbet, 1964), p. 190.
21. Calvin G. Rand, 'Two Meanings of Historicism in the Writings of Dilthey, Troeltsch and Meinecke', *Journal of the History of Ideas*, xxv (1964), 507.
22. *Gesammelte Schriften*, ii. 732.
23. R. G. Collingwood, *The Idea of History* (Oxford: Oxford University Press, 1961), p. 240. It is interesting that in the context Collingwood is attacking F. H. Bradley, whose 'The Presuppositions of Critical History', in his *Collected Essays* (Oxford: Oxford University Press, 1935), i. 1-53, had grown out of his interest in the credibility of the biblical narratives, and in particular their miraculous element.
24. See above, p. 99.
25. See below, p. 105.
26. Cf. the remark of Wittgenstein: 'Suppose some adult had told a child that he had been on the moon. The child tells me the story, and I say it was only a joke, the man hadn't been on the moon; no one has ever been on the moon; the moon is a long way off and it is impossible to climb up there or fly there. If now the child insists, saying perhaps there is a way of getting there which I don't know, etc. what reply could I make to him? What reply could I make to the adults of a tribe who believe that people sometimes go to the moon (perhaps that is how they interpret their dreams) and who indeed grant that there are no ordinary means of climbing up to it or flying there? But a child will not ordinarily stick to such a belief and *will be convinced by what we tell him seriously.*' See Ludwig Wittgenstein, *On Certainty* (New York: Harper and Row, 1972) p. 16e, para. 106. (emphasis mine). The imaginary tribe postulated here is a very different one from the one postulated by Wittgenstein. The role of trusted testimony about the real moon landings is well illustrated in the following story reported to me by Professor Wiles from America. 'Our hosts on arrival told me a story ... An elderly black woman who worked for them in Philadelphia commented on what an impressive show the TV had put on with the moon landings and expressed wonder that they had succeeded in making it look as if it were real. For a long time she wouldn't believe they were real but eventually said "Well, Mrs. Winslow, over many years you have never lied to me before, so I suppose it must be so!"' Personal communication from Professor Maurice Wiles, dated 9 Feb. 1977.
27. *Gesammelte Schriften*, ii. 733. The interrelation between analogy and correlation is well illustrated by Nineham: 'Consider a historian attempting to decide whether in a particular campaign a general marched an army of a certain size across a certain tract of desert, as he is alleged to have done. The historian concludes that he did not do so in view of the number and size of the oases in the desert concerned, which could not possibly have produced sufficient water for even a tenth of the number of troops supposed to have been involved. The

conclusion seems sound enough but of course it presupposes that the oases in question were producing at the particular time roughly the same amount of water they are known to produce at all other times.' Dennis Nineham, *The Use and Abuse of the Bible* (London: Macmillan, 1976), p. 34. This positive way of relating analogy and correlation seems to me to be missed by Wolfhart Pannenberg and those who accept his criticisms of Troeltsch. See Wolfhart Pannenberg, *Basic Questions in Theology* (London: SCM, 1970), i. 43-50; also Colin Brown, 'History and the Believer', in *History, Faith and Criticism*, ed. Colin Brown (London: Inter-Varsity Press, 1976), pp. 171-4.

28.   Van A. Harvey, *The Historian and the Believer* (Toronto: Macmillan, 1969), p. 15.

29.   Thus he writes: 'I contest the universal applicability of the causal view, in the sense of a closed system of necessary causes and effects, as far as historical phenomena and the entire compass of human events are concerned.' *The Absoluteness of Christianity*, p. 31.

30.   As I understand it, this is the pattern of explanation utilized in paradigm empirical sciences such as physics and chemistry as elucidated in recent years by Hempel, Braithwaite, Popper, and others. Although there are uncertain points about scientific explanation, this is the pattern of explanation that most philosophers of science would accept as accurate.

31.   Troeltsch, 'Historiography', p. 719.

32.   This is a matter of some controversy in philosophy. However a large body of opinion adopts the position espoused here. Thus R. S. Peters reminds us: 'Nobody has yet demonstrated that explanations given in terms of these logically different types of concept are reducible to each other or that one is deducible from the other.' R. S. Peters, *Ethics and Education* (London: Allen and Unwin, 1970), p. 283.

32.   'Historiography', p. 719.

34.   This network of explanation would not be enough to explain all events in history. It would not, for example, explain the occurrence of inflation. But it is comprehensive enough to cover the kind of events at issue in this study.

35.   This distinction can be expressed very briefly. Care should be taken not to allow this to detract from its cruciality in the argument developed later.

36.   Quoted from *Zeitschrift für Theologie und Kirche*, viii (1898), 5, in A. O. Dyson, 'History in the Philosophy and Theology of Ernst Troeltsch', p. 209. John Macquarrie suggests that Troeltsch was not an extremist and that 'he explicitly rejected a purely naturalistic approach to history', *The Scope of Demythologising* (London: SCM, 1960), p. 66. But this is not necessarily incompatible with what is said here, for Troeltsch did claim to see God at work in the events of history within the framework of an Idealist metaphysics.

37.   That the explanation is not scientific does not alter this fact. As I have attempted to show, theological discourse about direct divine action is factual and explanatory.

38. For the overall character of Troeltsch's theology and his relation to nineteenth-century theology I am much indebted to A. O. Dyson's 'History in the Philosophy and Theology of Ernst Troeltsch'. That Schleiermacher was opposed to divine intervention is made clear by Gordon D. Kaufman in 'On the Meaning of "Act of God"', in *God the Problem* (Cambridge, Mass.: Harvard University Press, 1972), p. 131.

39. Basil Mitchell, *The Justification of Religious Belief* (London: Macmillan, 1973), p. 151-2. That the door should be left open for extra-scientific explanations is also suggested by Macquarrie in *The Scope of Demythologising*, p. 71. That Troeltsch made the move from a conceptual point about the logic of history to a disputable metaphysical thesis is made clear by the quotation given above, p. 108.

40. Kaufman, *God the Problem*, pp. 134-5.

41. 'Historiography', p. 721.

42. Ibid.

43. He can, of course, report that others claim to see God act.

CHAPTER 6

1. Van A. Harvey, *The Historian and the Believer* (Toronto: Macmillan, 1969), pp. 1-9.

2. Ibid., p. 33.

3. Ibid., p. 34.

4. Ibid., p. 84.

5. Ibid., p. 49.

6. Ibid., p. 55.

7. Ibid., p. 62.

8. Ibid., p. 115.

9. Ibid., p. 34.

10. See above, ch. 5, n. 6.

11. He devotes an entire chapter (ch. 4) of *The Historian and the Believer* to this topic.

12. In some contexts this description would not be acceptable; some would reject it outright. It is meant here as a minimal description and does not rule out at all an element of mystery. I would accept Brown's statement: 'Our earliest ancestors in the faith proclaimed a bodily resurrection in the sense that they did not think that Jesus' body had corrupted in the tomb. However, this is equally important, Jesus' risen body was no longer a body as we know bodies, bound by dimensions of space and time.' Raymond E. Brown, *The Virginal Conception and Bodily Resurrection of Jesus* (London: Chapman, 1973), pp. 127-8. This should be kept in mind throughout the discussion.

13. *The Historian and the Believer*, p. 88.

14. Quoted by Harvey, ibid., p. 10. The point is also made by Harvey in his own terms, ibid., p. 88.

15. Ibid., p. 123-4.

16. Ibid., p. 112.

17. Ibid., p. 113.
18. Ibid., p. 118.
19. Ibid., p. 122.
20. Ibid., p. 111.
21. Ibid., p. 103.
22. Ibid., p. 123.
23. Ibid., p. 68.
24. Ibid., p. 114.
25. Ibid., p. 237.
26. Ibid., p. 115.
27. See, e.g., Ronald J. Sider, 'The Historian, the Miraculous and Post-Newtonian Man', *Scottish Journal of Theology*, xxv (1972), 311. It should be noted, however, that Sider does not confine his criticisms to the kind described here.
28. *The Historian and the Believer*, p. 115.
29. This is ignored by Harvey in his discussion of the autonomy of the historian. See *The Historian and the Believer*, pp. 39-42.
30. Ibid., p. 81.
31. Ibid., p. 80, my emphasis.
32. See above, pp. 33-5.
33. This is not an uncommon way of dismissing the views of Troeltsch and Harvey.
34. *The Historian and the Believer*, p. 229.
35. See above, pp. 60-1.
36. See above, p. 52.
37. *The Historian and the Believer*, pp. 107-10.
38. Ibid., p. 228.
39. See above, pp. 32-3.
40. Antony Flew, *Hume's Philosophy of Belief* (London: Routledge & Kegan Paul, 1961), p. 202.
41. See quotation above, p. 122.
42. Quoted by Harvey, *The Historian and the Believer*, p. 114.
43. That Harvey lumps such matters together indiscriminately may be due to the cultural relativist strand in his argument.
44. This needs to be qualified, for every age displays a certain craving for the extraordinary. For a contemporary illustration of this see Graham Massey, 'The Case of the Bermuda Triangle', *Listener*, 19 Feb. 1976, pp. 199-200.
45. 'The Historian, the Miraculous and Post-Newtonian Man', p. 316.
46. 'Never since the world began has it been heard that any one opened the eyes of a man born blind.' John 9: 32.
47. *The Historian and the Believer*, p. 119.
48. Ibid., p. 103.
49. Vico, the great Italian philosopher, did not think so, for example.
50. Cf. Butterfield's comment: 'Lord Acton once suggested that the truth of religion was so momentous an issue, and the controversies about it were so intense, that the critical methods were developing in ecclesiastical research before anybody thought of transposing them

into the field of modern history.' Herbert Butterfield, *Man on his Past* (Cambridge: Cambridge University Press, 1969), pp. 15-16.

51. It would be insensitive in the extreme to impugn the historical judge-ment of scholars like B. F. Wescott, F. J. A. Hort, J. B. Lightfoot, Sir Edwyn C. Hoskyns, A. C. Headlam, C. A. Briggs, T. W. Manson, H. H. Rowley, C. E. B. Cranfield, B. M. Metzger, F. F. Bruce, and C. F. D. Moule, all of whom accepted a relatively traditional version of Christianity.

52. *The Historian and the Believer*, pp. 229-30.

53. Ibid., p. 37, n. 35.

54. Thus A. R. Vidler writes: 'while it may seem to undergraduates who are reading for the theological tripos that the documentary records of Christian origins are pretty substantial and extensive, yet in com-parison with the import of their subject matter they are all too frag-mentary. I remember an eminent New Testament scholar saying to me that the period before A.D.170 is rather like the prehistory of Christianity, and that we have sufficient documentation for a history proper only after that date. I think there is something in that analogy. It does not of course mean that we can reach no conclusions about the earlier period, but the comparative fragmentariness of the surviv-ing records accounts in part for the variety of ways in which they can be interpreted.' 'Historical Objections', in *Objections to Christian Belief*, ed. D. M. Mackinnon (London: Constable, 1963), p. 68.

55. Thus F. Gerald Downing writes: 'When the man in the study group or the girl doing scripture O-levels or the woman with grown children taking R.E. subsidiary in her mature student's teacher training find this plethora of conclusions backed by careful but largely invisible scholarly work, scepticism flourishes. All the complicated theories you are expected to follow and memorise and reproduce still lead to the ancient texts saying what anyone wants them to say.' *The Past is all we have* (London: SCM, 1975), p. 31.

56. *The Historian and the Believer*, p. 18.

57. Such a charge may simply evoke the counter-charge that there is much unbelief corrupting his own historical judgement or that of those authorities he relies on. This just grinds the argument to a halt.

58. To argue that it can is by no means a minority position in current New Testament scholarship. Also, other considerations such as the change in the disciples, the rise of the Church, the failure of the opposition to produce Jesus's body, would be relevant. As I want only to sketch the character of the argument, there is no need to go into such material in detail.

59. Cf. Swinburne's definition of a miracle as 'an event of an extra-ordinary kind, brought about by a god, and of religious significance.' See Richard Swinburne, *The Concept of Miracle* (London: Mac-millan, 1970), p. 1.

60. This is the term suggested by Harvey, *The Historian and the Believer*, p. 116. I recognize that I have myself used the term 'intervention' in this study.

61. See above, ch. 3.
62. Compare this with the rebuttal suggested by Pannenberg. He appealed to the future general resurrection of all men in order to make the resurrection of Jesus plausible. This in turn was grounded in the anthropological and philosophical claim that men cannot understand themselves as men without the conception of a resurrection from the dead. See Wolfhart Pannenberg, 'Did Jesus really rise from the Dead?', in *New Testament Issues*, ed. Richard Batey (London: SCM, 1970), pp. 107-8. There are at least two problems with this view: (1) it is surely false to say that the future general resurrection of all men is the obvious philosophical truth about the human condition that Pannenberg thinks it is; (2) that all men will rise in the future from the dead does not provide a warrant for the claim that a particular person has risen from the dead on the third day after his death.
63. A. E. Taylor, *Philosophical Studies* (London: Macmillan, 1934), p. 361.
64. See Harvey, *The Historian and the Believer*, p. 116.
65. Acts 2: 24.
66. D. M. McKay, *The Clockwork Image* (London: Inter-Varsity Press, 1974), p. 64.
67. This was the burden of the argument in ch. 1 above.
68. Merold Westphal, review of *The Historian and the Believer* in *Religious Studies*, xi (1967), 280.
69. Strictly speaking, the empty tomb will only be seen as a necessary condition if the body of the risen Jesus is understood to have been the same as that which had been laid in the tomb.
70. See Hugh Trevor-Roper's review of C. H. Dodd's *The Founder of Christianity* in the *Spectator*, 23 Jan. 1971, pp. 123-4.
71. Harvey, in the preface, points out that the basic intention behind *The Historian and the Believer* was theological, and he does explicitly take up the question of revelation in the final chapter. But neither of these points make up for the gross insensitivity he displays to the theological context of belief in the resurrection of Jesus.
72. H. H. Rowley, *The Faith of Israel* (London: SCM, 1956), p. 58.,
73. See below, ch. 7.

CHAPTER 7

1. T. A. Roberts, *History and Christian Apologetic* (London: SPCK, 1960), p. 153.
2. Ibid., p. 150.
3. Ibid.
4. Ibid.
5. T. A. Roberts, 'Gospel Historicity, Some Philosophical Observations', *Religious Studies*, i (1965-6), 189.
6. *History and Christian Apologetic*, p. 149.
7. Ibid., p. 170.
8. Ibid.
9. Ibid., p. 173.

10. Ibid., p. 160.
11. Ibid.
12. Ibid.
13. 'Gospel Historicity, Some Philosophical Observations', p. 200. Emphasis as in the original.
14. Ibid., p. 201.
15. Ibid.
16. Ibid., p. 200.
17. Ibid., p. 201.
18. Ibid.
19. See above, p. 67. It should also be said that it is only with great reserve, if at all, that a phrase like 'religious genius' should be applied to such figures as Jeremiah, Jesus, or Paul if we identify these as paradigm figures of the religious life. Such a predicate overlooks their possible direct dependence on divine activity for their positive religious value. Thus Basil Mitchell writes: 'It would not be so much false, as inappropriate and incongruous to call St. Paul or St. Augustine or St. Vincent de Paul great men. We can talk about the giants of literature, but scarcely about the giants of religion. St. Paul may have started life as a "religious genius"; but he became a "saint".' See 'The Grace of God', in *Faith and Logic*, ed. Basil Mitchell (London: Allen and Unwin, 1957), p. 172.
20. See above, p. 55.
21. See below, p. 161.
22. I am indebted to Phyllis McGinley for this example. See her *Saint-Watching* (London: Collins, 1970), p. 69.
23. e.g. D. E. Nineham in 'The Lessons of the Past for the Present', *The Church's Use of the Bible*, ed. D. E. Nineham (London: SPCK, 1963), p. 155.
24. 'Gospel Historicity, Some Philosophical Observations', p. 200.
25. Ibid., p. 189.
26. One could expand the notion of historiography to cover this principle, but I am working here with Roberts's concept. It does seem odd to class it as a technique.
27. As Collingwood pointed out, people are liable to 'blow up right in your face', when challenged, and are 'apt to be ticklish' about this kind of commitment. See R. G. Collingwood, *An Essay on Metaphysics* (Oxford: Clarendon Press, 1940), p. 31.
28. See above, p. 120. We do not, of course, have a recipe in the sense that we can specify without difficulty the meaning of the resurrection of Jesus.
29. This is sometimes taken as the only legitimate approach to all stories of miracle. See, for example, F. Gerald Downing's *The Past is all we Have* (London: SCM, 1975), pp. 23-4.
30. Cf. Austin Farrer's comment: 'What Christians find in Christ through faith inclines them at certain points to accept with regard to him testimony about matters of fact which would be inconclusive if offered with regard to any other man. The Christian who refused

to take that step would in my opinion be pedantic and irrational, like a man who required the same guarantee for trusting a friend which he would require for trusting a stranger. Thus it is possible through faith and evidence together, and through neither alone, to believe that Christ really and corporeally rose from the dead, not merely that his death on the cross had a silver lining significant for our salvation.' See his 'An English Appreciation', in *Kerygma and Myth*, ed. Hans Werner Bartsch (New York: Harper and Row, 1961), p. 220. This point is also made by D. E. Nineham, 'The Lessons of the Past for the Present', p. 156, n. 1.

31.   Care must be taken here not to belittle the fact that claims to resurrection outside this have been believed by Christians, e.g. by Irenaus. They seem, in fact, to have been accepted by many Fathers in the late second century. It would undercut Roberts's argument if they were accepted as genuine. As I want to take his case at its strongest, I ignore this possibility here.

32.   This point must not be exaggerated, for the philosopher may have to rule that such arguments do not make sense and therefore cannot proceed. My point is that a determined attempt should be made to try and map what the argument is. Roberts seems to have given up too quickly because he ignores or rules out the role of theology in such arguments.

33.   See his review of *The Historian and the Believer* in *Religious Studies*, vii (1971), 255-7.

34.   I presume that Roberts has in mind the empiricism of thinkers like Stephen Toulmin and Patrick Gardiner.

35.   'It would take too long to substantiate this point in detail here, but what I want to suggest is that in his book we have an unresolved conflict between the empiricist and idealist views of history. Further, I would maintain that the author himself is not aware of the conflict and it is very important for the future of New Testament scholarship that this conflict be resolved in favour, generally speaking, of the idealist position.' *Religious Studies*, vii (1971), 256-7.

36.   'When New Testament Scholars such as Knox and Dodd, or apologists like Alan Richardson, have seized on the 'no-fact-without-interpretation' slogan, which is taken to summarise crudely the idealist view of history, and turned it to their own theological purpose, they have failed to grasp the subtle metaphysical interpretation of reality which is at the "root of idealism".' Ibid., p. 255.

37.   The issue is, of course, nothing new. It was set out long ago in Hume's discussion of miracles.

38.   See *History and Christian Apologetic*, p. 173.

39.   See above, p. 144.

40.   See *History and Christian Apologetic*, p. 173.

41.   See above, ch. 6, n. 50.

42.   See *Religious Studies*, vii (1971), 253.

43.   See above, p. 142.

44.   'The Lessons of the Past for the Present', p. 156, n. 1.

45. An excellent example is J. H. Plumb, who has made it clear that he believes that the idea of progress should be central to history. For him, 'it ought to be the prime duty of the historian to investigate this process, to describe it, to attempt an explanation of how it came about, and for this theme to be their social purpose'. 'The Historian's Dilemma', in *Crisis in the Humanities*, ed. J. H. Plumb (London: Penguin, 1964), pp. 42-3. Let him who will cast doubt on his stature as a historian. It is interesting to record that Plumb is quite happy to apply the term 'historian' to both Spengler and Toynbee despite the searching criticism he applies to them. Because of the presence of metaphysical claims in historical narrative I find Troeltsch's distinction between two types of interest very helpful. See above, pp. 95-8.

46. Sir Isaiah Berlin, 'The Concept of Scientific History', in *Philosophical Analysis and History*, ed. William H. Dray (New York: Harper and Row, 1966), p. 24. See also ibid., p. 38.

47. See above, p. 95.

48. See Berlin, 'The Concept of Scientific History', p. 5.

49. See R. G. Collingwood, *The Idea of History* (Oxford: Oxford University Press, 1961), p. 9.

CHAPTER 8

1. This is made very clear by Patrick Gardiner in *The Nature of Historical Explanation* (Oxford: Oxford University Press, 1961), pp. 10-12. This insight is skilfully applied to the problem of freedom and grace by J. R. Lucas in *Freedom and Grace* (London: SPCK, 1976), pp. 1-15.

2. It should be noted that I am not taking sides in the debate about what happened.

3. R. G. Swinburne, 'The Argument from Design', *Philosophy*, xlii (1968), 203-4.

4. Ibid., p. 202.

5. For this distinction I am indebted to Guy Robinson, 'Miracles', *Ratio*, ix (1967), 158-60.

6. In what follows I am much indebted to R. G. Swinburne, *The Concept of Miracle* (London: Macmillan, 1970), ch. 3.

7. It cannot be stressed too much that the accepting of a theological explanation need not be arbitrary or a matter of whim. This is too readily assumed by many. Consider, for example, Guy Robinson's comment: 'Scientific development would either be stopped or else made completely capricious, because it would necessarily be a matter of whim whether one invoked the concept of miracle ... to explain an awkward result or, on the other hand, accepted the result as evidence of the need to modify the theory one was investigating.' 'Miracles', p. 159.

8. H. H. Rowley, *the Relevance of the Bible* (London: James Clarke, 1941), p. 115.

9. Ibid., p. 116.

10. Cf. the comment of Danto: 'A believer might ... take some comfort from the fact that "God made the world" and "The world was not caused" are quite compatible if the former describes a basic action.' See Arthur Danto, 'What We can Do', in *Readings in the Theory of Action*, ed. Norman S. Care and Charles Landesman (Bloomington: Indiana University Press, 1968), p. 125.

11. See above, p. 171.

12. See Malcolm L. Diamond, 'Miracles', *Relgious Studies*, ix (1973), 307-24. His position has also been presented in ch. 4 of his *Contemporary Philosophy and Religious Thought* (New York: McGraw-Hill, 1974).

13. 'Miracles', p. 311.

14. Diamond uses the term 'supernaturalist' to describe this kind of interpretation. As I have avoided this term throughout, I have ommitted it where possible in the exposition here.

15. Diamond, 'Miracles', p. 315.

16. Ibid., p. 320.

17. Ibid., p. 321.

18. Ibid.

19. Ibid., p. 322.

20. Ibid., p. 324.

21. Ibid.

22. Diamond's choice of Austin Farrer at this point is surely inappropriate in the extreme.

23. Diamond has in mind here such factors as the principle of indeterminacy, the theory-saturated character of scientific observations, Thomas Kuhn's subjectivistic view of scientific revolutions, and the downgrading of the element of prediction in scientific work by some philosophers of science. 'Miracles', p. 308.

24. Presumably, this is the position adopted by the existentialists.

25. I assume at this point that the theist relies on some account of analogy to secure the meaning of discourse about God.

26. See above, n. 20.

27. Thus Diamond has the following as part of the dialogue in his scenario: 'The Pope: Fine, from what I hear you're just the man to do it. Go ahead.' This is addressed to the scientists. See 'Miracles', p. 321.

28. Cf. Ninian Smart's comment: 'it is true indeed that a doctrine which explains miracles as due to God's action does not have any predictive value *in regard to further miracles*. Yet it might have predictive value in other contexts, regarding the course of history, for instance. By attaching miracle to a whole network of doctrines, some of which concern the future (for instance, they concern what in human life conduces to salvation, to the vision of God, and so forth), it implicates in a 'theory' which does have predictive value - and to this extent there is an analogy with scientific explanation.' *Philosophers and Religious Truth* (London: SCM, 1969), pp. 41-2. The emphasis is as in the original.

29. Maurice Wiles has stated a more moderate version of the argument developed by Diamond as follows: 'The experience of divine guidance

or divine providence is so frequent and so fundamental to Christian experience that if it were to be understood as always implying special divine causation (however possible theoretically that may be) the occurrences of such activity would have to be so numerous as to make nonsense of our normal understanding of the relative independence of causation within the world.' *The Remaking of Christian Doctrine* (London: SCM, 1974), pp. 37-8. Three comments are in order concerning this version of the argument: (1) it is not clear that all Christian discourse about guidance and providence does imply special divine causation. Much of it may not, and only detailed analysis will reveal how much. (2) A clear distinction needs to be made between non-miraculous and miraculous intervention. See above, p. 28. It is only the latter which can be used to support Wiles's moderate claims, and I suspect that most divine guidance that implies special divine causation does not fall within this class. (3) This leaves sufficient scope for as much independent causation as is necessary for the scientific enterprise. At any rate, it is surely precarious to say it does not.

30. Diamond, 'Miracles', p. 323.

INDEX

Index

DATE DUE

A.L.L. CAT. NO. 30501